To- Marie
love

SWEETS ON A SUNDAY

by

Shelagh Flynn

Bloomington, IN   Milton Keynes, UK

authorHOUSE®

AuthorHouse™
1663 Liberty Drive, Suite 200
Bloomington, IN 47403
www.authorhouse.com
Phone: 1-800-839-8640

AuthorHouse™ UK Ltd.
500 Avebury Boulevard
Central Milton Keynes, MK9 2BE
www.authorhouse.co.uk
Phone: 0800 1974150

First published by AuthorHouse 5/4/2007

Printed in the United States of America
Bloomington, Indiana

This book is printed on acid-free paper.

ISBN: 978-1-4259-9139-5 (sc)

This book is dedicated to my very special family.

My husband Peter, our son Darren and daughter Adele.

My brother Tony and my sisters Pat and Joyce.

To my nieces Angela and Tina and my nephews Neil and Ian.

My thanks are endless.

To my husband Peter for his patience and his constant encouragement during the four years it took to write this book.

My daughter Adele for all her help.

Sharon McCormack, Social Worker, Leeds City Council who retrieved a monthly account of our lives in care from the City Archives dating back to 1947. Without these, I would not have been able to tell our story.

My wonderful relatives and friends for their support, especially, when I found it emotionally difficult to carry on writing.

Terry, a very special brother-in-law, for his support and always being there when I needed help, and those times were many. I could not have managed without you.

David Mayers, Lecturer at Bradford College, for his invaluable time, advice and encouragement and his son Thomas for the design of the book cover.

Roger Lowe, Solicitor, for his advice on legal matters.

Tobias and Verity Ward who would listen and be mesmerised at the stories I used to tell them about the times when we were in the Children's Home. "Have you started that book yet?" Tobias would ask every time I saw him. "One day I will," I would always answer.

Members of the East Leeds Writer's Group, especially Maureen Mason, who has helped me more than she will ever know. Pam Pennock, for steering my story in the right direction from the very beginning. Joyce Kirk for all her help, and finally to the rest of my friends in the Group - Phil, Eileen G, Margaret, May, Eileen H, Melody, Judith, Lynn, Dorothy and Audrey, for their continuous support and advice.

Additional thanks also to Maureen who gave permission to use her late brother, Bryan's photograph on my front cover.

Leeds City Council, Archives Department, for giving permission to use letters and forms from the case notes appropriate to our story.

Pauline Cooper, a reporter from the Yorkshire Evening Post, for beautifully writing about our story and her colleague, Andrew Hutchinson, for covering our family reunion with care and compassion. Thank you.

Finally, all those, who gave permission to use their names and stories.

This is a true story based on documented evidence.
Some fictitious characters have been created and some names have been
changed to protect identities.

Chapter 1

Alice, who was pregnant with her fifth child, locked the door for the very last time, dropped the key through the letterbox and set off walking with her four children in the pouring rain.

They had no idea where they were going. It was to be a very long journey.

This day would change their lives forever.

They walked all the way down York Road, crossing the road at the bottom, through Burmantofts, towards St James's Hospital. The two elder children were crying and complaining that their legs were hurting. Alice promised them that they would stop at the next bench and they could all have a rest. She could see a bench in the distance. They stopped, rested awhile and then set off walking again passing St James's Hospital. They continued along Harehills Road and then turned right at the bottom towards Roundhay Park.

Tony was now crying all the time.

"Where are we going?" he asked his mother, "I'm cold and my legs ache."

"We're going somewhere where you'll be warm, and when you get there, there'll be something nice to eat for all of you," Alice replied.

She lifted him up and sat him beside Pat on the front of the pram. Under the hood, protected from the rain, Joyce was fast asleep. Alice saw another bench near the park, where they rested again.

"We're nearly there, just a short walk away," she told her children, as they set off walking again.

Finally, they stopped at some black painted wrought iron gates. She opened the gates and walked down the drive to the house. It was Street Lane Children's Home. She stopped just outside of the house, put the brake on the pram and lifted Tony down. He held the pram handle on the left side with Shelagh still holding onto the other side. Alice entered into a small arched vestibule and rang the doorbell by the side of the door, then returned to be with her children.

Within minutes, a friendly young woman answered the door. Tony, who had previously complained of his legs aching, ran around the back of Alice and held onto her coat, peeping with one eye, and frowning at the woman he didn't know. Shelagh let go of the pram handle and grabbed hold of her mother's hand. She was very nervous not knowing why they were there.

"Could someone please help my children and me?" Alice asked the young woman who answered the door. "I have been evicted from my home and I am desperate. I have four children and I am pregnant again."

"Eeh lass you look all done in, come on in, I'll give you a hand with the pram," was the kind reply.

She invited Alice into the house, and helped to lift the pram into the hallway. They were all shown into a small bright waiting room. The rain had now stopped and the sun was shining through the one large window that looked out onto the main road. Eagerly, Alice sat down on a chair. She was exhausted. Pat and Joyce were quite happily sitting in the pram. Shelagh and Tony sat on the floor beside their mother. They were tired, cold, wet and hungry. Tony began to cry.

"Why are we here?" he asked his mother, his bottom lip quivering. "I want to go back home. I don't like it here."

Alice told her children they would not be going back to the old house again, but not to worry, as everything would be all right. Shelagh did not like hearing her brother cry and put her arm around his shoulder to comfort him. She herself was wondering why they were there.

2

After a while, a middle-aged woman came into the waiting room. She introduced herself as Miss Smith, Matron of the Children's Home. She was tall, with neat, short brown hair. She wore a long-sleeved, three-quarter length black dress, black stockings and black lace-up shoes. She had a long chain around her waist with keys attached. She smiled at Alice and the children.

She knelt on the floor beside Shelagh and Tony. They were very nervous. She held out both hands to them. They looked at each other before Shelagh reached out first and held one hand. She thought Miss Smith's hand was soft and warm. Then she looked up into a kind face with blue eyes. After a few moments, Tony held the other hand.

Joyce was now sitting up in the pram. Pat was still happily sat at the front. Miss Smith spoke to both of them in baby talk. They laughed and giggled at her. Alice began to cry uncontrollably.

"Don't worry," said Miss Smith, "I'm here to help you and your children," then asked to be excused for a few moments.

She returned a few minutes later with two young women, and asked the older children if they would like to have a look around the big house while she talked to their mother. They looked at Alice for her approval and she nodded. One of the young women wheeled the pram with Pat and Joyce out of the waiting room. The other young woman took Shelagh and Tony by the hand and told them her name was Anne.

Miss Smith turned to Alice. "Let's go into the kitchen where it's warm. I'll put your coat and scarf on the clothes airer in front of the fire to dry." She followed Miss Smith from the small waiting room down the hall into the kitchen.

"I'll make us a nice cup of tea, and then we'll have a chat. Please sit down," she said, as she pulled out a chair from under the table.

"Why don't you wipe your face?" she asked softly, handing Alice a warm, wet flannel and a small hand towel. "It will freshen you up and make you feel better." She placed two cups of tea on the table and sat down beside Alice, taking her hand.

"Now," she said softly, looking into Alice's tired worried face, "tell me what brought you and your children here today?"

"I don't know where to start," replied Alice. Then, pausing for a moment, she said, "I really don't know where to begin."

"Start from the beginning, the very beginning, that's usually the best, don't leave anything out, tell me everything," smiled Miss Smith, encouragingly.

Nervously her story began to unfold.

Chapter 2

Times were hard for many families after the Second World War. Robert and Alice Gregson, who lived in the Leeds 9 area, were one such family. Home for this family was a one-up one-down, back-to-back terrace house, sharing a toilet halfway down the street with neighbours. It was just one of hundreds of houses in that area. Row after row of cobbled streets stretched in all directions. Many of these houses have now been replaced by modern homes.

There were no gardens for the children to play in; just two stone steps leading from the flagged pavement directly into the only room. The most dominant feature of the room was a large black-leaded cast iron fireplace that almost covered an entire wall of the room. The fire was heated by coal and anything else that would burn. The heat from the fire heated the oven. An iron kettle, full of hot water, always sat on top of a shelf directly above the fire. A mantelpiece ran the full width of the fireplace, and underneath, a washing-line stretched from one end to the other.

With three small children, there was always washing hung to dry that had been washed by hand. There were few washing machines in those days. A large metal mesh fireguard wrapped around the open hearth that always seemed to have nappies drying on it. In the hearth stood a half-filled bucket of the cheapest coal, and alongside a companion set, which consisted of a small brush, shovel, poker and coal tongs hanging from a chrome stand. In the middle of the room stood a square scrubbed wooden table with four chairs, two worn fireside chairs and a handmade clip rug lay on the floor in front of the fire. To the right of the fireplace, in front of the only window, which looked directly onto the street, stood a large square white pot sink, with its single cold-water tap where all the daily washing was done. A flight of steps through a door at the far side of the room led upstairs to the bedroom, where everyone slept in one bed. When the children complained of being cold, overcoats would be used as extra blankets.

Alice Gregson was a good-looking woman, with blonde hair, blue eyes, and stood five foot four inches tall. She was twenty-six years old, had three children and was expecting another baby. Shelagh was the eldest, almost four. Tony was two and a half, then came Pat, just twenty months old. Pat was a sickly child who cried a lot and needed lots of attention. She spent most of the time playing in her pram. Shelagh and Tony were two normal happy children who occupied themselves by playing on the flags outside their house. Marbles or taws, as the local kids called them, was a game that kept them happy for hours. Taws were played in the edge of the gutter, as they would roll along the side and not get lost unless they were too close to a grate.

Tony particularly loved playing with his Meccano Set. He and Shelagh played many a happy hour building different models. The children's father, Robert Gregson, was a handsome man. He was twenty-eight, six foot three inches tall, had piercing blue eyes and black wavy hair.

Sometimes he would sit in the doorway on the top step, with Shelagh on one knee and Tony on the other, teaching them nursery rhymes or telling them funny stories and they would laugh until their sides ached. Alice would listen to them and smile as she prepared tea for them all.

Robert was not very good at working. He was always in and out of different jobs and didn't always bring home the money he earned. Robert was also a gambler, and sometimes would not come home for days at a time. Often the rent would not be paid for weeks and the children were not fed as often as they should have been.

Alice was one of twelve children. Her parent's brothers and sisters lived not too far away, so it became a regular thing for them to help when she had no money. They would bring food, coal for the fire and second-hand clothes for the children.

Alice was attending the local antenatal clinic. She had decided to have a home confinement for her fourth baby. When she was eight months pregnant, she asked the doctor at the clinic if there was any way the Council could take care of her three children while she had her baby at home. Doctor Swain, Head of Harehills Clinic, wrote to Leeds City Council's, Social Services, asking if they would support one of his patients who needed help. He gave them all the relevant information and asked if the children could be taken into care for a few weeks.

Leeds City Council sent all the appropriate forms for Robert to sign and asked him to take his three children to the Care of Children Office, in Woodhouse Lane.

On the 18 August 1947, Robert took and handed over his three children. He signed to say that he consented for them to be taken into care. It was Shelagh's fourth birthday.

Alice gave birth to a little girl, Joyce, the following month, and after a while, Shelagh, Tony and Pat returned to their parents.

Shelagh was registered at All Saints School, in York Road. The headmistress was called Mrs Redpath. The school was enclosed in a large yard surrounded by tall blue fencing. Painted on the fencing were large golden sheaves of corn above which the name Hemingway's Brewery was painted in gold.

All the children who went to the school attended a short church service every morning. Shelagh enjoyed school and was always willing to do anything asked of her and more. She never wanted to go home, always finding any excuse to stay.

Months passed, and Alice continued to struggle with her four children in the one-up and one-down little house, living below the breadline as many other families did in those days.

Robert had not changed, still passing from one job to another. Without the help of her parents, Alice and her children would not have survived. They had told her many times that if things got too bad she could go home and live with them. When she was almost at the end of her tether, she received the letter she

7

had been dreading. It was from her landlord. She could not remember the last time she had paid any rent. The landlord had warned her many times that if she did not keep up with her payments then she would have to leave. The letter was giving her an eviction date. She had hoped that, as she had four children, he would take pity on her and give her a little more time, but it was not to be. Her hands were shaking as she read the letter repeatedly and she began to cry. Alice had not seen Robert for days. She did not know if he was coming home or not, and if he did, would he have any money. There were no guarantees.

Pat was sitting in a corner crying. Joyce at nine months old was asleep in her pram. Shelagh and Tony were playing outside and she was pregnant yet again.

On the day she was to be evicted, she decided enough was enough. She couldn't take any more. She couldn't continue to take food, coal, money or pity from anyone any longer. She wrapped up Joyce, who was nine months old, in a blanket and put her back into her pram. Then she dressed Pat, and sat her on the front of the pram. She was just two years old. Moving on to Tony, who was three and a half, she continued with the task, then turned to Shelagh, who at four and a half years old still needed some help dressing. Looking around her little home, she remembered the good times, and the hard times. As she glanced out of the window, she saw it was raining heavily. She put on her coat, tied a scarf around her head and then lifted the pram outside. Shelagh held one side of the pram handle, Tony the other.

Locking the door, Alice put the key through the letterbox, and looking at her children, wondered if what she was about to do was the right thing. She had thought long and hard about this, and with tears in her eyes, she decided it was.

CITY OF LEEDS SOCIAL WELFARE COMMITTEE

I, the undersigned, hereby make
application for *my Children*
Shelagh Anthony & Patricia
to be admitted, as a temporary arrangement
to the Children's Homes under the control
of the Social Welfare Committee on account
of *wife being confined*
and undertake to remove him/her/them from
the Homes at the earliest possible moment
and, in any event, within seven days of
receiving a written request from the
Director of Social Welfare

Signed

Date *18 - 8 - 47*

Witness *W. Lockwood*

Chapter 3

One warm, sunny autumn morning, after having had a warm relaxing foam bath, I sat with my dressing gown on at the kitchen table, buttering toast for breakfast. Mrs Tate was pouring tea from a white flowered china teapot into three matching china mugs.

"Come and get your breakfast," she shouted through the open kitchen door into the garden.

"It'll get cold."

Mr Tate walked into the kitchen and over to the sink to wash his hands, then looked up at the clock on the wall.

"You'll be Mrs Peter Flynn in a few hours time," he said smiling. "Are you still nervous?"

"Don't keep telling her Fred, she's nervous enough without you reminding her. Just sit down and eat your breakfast."

When all the breakfast pots had been washed, dried and put away, I had a few minutes left for a quick cup of tea before going upstairs to put on my wedding dress.

It had been a year ago, when I had nowhere to live, that Mr and Mrs Tate had kindly given me a home, they had cared for me, and made me part of their family. Mrs Tate had taught me how to cook, bake and even wallpaper!

I had grown to care for them and I knew I would never forget the kindness that they had shown me over the past year. Mr and Mrs Tate were best friends and neighbours of Charlie and Hilda Flynn, Peter's father and mother. They lived on the opposite side of the Avenue.

I heard the front door open and close.

"Thought I'd come and give you a hand to put your dress on," shouted Elaine, as she walked though the lounge and into the kitchen where they were sitting still chatting. Elaine was the daughter of Mr and Mrs Tate.

"Wish I'd have had a day like today when I got married. It chucked it down! The sun's shining and it's lovely and warm. The Avenue's full of autumn leaves; it looks like a picture postcard. Somebody up there must like you," said Elaine smiling wistfully.

"And about time too," said Mrs Tate, lifting up her head and looking towards the ceiling. "Have you seen the time?" said Elaine, looking up at the clock on the kitchen wall.

"Time you were getting ready; don't want you to be late. Off you go upstairs you two, I'll be up shortly," said Mrs Tate.

"Ooh your dress is lovely," said Elaine, looking at the full-length, long-sleeved white brocade dress spread out on the Tate's double bed.

"It isn't mine," Shelagh shouted from the bathroom, "I've borrowed it from my best friend Mary. The veil to match is hanging up at the back of the door."

"Bob's making a good job of his car for the wedding, come and have a look," Elaine shouted, Shelagh quickly finished cleaning her teeth and ran to join Elaine, who had lifted the net curtain to one side and opened the window.

"You've done a good job there," Elaine shouted down to Bob. The blue and white Ford Zephyr Zodiac sparkled. It had been neatly trimmed with white ribbons and the seating inside covered with white cotton sheets.

Bob, who was married to Pat, Peter's sister, was going to be their chauffeur and Peter's best man.

"Do you think so?" he said smugly, lifting up his shoulders and sticking out his chest.

There was a knock at the bedroom door.

"Can I come in?" shouted Mr Tate.

"You can now," answered Mrs Tate.

"Eeh you look lovely. If I were twenty years younger, I'd marry yer meself."

That made me blush.

"I'll just dab you with a bit of my best perfume, and then you're done," Mrs Tate fussed.

Uncle Harry, one of my mother's older brothers, who was giving me away, was waiting for me downstairs. Friends and neighbours had gathered to watch as he helped me down the steps and into Bob's car.

"I now pronounce you man and wife," said Father Brannigan. Gently lifting my veil,

Peter kissed me softly, and when I looked into his eyes, I knew for the first time in my life how it felt to be loved and valued unconditionally. Suddenly I felt normal, as though a great weight had been lifted from my shoulders. At last, I belonged to someone. Never again would I be a nobody, belonging to no one. As I walked from the altar to the vestry on my husband's arm, my feet never touched the ground. I was walking on air. Inside the vestry, we looked into each other's eyes. Peter wrapped his arms around me and whispered in my ear,

"I love you, and you look beautiful." He lifted me high into the air and swung me round and round.

After the photographer had taken all the photographs, everyone made their way to the church hall for the reception.

"Who ever got this ready for you Hilda has done you proud," said May, Hilda's older sister as they walked into the church hall.

"It's lovely and clean and the tables are set out beautifully."

"It wants to be," replied Hilda, "Shelagh and me spent hours in here last night, mopping the floor, washing chairs and cleaning windowsills. Later Charlie and our Peter came to give us a hand after they had been to the pub for a few pints. Must have been eleven before they got here. Anyway, between the four of us, we got it all ready. It must have been twelve before we finished. I must say it does look nice," she said proudly.

While everyone was eating, laughing and chattering between themselves, I sat at the head of the table, arms folded, watching everyone. The whole day had been like a dream, I sat with my hands resting on the table, stroking and showing off my shiny new wedding ring. I looked at Peter sitting beside me whom I loved dearly, then across at my mother and father-in-law, Hilda and Charlie, and my sister-in-law Pat with her husband Bob. How proud I was to be a part of a real happy family. Then I looked at my uncle Harry, auntie Ethel and cousin Pat, who was feeding her new baby. Beside her Belinda, her four-year-old daughter was tucking in to jelly and ice cream, and there was Malcolm, who was laughing at his daughter, who was managing to get more on her face than actually went into her mouth. I looked proudly at my brother Tony and two sisters Pat and Joyce who were talking and laughing together.

My thoughts wandered to the house that Peter and I had bought not too far away. The deposit that we had saved so hard for was not enough, so Peter borrowed a hundred pounds from work, which had to be paid back at two pounds a week. Tonight, I would go back to my house, no 'our house,' and I would sleep in a bed that no one had slept in before. I had always slept in beds where someone else had slept before me, and there had been plenty of them. Most of the rooms in our house were empty. I didn't care. Now I'll be able to make a cup of tea whenever I wanted to without ever having to ask anyone's permission. I couldn't wait. Hilda had given us two fireside chairs and a clip rug. "I couldn't wait for us to sit in our house," I thought, sitting in our chairs in front of a cosy warm fire. I looked at Tony, Pat and Joyce who were still talking and laughing. It was around a fire that we had sat when we had been separated sixteen years ago. So much had happened to us since that day. The memories came flooding back, the long walk to Street Lane, when Anne took us out of the waiting room to show us around the big house, leaving Matron to talk to our mother.

That was the day we all went into care.

Chapter 4

First, Anne took Shelagh and Tony into the kitchen. The smell of food greeted them, which made them hungry. The kitchen was warm and cosy. A coal fire burned in the grate, with the usual cast iron oven at the side. Tony nudged Shelagh with his elbow.

"We have one of those at our house," he said, arching his shoulders and pointing to the fire.

In the centre of the kitchen, was a well-scrubbed wooden table with matching chairs. On the wall by the door stood an old dresser filled with crockery.

From the warm kitchen, Anne took them to the playroom, a long wide room with a polished lino floor. To the right of the room were four arched windows, whilst on the left side; a fireguard protected a burning fire. A square rug lay on the floor in front the fire. Dotted around the playroom were various toys. The two children's eyes lit up. Suddenly they weren't tired any longer. In one corner stood a small white rocking horse with red straps, and in another, a swing attached to a metal frame, a small slide and a metal framed seesaw with canvas seats. A dolls pram, a box with different coloured bricks, and lots more. The children looked up at Anne pleadingly and asked if they could play.

"Not for the moment," she replied, but promised that she would bring them back later. Their faces lit up with excitement at the thought of playing with all those toys. They climbed a long winding staircase and Anne led them to the bathroom, where there was a row of small sinks on one wall, and a toilet in the corner. A high bath on legs stood near the wall opposite the door.

By this time, Anne had managed to gain their confidence. She asked them if they would like a warm soapy bath, and afterwards, some new clothes and something to eat. They looked at each other and nodded.

While the bath water was running, Anne undressed them, and then lifted them in, one at each end. They were washed with a loofah, a long round rough sponge and a block of carbolic soap. Their hair was washed and cleaned with disinfectant shampoo. They were enjoying it so much they were allowed to play for a while. They played with the plastic toys, splashed soapy water at each other, blew bubbles and screeched with laughter. They loved every minute. There was water everywhere.

Eventually they were lifted out on to a wooden board, each wrapped in a large soft bath towel and dried vigorously. Their hair was brushed and then checked for lice with a nit comb. Anne then took them into the linen room, a long narrow room with wooden shelves from floor to ceiling. These were filled with clothes donated by various charities. They were then dressed in clean clothes and socks. One shelf had a box with shoes of different sizes. Anne found shoes to fit them both. By this time, they were both feeling really important and asked if they could show their new clothes to their mother. She took them back to Alice, who was now sitting in the warm kitchen with Pat on her knee. Joyce was asleep in her pram, which now had clean sheets, blanket and a pillowcase. Shelagh and Tony ran towards their mother. She quickly sat Pat on a chair beside her and opened her arms to catch them; hugging and kissing them both, and told them how lovely they looked as they walked up and down the kitchen and posed for her, showing off their new clothes. Pat eagerly joined her brother and sister and was now showing off her new clothes. Joyce, still asleep, was oblivious to all this.

When Miss Smith came into the kitchen, the children ran and sat on the chairs around the table. She asked them if they were hungry and would like something to eat. They nodded and said eagerly.

"Yes please." It had been a long time since they had eaten. They were all given a hot meal and a glass of milk. They were so hungry they ate everything on their plates.

After they had eaten, Alice told the children she wanted to talk to them. First, she asked them if they were enjoying themselves. They looked at each other, smiled and nodded. Then she pointed to the burning coal fire, saying how warm and cosy it was. They were wearing new clothes, and had eaten a hot meal. Alice told them she had not been able to look after them properly for a long time and explained to them that she wanted them to stay here for a while as she was going away to have another baby. She would get a bigger house, come back for them and they would all be back together again. She knew that if she left them at Street Lane they would be warm and clean and have plenty to eat. More importantly, they would all be together. As Shelagh was the eldest, Alice asked her to take care of her brother and sisters. She asked them all to be good children, and gave each child a big hug and a kiss and promised they would all be back together soon. Alice started to cry, and opening her handbag for a handkerchief, she noticed she had forgotten to give Miss Smith the children's ration books and identity cards. She put them on the table.

She did not want the children to see her crying any more, and quickly began to walk away from them. By the time she had reached the door; her eyes were blinded with tears. Alice walked out heartbroken.

The children's lives were to change from that day on.

Chapter 5

It had stopped raining when Alice left the Street Lane Home. She walked a while, and sat on the same bench where she had been with the children. So much had happened since that morning. She would miss them dreadfully but she knew that they would be well taken care of until they could all be together again.

After two tram journeys, she arrived at South Lodge in Hunslet. The Master of South Lodge was expecting her. Miss Smith, the Street Lane Matron, had arranged for Alice to stay there until she had her baby.

South Lodge was home for women who, like Alice, needed help.

Chapter 6

After Alice had left, as promised, Anne took the children to the playroom, Joyce was now wide awake and sitting up in her pram. The hood was folded down neatly behind her. She was hooked to each side of the pram with a baby harness and a pillow was cosily tucked behind her back. She was happily gurgling and chewing on a teething ring. Other toys had been put in her pram for her to play with, coloured bricks, rattles and soft toys. Pat toddled over to the small white rocking horse. Shelagh ran after her and lifted her on, gave her the red reins to hold onto, and gave her a ride. Tony was playing happily on the swing. They ran around the room, playing with everything they could see. The children were screeching with laughter and thoroughly enjoying themselves. Shelagh ran to look out of one of the windows and gasped,

"Tony come and look." Tony joined her. Faces and hands were pressed against the window. Directly outside the window was a neatly cut lawn, with flowers of all colours around the edges. The only grass and flowers they had seen had been in storybooks.

"Real flowers!" Tony shouted.

Hearing the door handle turn, they stopped what they were doing, looked at each other and then looked at the door. Shelagh grabbed Pat out of the sand pit and ran to sit on the carpet in front of the fire where Tony was already sitting. Joyce had thrown all her toys over the side of the pram onto the floor, and was now bored and crying. Miss Smith came into the playroom, took Joyce out of the pram, picked up a small chair that was in a corner of the room and sat down beside the children with Joyce, who had now stopped crying. She explained to them that Street Lane was a short stay assessment centre. They would only be there for a short time until somewhere else was found. Unfortunately, they might have to be separated for a while, but emphasised that it would not be for long and eventually they would all be back together with their mother, father, and a new baby brother or sister.

"However," she said, "there was one place at Rothwell Children's Home for Girls and whoever puts their hand up first, I will give them an apple and orange." Shelagh's hand went up first. She would go to Rothwell in the next few days. Miss Smith told Shelagh that before she left, she would like her to be seen by a doctor.

Doctor Davies said her hair was nit free, and that she was healthy enough to be sent on to Rothwell Children's Home for Girls. He was concerned that she had a large bald patch on the top and down the right side of her head. Miss Smith, who was helping Doctor Davies, was aware of this problem. She explained that it was a meat fat scald caused by an accident in the family home. When she was a small baby, she had been laid in her pram inside the house, by the side of the fire. Her father Robert had taken the meat out of the oven and as he was carrying it to the table he tripped and lost his balance, the fat from the meat spilt on top of her head, leaving a large scald. She still has the scar to this day.

Doctor Davies later passed Tony fit and healthy. Pat was found to be a little underweight and under nourished. Joyce was passed a healthy baby. He documented that all the children were nit free and were all healthy enough to be sent onto children's homes.

Tony was found a place in North Park Avenue Children's Home for Boys at Moortown. Pat and Joyce were to be sent to St Angela's Nursery for Babies, part of Street Lane Home. They were all now under the care of Leeds City Council's, Care of Children's Department.

Each child now had their own Children's Care Officer. Miss Baker was to be Shelagh's.

A few days later, Miss Baker arrived to take Shelagh to Rothwell Children's Home. She was a middle-aged woman with short silver hair rolled up around the back. She wore a dark brown tweed suit, a white silk blouse, seamed stockings and brown lace-up shoes.

"You will like it there," she told Shelagh, "there'll be lots of other children to play with and they have a playroom with swings, slides, dolls prams and lots more."

Shelagh bade a sad goodbye to her brother and sisters and promised that she would see them soon. Miss Baker held her hand as they walked along the driveway, and then lifted her into the car, sitting her on the front seat. It was the first time Shelagh had been in a car. She was smiling and looking out of the window, watching people walking while she was being driven. She felt rather important. It was a lovely warm, sunny day, not a bit like the day they had arrived at Street Lane, when it was cold and raining.

Arriving at Rothwell Children's Home, Miss Baker parked her car in the drive, lifted Shelagh out and held her hand as they walked down the driveway to the back of the house. They could hear children shouting and laughing as they walked to the back door. Lots of girls of all ages could be seen playing in a nearby field. Miss Baker knocked on the door. A small, round, friendly woman appeared. She was wearing a paisley patterned overall over her dress, her hair neatly tucked under a hairnet. Her overall and hands were covered with flour. She introduced herself as Clara, and said she was the cook, pointing towards the kitchen table where she had been rolling out pastry with a long wooden rolling pin. She told them that she was preparing a meat and potato pie for the evening meal. She asked them if they would like to sit down on one of the chairs that she pulled out from under the table. She washed her hands, made them refreshments and asked to be excused while she went to tell Matron they had arrived.

A few minutes later, Matron entered the kitchen and introduced herself as Mrs Wood.

"Hello," she said to Miss Baker, then she sat beside Shelagh, who was sitting quietly and nervously holding both hands together on her knees under the table, head on her chin, looking down at the floor in between her swinging legs. Shelagh's thoughts went back to Street Lane, thinking about the apple and orange she had been given to come here. Slowly she lifted her head and looked into the face of a softly spoken woman who was telling her of all the good things she would like whilst she was here. Mrs Wood reminded Shelagh of Miss Smith at Street Lane whom she liked and trusted; so she decided she liked her too. Mrs Wood asked if she would like to play on the field with the other girls. Shelagh wasn't sure, as she did not know them and was not certain that they would like her. She frowned and nodded slowly. Matron stepped outside the kitchen and shouted to two older girls. They came running into the kitchen and said "hello" to Miss Baker and Shelagh, introducing themselves as Janet and Jean. They asked Shelagh if she would like to play with them. She looked up at them shyly, and slowly nodded. They took her by her hands and led her towards the field, while Miss Baker brought Mrs Wood up to date on Shelagh's background. Miss Baker gave her a ration book, an identity card, and a form headed 'Care of Children for Inter-Department Notification', which showed Shelagh's name and date of birth – 18 October 1943. The form was dated July 1947.

Three years later, her date of birth was found to be incorrect.

Jean and Janet were playing happily on the field trying to teach Shelagh how to skip. She couldn't skip for toffee and everyone was laughing at her, and she was laughing with them too. Then a few more children joined them as they began to play, 'Ring a Ring o' Roses'. She liked that.

Before she left, Miss Baker walked towards Shelagh to say goodbye. Shelagh ran towards her.

"When will I see my mum and dad and my brother and sisters again?" she asked. She was missing them already.

Miss Baker told her it would not be for very long, and until then, Rothwell was to be her home and she would visit her every few weeks. Shelagh watched and followed her as she walked up the drive and got into her car. She drove away, waving to her as she passed. Shelagh started to cry so much she couldn't stop.

"Come and play with us," shouted Janet, skipping up the drive.

"Yes," said Jean, "don't worry, everyone cries at first. You'll be alright, we'll look after you."

They slowly turned her around, put their arms around her shoulders and headed back towards the playing field.

Clara stepped from the kitchen and rang a wooden handled, brass bell, which was almost as big as she was. Children of all shapes, sizes and ages ran towards the house.

"Tea time," Janet announced.

"Can I sit near you?" Shelagh asked

"Course you can," she replied.

The dining room was a long narrow room with two long tables down the centre, with chairs tucked underneath. On one wall were rows of small lockers, one for each child. Behind the door stood a tall dark wooden bookcase filled with old books of different colours and sizes, together with a small table in one corner for Mrs Wood and her staff. Next to Mrs Wood's table, a serving table was placed against the wall, above which two small sliding doors led directly into the kitchen. Large pans of food would be passed through on to the serving table. Noisy, hungry children ran to their seats. Shelagh sat quietly and nervously at the top of the table beside Jean.

"What's your name?" shouted one child.

"How old are you, why are you here?" shouted one of the other children.

"Just ignore them," said Jean, "and eat your dinner."

The questions continued.

"Is your mother and father dead?"

"Have you any brothers or sisters?"

"Where are they?"

"How long have you come for?"

"Now that's enough," Mrs Wood said angrily. "She's only been here for a short time, so give her a chance to settle in. Get on with your dinner and leave her alone."

The dining room went quiet. After a few moments, the children continued their usual loud chattering and laughing between themselves. Jean ate all her meat and potato pie, with potatoes, cabbage and gravy. She noticed Shelagh had stopped eating and was sitting quietly holding her hands together on her lap under the table.

"Eat your dinner," she encouraged.

"Don't want it, don't like it," Shelagh muttered.

"Don't like it?" said Jean.

"Don't like what?" she continued.

"That," said Shelagh pointing towards the meat and pulling a face "makes me gip." My mother never gave me meat. She knows I don't like it and won't eat it."

"Can I have it?" said Jean promptly, exchanging plates and eating what was left.

For the rest of the evening Shelagh never left Jean's side. Mrs Wood had asked Jean to keep an eye on her and take responsibility for her until she settled in and could fend for herself.

After tea, the two girls showed Shelagh around the big house. Janet and Jean lifted her high into the air as they swung her up and around the open staircase, making her laugh and giggle.

The top of the staircase opened onto a wide landing with closed doors on either side.

"This is where you'll be sleeping," said Janet, opening one of the doors.

The dormitory was long and wide. On the back and two side walls, were rows of high, round headed, cast iron bedsteads. Each bed was neatly made, with one pillow covered with a white cotton pillowcase, white cotton sheets, and one thick grey blanket edged with red blanket-stitching. On the bottom wall, a window looked onto the playing field. Placed underneath the window was a small chest of drawers, one drawer for each child.

"This one is for you," said Jean, climbing onto a bed.

Janet lifted Shelagh up to sit beside Jean.

"This bed is nearest to the bathroom. If you want to use the toilet, it's over there," she indicated pointing to a door opposite. Jean jumped down from the bed and lifted Shelagh down. Shelagh looked up at the high bed and wondered how she would get in, or out. Janet knew what she was thinking and said that when it was time for bed she would give her a lift.

At bedtime, she was given an ankle length, long sleeved flannelette nightdress to wear. The clothes she was wearing were taken away. She could not sleep when she was put to bed. She really did not want to be there, but finally fell asleep.

She woke up to the noise of half dressed children shouting and running backwards and forwards, in and out of the dormitory. She lay still for a moment, peeping over the blankets, frightened, not knowing what to do. She noticed a neat pile of clothes on the end of her bed. Still not sure what to do, she slid down the side of the bed, still frightened and bewildered, sat on the floor at the top end of the bed with her back against the wall, her knees close to her chest, watching different sized feet and legs running backwards and forwards through the gap at the bottom.

Her heart was pounding. She wished she were back home with her mother, father, brother and sisters. She was about to start crying again, when Jean's head appeared under the bed. She held out her hand and took her across the landing into the bathroom. On the right hand side of the bathroom were rows of towels on hooks, with a row of flannels above. Each one had an embroidered number in a corner. Jean told Shelagh that hers was number four.

"Just remember how old you are," she insisted.

On the bottom wall, under the windows, were a row of sinks, above which stood a row of numbered toothbrushes. Small cut pieces of carbolic soap and round tins of powdered toothpaste were dotted around the sinks.

Children of all shapes and sizes were chattering and laughing together. Some stopped to say hello to the new girl. Jean helped her wash, dry herself and clean her teeth with her number four flannel, towel and toothbrush. Then it was back to the dormitory where she dressed her in the clothes that were at the end of her bed, a vest, a pair of silk knickers, a liberty bodice, a long-sleeved jumper, a cotton smock, shoes and socks.

Down in the dining room, Shelagh sat on the same chair that she had sat on the previous day between the two older girls. Breakfast was one ladle of porridge with a small white enamelled mug filled with cocoa. In the middle of the table were plates of buttered bread for the children to help themselves. Each child had a small plate, knife and spoon, and on each plate, a teaspoon of marmalade. Shelagh had never seen so much bread. She thought she might like it here for a while after all. After breakfast, an assistant took her upstairs to the linen room.

In the long narrow room were wooden shelves on either side, reaching from floor to ceiling. She was given a white blouse, a burgundy coloured skirt and blazer, a school hat, some underwear and socks.

Shelagh would attend Rothwell School with the rest of the girls and was not afraid as she recalled her days at All Saints in York Road, which she remembered as happy days. The school was quite a long walk away, so all the children were lined up in twos, the younger children in front, with a carer to supervise, and the older ones at the back. It was the same when they were coming home.

Weeks went by and she seemed to settle and make new friends and learnt to skip and play ball on the playing field round the back of the home.

She missed her family, but still believed that one day they would all be back together again.

Chapter 7

Weeks passed into months and with no word from Robert, Alice began to despair.

"What am I going to do?" she said to the Master. "How can I find him? I've written to places he might be, he must be somewhere. He must be in trouble. I can't stand this any longer. I haven't seen my children for three months. I daren't visit and if I do, I will have to leave them. They've never been parted from me before. I'm soon to have another baby and all this is making me ill. What shall I do, who can help me?"

"That's enough," said the Master, holding up one hand.

"Let's think about it. Tell you what, why don't I go make us a cup of tea, then we'll sit down and talk about it."

"Have you thought of anything?" she shouted, as he walked towards her carrying two mugs of tea, which he placed on the kitchen table. He sat beside her, elbows bent, his chin cupped in both hands.

"Why don't you write a letter?" he urged her. "Yes, maybe that's what you should do. Write a letter to the Social Welfare, tell them how you feel, and ask for help. I don't know if they'll be able to help, but you can try, you've nothing to lose. I'll help you if you like."

Alice wrote, asking them if they could find Robert, and if they couldn't, would they ask the police to put out a warrant for his arrest.

"You are my last hope. Please help me."

Chapter 8

One cold, snowy winter's day in January, all the children were playing in the field at Rothwell Children's Home, making snowmen and throwing snowballs at each other. Their laughter and screeching could be heard in the kitchen.

"Shelagh," Clara shouted.

"Matron wants to see you in her office."

Wondering whether she had done something wrong, Shelagh went along to see her.

"Come in dear and sit down," she smiled, "your daddy has just telephoned to ask if he can take you out for the day next Saturday. Would you like to go?"

Her little face lit up.

"Oh yes please!" she answered.

She had thought that he had forgotten all about her. She ran out of Matron's office, across the hall and through the kitchen.

"Stop running or you'll fall!" shouted Clara.

"I'm going out with my daddy next week," she shouted to everyone, "can't wait."

"Wish I had a dad to take me out," said Jean, "my mum and dad are dead. They were sick, Matron said they had TB."

For the rest of the day Shelagh skipped around the field saying repeatedly,

"My daddy's taking me out. My daddy's taking me out."

The night before he was due to come for her, she lay awake for hours wondering where they would go and what they would do for a whole day. The following morning, she sat on a bench at the front of the house, never taking her eyes off the gate. The waiting seemed endless, and then she saw him. She ran as fast as her legs would go, jumping up at him, throwing her arms around his shoulders and wrapping her legs around his waist, she wouldn't stop kissing him.

"I've missed you so much," he said, whispering in her ear.

"And I thought you had forgotten me," sighed Shelagh, "have you come to take me home?"

"Not just yet," he replied, quickly changing the subject, "I thought we might go and see your grandma. Would you like that?" She nodded her head, a little disappointed.

"And when we get there," he carried on, "there's a surprise birthday present for you, seeing as I couldn't get to see you on your birthday. Bet you thought I'd forgotten that too." The thought of a present brought a smile to Shelagh's face.

"And how old are you now?" he said, testing her to see if she knew.

"Five," she said smugly, tilting her head to one side, then spreading her fingers as she held up her hand for him to see.

They took a tram to Leeds centre and then another to Seacroft, where her grandmother lived.

As they approached the garden gate, Grandma Gregson came out to meet them. She bent down and gave Shelagh a big hug.

"I've missed you," she whispered in her ear

The smell of home cooking greeted them as they reached the door. Grandma smiled encouragingly,

"I've made a really lovely dinner for all of us." She held Shelagh's hand as they walked into the house, through a small square hall into a neat and tidy sitting room. On the centre wall was a cream tiled fireplace with a fire burning in the grate. A half moon rug lay on the floor in front of the fire. Positioned around the fire were two green leather armchairs. A polished drop-leafed table stood under the window that overlooked a small back garden. On the back wall was a long polished sideboard; a white, cotton embroidered runner lay on top. In the middle of the sideboard stood a large ornamental Alsatian dog.

"There's your present, over there," said her father, pointing towards a brown paper parcel tied up with string, on top of the table.

"You can open it if you like."

She ran over to the table, tearing open the paper in seconds.

"Ooh, can I wear them now?" she said excitedly, unwrapping a long, soft, red, woolly scarf with a fluffy red pompom on each end, and a matching pair of red mittens.

"We'll go for a walk after dinner and then you can wear them," he smiled.

"And here's a little present from me," said Grandma, handing her a small round tin of sweets. "You can have some after dinner."

After they had eaten a lovely meal, Shelagh and her father walked hand in hand to the local park, Shelagh proudly wearing her new scarf and mittens. He pushed her on the swings, and caught her as she slid down and off the small slide. They sat at either end of the seesaw, and played on the roundabout together,

"My turn!" he shouted, running towards the bigger swings that were there for the older children. He scooped her up into his arms as she ran towards him, and then, holding her tightly with one arm, began to swing. The higher they swung the louder they laughed. They were laughing so loud, the rest of the children in the park were laughing at them.

"Time to go back to grandmas," said her father, "its getting dark."

After tea, Shelagh sat on her father's knee, and they sang nursery rhymes he had taught her previously. He told her the same funny stories that he used to tell, and they both laughed and laughed, grandma was laughing too. It was like old times. Shelagh didn't want this day to end. All too soon, however, it was time to go back to the Home.

"I don't want to go back, why do I have to go back? Why can't 1 stay here with you?" she pleaded.

"I'm working away and grandma is too old," said her father sadly. "When I come back, I promise I'll get a bigger house and we'll all be together, don't worry it won't be too long."

Shelagh indignantly pulled a face and her father sighed.

"My mam said that, and I haven't seen her for a long time, when will that be?"

"Soon," he replied, "soon, don't worry, soon."

Again they got the tram to Leeds centre, and then another to Rothwell. They got off near to the Home and walked the rest of the way. Shelagh held her father's hand tightly, and looked up at him as they walked under the gas lit lamp. He wore a black Crombie overcoat, and around his neck hung a long, white, tasselled, silk scarf. She thought how proud she was of him and how much she loved him.

"I'll see you again soon," he said, as he hugged and kissed her, and then handed her back into the safe hands of Mrs Wood. They waved at each other as he walked towards the gate. Turning the corner and out of sight, he began to cry.

Little was Shelagh to know that it would be the last time she would ever see her father.

Chapter 9

"I've got some good news for Shelagh," said Miss Baker to Mrs Wood, on her monthly visit to Rothwell Children's Home. "Mr and Mrs Crampton have asked if she can go and stay with them for a weekend. Mr Crampton is one of Mrs Gregson's older brothers. What do you think?"

"I think it will do her good," replied Mrs Wood, "she's been out with her father only once in nearly a year, and no one else has rung or been to see her. Yes I think she should go."

After seeing Miss Baker arrive and walk into the kitchen, Shelagh ran in from the playing field and into the kitchen, where Miss Baker was sitting at the table talking to Mrs Wood.

"I've got some news for you," Miss Baker said, with a big smile on her face. Shelagh's face lit up with excitement

"Have you come to take me home?" she said, jumping up and down.

"Your Uncle Harry and Auntie Ethel would like you to stay with them for a weekend," said Miss Baker, avoiding the question. Shelagh's face dropped. The disappointment was clear. She stood quietly looking down at the floor. "They have a little girl," Miss Baker continued, "her name is Pat. She's seven, just a bit older than you, and you'll be able to play with her." Shelagh stared at her and said nothing.

"And they have a baby boy, nine months old, his name's Terry and I know you like babies, and if you like it there, they said you can go stay with them during Easter Week. Shall I make arrangements for your Uncle Harry to pick you up next Saturday?"

Not sure whether she wanted to go or not, Shelagh slowly nodded, and walked out of the kitchen, back towards the playing field. It was not the news that she wanted to hear, and wondered again when that would be. Soon she hoped.

Later that evening, Mrs Wood was sitting relaxing in her armchair by the fire, reading the evening paper, when there was a knock at the door.

"Come in," she shouted, folding the newspaper down on her knee, and looking over the top of her glasses towards the door.

"Yes?" she said to Shelagh, who was standing just inside the door, holding her hands together behind her back.

"Janet sez if I go stay with my auntie and uncle at Easter, I won't get an Easter Egg," Shelagh said, with a frown on her face and concern in her voice.

"Did she now. Well you can go tell Janet she's wrong, I'll save you one, and you never know you might get one off your Auntie and Uncle as well. Now off you go," she grinned, giving her a wink and a smile.

Towards the end of Easter Week, Harry, Shelagh's uncle, was watching Pat, his daughter and Shelagh through the kitchen window, skipping in the cobbled back yard.

"I don't want to take her back to Rothwell," he said to his wife. Ethel was standing behind him at the kitchen table ironing. "You should have seen her face when I took her back and left her, it was awful and it upsets me. I've been thinking we could give her a home until our Alice gets on her feet, what do you think?" he asked.

"Well I've been thinking the same," said Ethel, "we'll have to make some changes. She won't be able to sleep with our Pat anymore. She'll have to have a bed of her own, but that's not a problem. Tell you what, I'll ask Miss Baker to come and see us. She'll tell us what to do."

Chapter 10

The following week, Miss Baker set off to see Mr and Mrs Crampton, who lived in a terraced house in the Beeston area of Leeds. Mrs Crampton was standing in the front garden, her arms folded, talking to the next-door neighbour over the privet hedge, when Miss Baker arrived and stepped through the gate carrying a briefcase. It was no surprise to her that she walked into a well presented front room, not unlike so many she had visited on previous occasions during the course of her work. In the centre of the room stood a brown three-piece leather suite, with a piano on the back wall. Through the room door, was a flight of stairs to the left, and coats hung on hooks to the right. A lovely smell of baking greeted her as she walked into the kitchen. She suddenly felt hungry. The kitchen was much the same as all large kitchens, with a black range fireplace, small gas cooker, a deep, white old pot sink, a sideboard, and wooden clothes airier suspended from the ceiling. A freshly made apple pie and a plate of jam tarts were cooling in the middle of the square wooden table.

"There's an awful lot of paperwork to do, and I'll have to have a look around, if that's all right with you," said Miss Baker.

"That's fine," replied Mrs Crampton, "I'll show you around first, then we can sit around the kitchen table and you can tell me what we need to do."

Outside the kitchen door, stone steps led down to a cobbled back yard. Hanging on a washing line that stretched across the yard, spotlessly clean white nappies were blowing in the wind. Behind a wooden latched door, under the steps, was the outside toilet, with cut pieces of newspaper tied with string hung on a hook on the inside of the door. Mr and Mrs Crampton's bedroom was directly above the kitchen, again clean and well presented. In the far corner, Terry was in his cot having his afternoon nap. The bath, where the weekly baths took place, was under the window. Pat's bedroom was above the front room, with a small chest of drawers under the window and a small wardrobe in the recess. Her bed stood in the corner.

"One of my friends has promised me a bedstead if Shelagh's allowed to come and live with us. We wondered if we could borrow a mattress and some bedding? We'd send it back when it's not needed any more," Mrs Crampton asked.

"I'll ask the Committee, when I put your application in and let you know," replied Miss Baker.

After they had eaten a piece of delicious freshly baked apple pie and drank a cup of tea, Miss Baker opened her briefcase and took out a handful of paperwork, laying it on the kitchen table.

"It won't be easy taking on board someone else's child Mrs Crampton," said Miss Baker, pausing for a moment, "it's a big responsibility, especially as you have two of your own. There are terms and conditions to be met and agreed, but I can see there should not be a problem, and it won't be for very long. Ultimately, Shelagh will be under the Care of Children's Department, and I'll visit every month to see how she's progressing. Would it be possible to take her to the Education Department in Great George Street every year for a medical? Asked Miss Baker.

"That's not a problem," replied Mrs Crampton, "I'll take her myself, she can also have the same doctor as us and I'm sure if you need references, he'll give us one and Harry could probably get one from work."

"We'll pay a boarding allowance of 13 shillings a week, plus 9 pence extra for Shelagh's pocket money, and also provide £2 and 12 shillings every three months for any new clothing she might need." Miss Baker further explained.

Pat came bounding into the kitchen from school.

"Is Shelagh coming to live with us?" she shouted in the direction of Miss Baker, "she can go to the same school as me, Rowland Road, and I'll be able to take her and bring her home. She can sleep in my bedroom and I'll look after her. When can she come?" she said excitedly.

"Soon I hope," replied Miss Baker.

After all the relevant forms were signed, Mrs Crampton walked Miss Baker to her car.

"What do you think our chances are?" Mrs Crampton asked.

"I can't see a problem, but I don't have the last say. It's up to the Care of Children Committee. I'll put my report in," she said, with a glint in her eye, "and I'll put a good word in for you. Why don't you give me a ring in a couple of weeks? Hopefully by then a decision will have been made, and I'll be able to tell you something positive." Miss Baker smiled at Mrs Crampton as she drove away.

Two weeks later Mrs Crampton telephoned Miss Baker.

"Good news," said Miss Baker, "the Committee has approved your request and agreed for Shelagh to be boarded out into your care. However, there are a few minor details to be dealt with before she can be discharged from Rothwell Children's Home. She will have to have a medical. I'll make sure she is issued with clothing, and oh, arrangements have been made for a new mattress to be delivered to your house next Wednesday. Hopefully, I'll make a date for her to be discharged the following Saturday. I'll bring her around lunchtime," she announced.

The day of Shelagh's discharge from Rothwell Children's Home finally arrived. She sat excitedly in the front garden on a bench next to Jean, facing the gate, and waiting for Miss Baker to arrive.

"I'm gunna miss you," said Jean, "but I might not be here much longer. Mrs Wood said a Mr and Mrs Walker are coming to have a look at me next week, and if they like me, I might be gunna live with them. Mrs Wood said I've got to be on my best behaviour, so with a bit of luck I might not be here much longer; I'm fed up of being here anyway."

As Miss Baker walked through the gates, Shelagh ran towards her and grabbed her hand. Together they walked into the home towards Mrs Wood's sitting room. After the papers were signed, it was time to leave. Mrs Wood gave Shelagh a brown paper parcel tied with string, containing articles of clothing, with a written list of contents. As they walked towards Miss Baker's car, Jean ran from the playing field to join them. The disappointment on Jean's face was clear. For the past year, she had taken care of Shelagh from the first day that she had arrived, and now that she was leaving, she would miss her dearly.

Miss Baker sat Shelagh on the front seat of her car, and put the parcel on her knee. As she drove away, Shelagh waved to Jean who was waving back, tears now rolling down her cheeks. Shelagh sighed, and wondered if she would ever see her again.

After what seemed an endless journey, they arrived in Beeston just before lunch. The smell of meat roasting in the oven greeted them as they walked in the front door. Mr Crampton was sitting in the armchair in the kitchen, facing the fire, playing with nine-month-old Terry, throwing him up in the air and catching him. Terry was laughing aloud. Mrs Crampton, standing at the small cooker stirring potatoes, invited Miss Baker to stay for lunch. Miss Baker could not resist the smell of roasting meat. Pat sat next to Shelagh and was constantly making a fuss of her, so excited she was to have a sister. After lunch, Miss Baker took a ration book, identity card and more paper work from her briefcase for Mr and Mrs Crampton to sign.

"I'm pleased to say Shelagh has passed her medical and is free of any contagious and infectious diseases, and here is a medical certificate to prove it," she announced. "We have supplied her with a list of clothes, but unfortunately we have not been able to find her a coat to fit her. However, as soon as one arrives at supplies in Easterly Road, I will call and deliver it, hopefully before my next visit."

After signing the foster care agreement papers, it was time for Miss Baker to leave. On her way out, she shouted goodbye to Shelagh, who was upstairs with Pat busy putting her clothes away.

"I'll be back next week," she shouted.

Shelagh was far too engrossed, what with all the excitement of having somewhere to live. Mrs Crampton walked with Miss Baker through the front door, towards her car.

"I normally visit once a month, but I'll be back next week to see how she's settling in, and if there are any problems, please get in touch with me," she said, as she drove away.

One week later, Miss Baker looked at Mrs Crampton's worried face.

"Is there a problem?" Miss Baker asked.

"Well yes there is," replied Mrs Crampton. "Harry and I are really worried about Shelagh. For the first few days, she was fine. After school, she played with Pat down in the yard, but then over the last few days she's become very withdrawn and very quiet. After school, she has tea, then takes herself outside and sits on the top step, and doesn't speak to anybody. Something's obviously worrying her. I've asked her what's wrong, and she just looks at me with those big sad blue eyes, and shakes her head. I don't want to push her. I was hoping by now she would have made new friends in the street. I do realise that she is only five years old and such a lot has happened to her in her short life. We were wondering if you would have a word with her?" she concluded.

"I'll go and join her on the top step and see if I can find out what's troubling her," said Miss Baker.

She found Shelagh just where Mrs Crampton said she would be, on the top step, chewing her nails while staring into space.

"Hello," Miss Baker said, reaching out to hold her hand. "Your Auntie and Uncle are really worried about you. Is something worrying you? Is it your new school?" Shelagh shrugged her shoulders.

"Do you like living here?" she continued, another shrug. Still holding her hand Miss Baker reached out for the other hand, turned Shelagh's face toward her and looked into the deepest saddest face she had ever seen a five year old possess.

"Now," said Miss Baker, "you and I have known each other for a long time, and if something is troubling you, I might be able to help, but I can't help you unless you tell me what's wrong." Shelagh turned her head towards the house, but still said nothing. "I won't tell your Auntie and Uncle," she said, sensing it was something to do with them, "it will be our little secret. Please tell me."

After looking towards the kitchen window for what seemed an eternity, Shelagh turned towards Miss Baker,

"You'll promise it will be our secret?" she asked.

"Yes of course," replied Miss Baker.

Shelagh glanced yet again towards the window, and then, leaning forward slowly, began to whisper very quietly.

"Now that I live in a real big house, won't I be able to see my brother and sisters anymore?" Miss Baker dropped her shoulders, and sighed with relief.

"Oh my dear, is that what it's all about," she answered, "did you really think you would not be able to see them again?" Shelagh nodded. "Why didn't you tell your Auntie Ethel when she asked you what was worrying you?" she asked.

"Cos I thought if I asked them, they would send me back to Rothwell Children's Home, and I didn't want to go back there, so I daren't ask," Shelagh blurted.

"You will always be able to visit your brother and sisters on visiting days just like before," assured Miss Baker. "I will make sure of that, and I know your Auntie will take you to see them. Tell you what, I promise you that every month I will arrange for you to see Tony, Pat and Joyce, but only if you promise me you'll go down those steps, go into the street and make new friends. Is that a deal?" Shelagh nodded. Her sad little face had now become a satisfied one. "Now I've got a surprise for you," said Miss Baker, "come back into the house and see what I have got for you." As they walked through the kitchen door, Miss Baker pointed to a parcel on a chair next to the sideboard. Shelagh rushed over to open the package. Inside was a green gabardine raincoat.

"Try it on," encouraged Miss Baker.

"It fits perfectly," said her Auntie Ethel, "you look lovely. Now you've got your very own coat for when it rains." Shelagh was elated and saying thank you to Miss Baker, as she ran upstairs to look at herself in the mirror.

Whilst she was gone, Miss Baker explained to Mrs Crampton what had been bothering her. She arranged to visit the following month, hoping by that time Shelagh would have made new friends.

After tea the following day, Shelagh nervously walked down the yard steps and opened the back gate, stepping into a long cobbled street. She stood against the wall on one leg with the other foot pressed against the wall, both hands behind her back looking up and down the street. A group of boys, at the far end, in the middle of the street, were playing cricket. Near to where she was standing, a boy and girl around the same age were knelt down, on the flags, playing taws. A pretty blonde girl, who looked the same age as Shelagh was riding up and down the other side of the street on a blue scooter.

"My name's Janice," she shouted, "do you want to have a ride on my scooter?"

From that day on, they became best friends and were inseparable.

Shelagh Flynn

CITY OF LEEDS ~~SOCIAL WELFARE~~ COMMITTEE.
CARE OF CHILDREN
(Boarding-out Sub-Committee)

I, the undersigned, having this day personally

examined...Shelagh Gregson............aged...5......years,
        Children's Homes,
residing at.137, Wood Lane, Rothwell Near Leeds hereby

certify that she is not suffering from any contagious or

infectious disease, and that her bodily health and mental

condition is good^x (with the exception that
        Nil
..............................) and that in my opinion, the case

is in all respects suitable for the administration of relief

by boarding-out.

Signed _____
Medical Officer.

Dated this ____25th____ day of ___April____ 1949.

40

CITY OF LEEDS
CARE OF CHILDREN COMMITTEE

CHILDREN'S HOMES

W. DAY.
Superintendent

F. DAY.
Matron.

Telephone 61870

Central Home,

123, Street Lane,

LEEDS, 8.

6th May, 194 9.

Dear Sir,

Shelagh Gregson.

With reference to your letter of the 29th ultimo I have to inform you that an outfit of clothing, comprising the undermentioned items, has been prepared for this girl and arrangements for her discharge from the Homes for boarding-out purposes can be made forthwith. It is pointed out that it has not been possible to provide a coat for Shelagh and it is presumed that arrangemnts will be made for the purchase of one as soon as convenient.

2 Dresses	2 Combs
3 prs Stockings	1 Hair brush
1 Beret	3 Pinafores
2 Liberty bodices	3 prs Shoes
3 Bloomers	1 Dressing gown
3 Vests	1 Cardigan
1 Tooth brush	6 Handkerchiefs
3 Nightgowns	1 Blazer

Yours faithfully,

Superintendent.

The Children's Officer,
Leeds, 2.

I . . . . of . . . .
do hereby agree with the Council of the County Borough of Leeds that
(a) I will receive . . . . . . Shelah . . . Gregson . . . . . into my home and
feed, clothe and look after her and bring her up as carefully
and kindly as i would a child of my own;
(b) I will help her to become a good citizen, send her to school -
work - and to church - chapel, and to arrange for recreation
suited to her age;
(c) I will look after her health and consult the doctor whenever
the child is ill, and in the event of her serious illness or
accident, I will also notify the Council immediately;
(d) I will provide for the cleaning, mending and renewal of her
clothing and its proper care;
(e) I will at all times permit any person authorised by the Home
Office or by the Council to see the child, her home and clothing, and I will attend to the advice of any such person;
(f) I will allow her to be removed from my home when required by
any person so authorised; and
(g) I will notify the Council within two weeks if I change my
address.

I make this agreement with the Council in consideration of my
receiving the sum of 13/- maintenance allowance per week. all re

I acknowledge having received Shelagh Gregson into my
home on the . . . . . 13th May 1949 . . . and agree that she brought
with her the following articles of clothing and personal possessions:-

No.	List of Clothing	No. Brought	No. Bought
1	Hats Beret		
	Coats		
	Raincoat		
	Gym Slip		
	Blouses		
2	Dresses		
3	Nightdresses or Pyjamas		
3	Vests		
3	Knickers		
2	Liberty Bodices		
3	Socks or Stockings		
2	Boots or Shoes		
	Slippers		
6	Handkerchiefs		
	Gloves		
3	Pinafores		
1+2	Brush and Comb		
1	Toothbrush		
	Suitcase		
1	Dressing gown		
1	Cardigan		
1	Blazer		

Signature of Foster . . . .

Address . . . .

Witness . . G. M. Baker . . . .

Address of Witness 229 Woodhouse Lane, Leeds 2
Children's Officer
229 Woodhouse Lane, Leeds

SHELAGH GREGSON.   "O.M.Baker".

16A   CITY OF LEEDS CARE OF CHILDREN COMMITTEE.

(1) APPLICATION-TO-ADOPT-A-CHILD.

(2)   "   FOR A BOARDED OUT CHILD. SHELAGH GREG

(3)   "   TO-BEFRIEND-A-CHILD-UNDER
           "UNCLES-AND-AUNTS"-SCHEME.

NAMES:-   , Ethel & Harry.

AGES:-

ADDRESS -   , Beeston.Leeds.11.

RELIGION:-   Church of England.

OCCUPATION - Machine Room Foreman at Messrs H.Moore & Co.Ltd.,
              Lady Pit Lane, Leeds.11.
INCOME:-   Approx. £7.0.0. per week.

ACCOMODATION:- Two bedrooms - attic - kitchen - living room.

GENERAL REMARKS:-
Mr. & Mrs.   want to have SHELAGH GREGSON boarded out in
their home - she is the daughter of Mr   sister who
was deserted by her husband.
Mr. & Mrs.   have two children of their own :-
          Patricia Ann - aged seven and a half years.
          Terence - age six months.
They are very fond of children and parioularly Shelagh.
Mrs.   appears to be a very pleasant kindly woman. Her o
little boy was seen and is obviously well cared-for.
          Mrs.   has a single bedstead for Shelagh wh
could share a room with Patricia , but she has not got a mattre
or bedding and asks whether assistance could be given by the
Committee to get the necessary bedding. She would be prepared
take on a loan or to have a mattress on loan.
          The home is clean and well furnished and it is
felt Shelagh would have a good home here. She would attend
Rowland Road School with Patricia who comes home for dinner,
          The following references were given:-

          Dr.   ,
          Victoria Housem,Dewsbury Road, Leeds.11.

          Mr.   ,
          c/o Messrs H.Moore & Co.Ltd.,
          Lady Pit Lane, Leeds.11.

CITY OF LEEDS
CARE OF CHILDREN COMMITTEE

CHILDREN'S HOMES

W. DAY.
Superintendent.
F. DAY.
Matron.

Telephone 61870

Central Home,
123, Street Lane,
LEEDS, 8.

26th April, 1949.

Dear Sir,

Shelagh Gregson - born 18.8.43.

I send you herewith a medical certificate of fitness for boarding-out in respect of the above-named child. I shall be glad of your instructions in connection with the discharge of Shelagh to the care of her Aunt, Mrs

Yours faithfully,

Superintendent.

The Children's Officer,
229, Woodhouse Lane,
Leeds, 2.

Chapter 11

Months later, mothers, young and old, were tending to the needs of their babies in the dining room at Wyther Hostel. Some were sitting in 'Shackleton style' chairs, feeding their babies, while others sat around the dining table, in the middle of the room, chatting. A smartly dressed, uniformed Matron, complete with white starched hat, came towards Alice, who was walking up and down, singing, cradling and rocking baby Robert to sleep.

"There's a 'phone call for you in my office," said Matron, "a Mr Parnell from Children's Care, would like to speak to you; I'll take Robert while you go and talk to him."

Alice instantly stopped singing, her face changed to fear, she could feel her heart beating. Something must be wrong. Something must have happened to the children. Why would he ring? She quickly handed over Robert, and ran towards the office. After what seemed a long time, Alice returned. Robert was now fast asleep in his pram in a corner of the room. She was trembling. Sheer panic and fear was evident.

"Whatever is the matter?" Matron asked.

"I cannot believe what Mr Parnell has just asked me," she gasped, "I just can't believe it." Matron took her by the arm and led her towards the table, sat her down, and again asked, "whatever is the matter?" Alice seemed to be in a state of shock. She sat with elbows on the table, face cupped in both hands, shaking her head.

"He's just asked me if I would allow my children to be fostered," she said eventually. "I know my eldest is alright, she's with my brother, and I know I haven't been to see the others since they went into care, and I know that's nearly a year, but that's only because I'm too scared to go. It breaks my heart just thinking of them. He obviously thinks I don't care and I don't want them. Well he's wrong, I do," she said emphatically. "He said they should be living in the community and that they should not still be in a children's home. He said foster parents are very carefully chosen, and the children will be well taken care of. He's asked me to let him know as soon as possible."

Alice jumped up and began pacing up and down the room, speaking to herself.

"What have I got to offer them? Nothing." She was now shouting and throwing both arms in the air. "Nothing," she shouted again, "I've been dreading this day. What am I supposed to do, what am I supposed to say?"

"Alice, put your coat on and go for a walk," Matron said, "you need to do some thinking. Find a bench, somewhere, anywhere. Sit down and think it over properly and when you come back we'll have a chat."

She walked to nearby Bramley Park, and found a bench to sit on. "I seem to do all my thinking on park benches," she thought to herself. The last time was when she had left her four young children at Street Lane. In the distance, she could see other mothers with young children playing on the swings. She could hear them laughing. She missed her own children dreadfully; they were always in her thoughts. "Joyce must be walking now; I wonder if she's talking? I wonder how many teeth she has?" she pondered, "I hope Pat has put some weight on, poor little thing. I hope Tony has some friends. He's not a very good mixer and he always loved to play with Shelagh. That Meccano Set was always on the flags outside our house." Suddenly a ball landed at her feet. A little boy, around Tony's age, came running towards her. She picked up the ball and gave it back to him.

"Thank you," he shouted, whilst running back towards his mother. The sound of his voice brought tears to her eyes, and she began to cry. Alice had not cried for a long time. She was now crying uncontrollably. The little boy's mother came towards her.

"Whatever is the matter?" she asked, "is there anything I can do?" She sat beside Alice and gave her a handkerchief. Eventually, Alice stopped crying. "Is there anything I can do?" the mother asked again.

"I'm fine now, but thank you for asking and for being so kind." Alice got up, wiped her eyes with the handkerchief, smoothed down her coat, straightened up her shoulders and set off walking back to the Hostel.

"Ready for a chat?" shouted Matron from the kitchen, seeing Alice hanging up her coat in the hallway. Alice nodded. "I'll make us a good strong cup of tea," smiled Matron, "then we'll go to my office. Hopefully we might get some peace and quiet there."

Alice followed Matron down the hall. Before she sat down, she was saying,

"I can't let someone else have my children. If I let them be fostered, I'll never get them back. They're my children, not anybody else's. What if they're fostered with some posh people? They'll get used to having things that I won't ever be able to give them, I won't allow it," she pronounced. "It's now time to do something about it before it's too late. First of all, I need somewhere to live. Do you think that if I wrote to the Housing Committee they would give me a house?" she asked hopefully.

"I don't know Alice. You haven't seen your husband in a long time, and they will worry who will pay the rent, but it's worth a try."

"I'll write to Mr Parnell," resolved Alice, "and tell him that after careful consideration; I don't wish to have my children fostered, my reason being that, in the near future, I have prospects of having a house through the Housing Committee, and hope to have my children back with me."

Chapter 12

On one of her many visits, Miss Baker asked Mrs Crampton if there were any problems, as she always did.

"No problems at all, in fact, quite the opposite," replied Mrs Crampton, "Harry and I have just been to Shelagh's first open day at school. Mrs Barker, Shelagh's teacher is very pleased with her. She said at first she was very quiet and withdrawn, but that was to be expected, what with everything that's happened, and also being her third school in one year. She's learning quickly now," Mrs Crampton continued. "She's reading well, can tell the time and tie her shoelaces. She's come on leaps and bounds. All the children have a nap in the afternoon, and Shelagh is the first to help set out the camp beds and put a blanket on each one. She's also been a class monitor a few times. Anyway, enough of that, I'll go give her a shout," said Mrs Crampton, "she'll be on the 'brick field' with little Janice Ward."

The end of the street looked over a wall down into a large playground containing two sets of swings, slides, seesaws and roundabouts, for both young and older children. Three brick walls surrounded the playground, hence the name 'brick field'. Children came from all around the area to play there. They nicknamed it the "brickie."

Mr Crampton had a small allotment just beyond the 'brick field' where he grew all his own flowers and vegetables. From his allotment, he could see and keep an eye on the children, whilst they were playing.

Shelagh ran as fast as she could down the street, flew up the yard steps into the kitchen and ran straight passed Miss Baker, who was sitting on a chair near the end of the sideboard.

"Look what I've got for my birthday," she shouted excitedly, opening the top drawer of the sideboard and lifting out a skipping rope. "A skipping rope all of my own. Come and see what I can do," she cried excitedly, grabbing Miss Baker's hand and pulling her towards the back yard, directing her to sit on the top step outside and watch. She did as she was asked and watched with enthusiasm as Shelagh began to show just how good she was at skipping. Miss Baker thought it was lovely to see her so happy. When she had stopped showing off, she sat next to Miss Baker on the top step. Now she had a serious look on her face.

"Do you know where my Mother is?" she asked.

"Why?" asked Miss Baker.

"Cos she didn't send me a birthday card, and she hasn't been to see me, so she can't know where I am, cos if she did, she would have been by now, so if you know where she lives, can you call on your way home and tell her where I am, then I know she'll come and see me." Miss Baker's heart was broken. She couldn't tell her that she knew where her mother was and didn't know why she hadn't been to see her daughter.

Chapter 13

In the corner of the dining room at Wyther Hostel, the tree was decorated beautifully for Christmas. Two women stood at opposite corners of the room, twisting cut pieces of coloured crepe paper, ready to be hung from the ceiling. Alice and other mothers were sitting at the table, licking, sticking and looping together the coloured pieces of paper, making a long chain. Matron entered the dining room, handing out the post.

"One for you," she said, handing Alice an official looking envelope.

After Matron had finished giving out the post, she glanced at Alice and noticed a worried expression on her face as she was reading her letter. "I'll be in my office if anyone needs me," said Matron, catching Alice's eye.

Moments later, Alice was knocking on Matron's door.

"Come in," she called.

"It's another letter from Mr Parnell," Alice began, "he keeps sending me letters, asking me to give permission for my children to be fostered. It's been months since that first telephone call. There's not a day goes by that I don't think about them. At night when it's dark, and everyone is asleep, I lie awake crying, wondering what to do. I've been refused a house from the Housing Committee, so it could be a long time before I'm in a position to give them a home. It doesn't matter what I want," she cried. "It's now what's best for them. He's right," she observed, "they deserve better, it's not their fault. He promises me that foster parents will be well chosen, and they will take very good care of them. I hope so; they could be with them a long time." Alice paused for a moment, held her face in her hands, struggling with the enormity of the situation. "I can't let them be adopted." Alice carried on, staring into space, wringing her hands together in anguish. "I'll lose them altogether, and they will lose each other, so I've decided I'm going to let them be fostered."

"I think you are making the right decision," said Matron, softly reaching out and taking hold of Alice's hands. "As you know, lots of the mothers here go out to work and leave their babies behind. We take very good care of them, so why don't you get yourself a job, Think positive and aim to get those children back. Start again, rebuild your life and hopefully in time you can apply for them back."

Chapter 14

Mr and Mrs Hillman, a young childless couple, had applied to be foster parents to a young child. After the Children's Care Committee had successfully approved them, arrangements were made for them to meet Miss Hudson at the St Angela's Nursery, on Street Lane, in the north of Leeds.

After a long journey from Ilkley, on a snowy winter's day, Mr and Mrs Hillman arrived at the nursery cold and wet. They were met by Miss Hudson, an officer to several children at the nursery, and shown into a warm, comfortable, sitting room and offered refreshments. Children's voices could be heard laughing and shouting from the playroom.

After they had biscuits and tea, they were eager to meet all the children. Miss Hudson led them down a long corridor and through a door at the bottom into the playroom. Children, up to five years old, were running around chasing each other, some playing on small slides and swings. Others were dotted around playing with different toys. An assistant was comforting a little girl who was crying and pointing towards another girl, saying she had pushed her down the slide. None of the children seemed to take any notice of Mr and Mrs Hillman, who sat with Miss Hudson around a table, under a large bay window, watching them play.

They were fascinated by all the children.

"What about the chubby little girl over there, in the blue dungarees, playing with a doll and pram?" said Mrs Hillman, "why is she here?"

"Her name is Joyce Gregson," Miss Hudson replied, "she was left here by her mother when she was nine months old, and we haven't heard from her or any her relatives since. She's now two and a half years old. She'd be a good choice, such a lovely child, no trouble, quite happy playing as you can see."

"Is she potty trained?" enquired Mrs Hillman.

"During the day she's dry," answered the officer, a little taken aback at the question, "only needs a nappy at night."

"I didn't really want a child still in nappies, can't be doing with all that mess," Mrs Hillman responded, pulling a face and shaking her head. "Although she is such a cutie, I suppose one nappy at night is not that bad," she said, still staring at Joyce.

"Have you thought about taking two children?" asked Miss Hudson. That's her sister Pat over there, standing beside the sandpit, holding a bucket and spade. She's four next week."

"Do you mean the skinny one?" asked Mr Hillman.

"Yes, we didn't really want to separate them," Miss Hudson replied, "they do have an older sister and brother who have already been separated, although they do all meet regularly on visiting days and it would be nice if the two could stay together."

"Well I suppose it's as cheap to feed two as it is one," said Mrs Hillman, looking backwards and forwards at the two girls.

"We'll pay you two boarding out allowances and give extra for the girls' pocket money, and every three months, we'll send you a clothing allowance for each child to buy any new clothes they might need, so that should help financially," Miss Hudson announced, looking at Mrs Hillman eager to please her.

"I could take Pat to work with me," suggested Mr Hillman, "the fresh air will put some colour in her cheeks, and make them little legs stronger."

He went on to explain that they lived in the country on a large estate, and rented a beautiful cottage from his employer and, in return, he took care of the grounds.

Pat had now abandoned her bucket and spade and was walking towards Joyce.

"What are those spots on Pat's face?" enquired Mrs Hillman pulling a face.

"Oh it's only impetigo," Miss Hudson replied quickly, "she's not been very well lately. Our doctor has seen her, and it's infectious, but it should clear in a week or two. I can assure you that both girls will be given a medical before they are discharged into your care."

"I would prefer our doctor to give them a medical," said Mrs Hillman, looking a little worried. "I'll make the necessary arrangements for our doctor to come here, if that's all right." Mrs Hillman paused for a moment, and then looked at Pat and Joyce. "Just one more question, are the children legitimate?" she asked.

"Yes," replied Miss Hudson, emphatically. Mrs Hillman seemed satisfied.

"Then we'll take them subject to a medical," she concluded.

Two weeks later, Joyce was discharged into their care. It was decided Pat would not be discharged until the impetigo had cleared.

Mr Parnell, Head of Children's Care, always took a keen interest in all the children in his care. He liked to put faces to names, so he visited them whenever he could. He had heard from Miss Hudson that Mrs Hillman had been a little fussy when choosing the children so a little worried and concerned, he decided he would personally take Pat on the day of her discharge. The snow had cleared, and the sun was shining as he drove through the beautiful countryside. Pat was sitting on the seat beside him, enjoying the ride, and every cow and sheep she saw, she shouted and pointed excitedly. When they arrived at the house, he was very impressed. Brooklands Cottage was just like a picture postcard, with a thatched roof, well-tended gardens and a small allotment, where Mr Hillman grew all his own vegetables. His worries disappeared when he saw Mrs Hillman sitting in the garden throwing a ball backwards and forwards to Joyce, who was dropping it more often than she caught it, and they were laughing. Pat quickly took off her hat and coat and dropped them on the lawn. Joyce's face lit up when she saw Pat running towards her, eager to join in. Mr Parnell was delighted to see that Mrs Hillman seemed to be growing very fond of Joyce. He felt happy that the girls would be well taken care of. He knew

Mrs Hillman had no experience with small children, so he told her that if she needed any help or advice, to contact him at his office in Leeds.

Before he left, he gave Mrs Hillman a list of dates and times of visiting days for Pat and Joyce to meet their older sister and brother. He drove away a contented man and wondered if he would ever see the girls again.

They would now be under the care of Bradford City Council.

Chapter 15

Unbeknown to Shelagh and Janice, Miss Baker was leaning with her arms folded on top of the 'brick field' wall, watching them smear candle grease the full length of the small slide to make it more slippery and faster. The loud sound of their laughter made her smile as they slid down and off the end of the slide again and again and again. As they ran towards the roundabout, after they had had enough of the slide, Shelagh saw Miss Baker watching them, so she ran around the bottom of the wall, and stood beside her.

After a short conversation, Miss Baker sensed she would rather be playing with Janice than talk to her. That pleased her, as she wanted to talk to Mrs Crampton without Shelagh being there.

"Off you go and play on the 'brick field' and I'll see you next month," she laughed.

Miss Baker set off walking down the cobbled back street.

"We were wondering if any of your relatives would take Tony to live with them?" she asked Mrs Crampton. "The two younger children are now boarded out and we would rather he lived with his own relatives, I wonder if you could ask around the family, or indeed anyone else?"

"I'll tell you what," suggested Mrs Crampton, "everyone visits my mother-in-law, the children's grandmother, on a Sunday, so we'll make a special visit and ask everyone, and I'll give you a ring Monday."

"Please don't mention it in front of Shelagh," implored Miss Baker, "you know how she is with her brother and sister. We wouldn't want to get her hopes up, would we?"

As promised, Mrs Crampton rang Miss Baker on Monday morning.

"I'm really sorry," she said, "most of the family are out at work all day, and it's felt the children's grandmother is too old to take care of a small boy. She already looks after her elderly, blind husband, and that's enough. So I'm sorry the answer is no, but I'll let you know if anything changes."

"Not to worry," said Miss Baker, "I'm sure someone will come along soon. Thank you for letting me know." She had secretly thought that would be the answer, and after all nobody had been to see the children all the time they had been in care. However, it was worth a try.

Chapter 16

A few weeks later, Mr and Mrs Hawkins applied to Children's Care to foster a young boy. After they had been accepted through the usual channels, Miss Turner, Children's Care Officer, arranged to meet them at the North Park Grange Children's Home for Boys.

On the day of their arrival, Miss Turner could see that they were eager to see all the children. She led them straight away to the big, square playroom. An assistant was in the middle of the room playing, Ring-a-ring-o'roses, with a group of boys. Another group of boys were sitting at a table, helped by another assistant, to cut out paper animals from glossy magazines, and then paste them, with flour and water, into their scrapbooks.

The couple sat quietly for a long time, watching the children play. Mrs Hawkins sat occasionally shaking her head, with a look of concern on her face.

"What about that little boy over there, sat on the floor in the corner of the room, with his back against the wall?" she asked, "the one sitting under the window with his legs crossed. He seems to be in a world of his own, playing with that Meccano Set," she observed.

"That's Tony Gregson, he's five," Miss Turner replied, "and he's been here since he was three, and neither parents nor any relatives have been to see him. He's a very withdrawn little boy," she continued, "and doesn't mix very well, likes to play on his own, always frowning, never smiles, and mistrusts everybody."

Mrs Hawkins took off her coat and handed it to her husband.

"For years we've wanted children of our own, but that seems not to be," said Mr Hawkins, watching his wife walk over to Tony and sit on the floor beside him. "We've decided we could give a child a good home. We live in a lovely three-bedroom house in the Beeston area of Leeds. My wife's elderly mother lives with us. She has the second bedroom, so we do have a spare room. It's so sad," he said, holding his chin and shaking his head as he looked around the room at children playing. "It looks as though she's taken a shine to that little boy," he concluded, looking over at his wife.

"My name's Mrs Hawkins, what is yours?" she whispered, leaning towards Tony. He ignored her and carried on playing with his Meccano Set as though she wasn't there. "Is that a car you're making?" she enquired, watching his small fingers attach a wheel to the object in his hand. Still Tony chose to say nothing. "We've got a car." Still Tony chose to ignore her. "Would you like a ride in our car?"

He stopped what he was doing for a moment, and without moving, he lifted his eyes and looked into her kind face. Now she had his attention. "My husband and I, Mr Hawkins over there, sat with Miss Turner, have a lovely big car," she beamed, "would you like us to take you for a ride, and we could take you to our home for tea, and then you could have a ride back. Would you like that?"

Tony glanced towards Miss Turner. "Shall I ask Miss Turner to make arrangements for you to come for tea next Saturday, and you can bring your Meccano Set with you. Would you like that?" she asked him again. He nodded, still looking at Miss Turner.

"That's the little boy for us," she said to Miss Turner emphatically. "What that child needs is lots of love and kind care and attention," she continued. "We can give him that, and in time he'll learn to trust us. We'll have the child we've always wanted, and you can play football with him in that big back garden," she said smiling, looking appealingly at her husband. "My mother's going to love him. He's going to get spoilt. If we had enough room, we would take them all. Can we take him now?" she asked, with a cheeky grin on her face.

"Organising a full clothing outfit and a medical won't take long," Miss Turner assured, "it's all the paperwork. I'll rush it through as quickly as I can, and yes, I think it will be a good idea for him to spend the afternoon with you next Saturday. It will give him a chance to get to know you before he's discharged," said Miss Turner.

When Mrs Hawkins arrived at the Home the following Saturday, Tony was sitting, swinging his legs, on the highly polished wooden bench in the hall, wearing his best clothes. This comprised of a grey peaked cap, white shirt, grey blazer, knee length grey trousers, held up with red and black striped braces, and polished black lace-up ankle boots. On his knees, he held his beloved Meccano Set. He clasped Mrs Hawkins's hand as they walked towards the car where Mr Hawkins was sitting in the driver's seat, waiting for them.

"Have a good time," shouted Mrs Wilson, the Matron, "and don't forget to be back by seven o'clock this evening."

"Look what I've got," said Tony on his return, showing Mrs Wilson a new football.

"My mother's bought him that, I told you she'd spoil him." said Mrs Hawkins knowingly.

"Time for bed," announced Mrs Wilson to Tony. He climbed up the wide-open staircase holding his Meccano Set and his new ball. As Mrs Hawkins waved at him, he gave her a half-hearted wave back.

A few days later, Tony was discharged into their care.

Chapter 17

When Miss Hudson arrived for work on Monday morning, she was surprised to find Mr Parnell pacing up and down in her office.

"Is there anything wrong?" she asked.

"Yes there is!" he said, shaking his head and looking very worried. "Miss Clark, Children's Care Officer of the two younger Gregson sisters, is most concerned and a bit baffled. She has rung me this morning from her Bradford office. A neighbour of the Hillmans had rung her saying Mr and Mrs Hillman and the girls have moved out of that beautiful cottage a few weeks ago, and she doesn't know where they are. Miss Clark doesn't understand why they've moved and not informed her. They've only had the girls a few months."

"They must have left a forwarding address with a neighbour or someone," said Miss Hudson, "they can't just have disappeared into thin air with two children. They must be somewhere."

With a troubled look on his face, Mr Parnell nodded, and carried on.

"The lady that rang Miss Clark said she'd heard that they'd moved into a fish and chip shop called Robinson, Robertson, or Roberts, or a name sounding something like that, in the Meanwood area of Leeds." He scowled and paused for a moment.

"I don't understand," he said, holding his chin in his hand, shaking his head and looking very puzzled. "They all seemed perfectly happy when I took Pat across."

"Don't look so worried, insisted Miss Hudson; I've known the girls for a long time. Why don't you go back to your office and leave it with me. I'll find them. I'll start with the telephone directory," she said, with a positive look on her face.

Miss Hillman held her hands to her face, and gasped with surprise when she saw Miss Hudson on her doorstep. For a moment, she was lost for words.

I can explain," she said, her lips quivering nervously, and then leading the way up the steps and into a flat above the shop.

"Where are the girls?" asked an anxious Miss Hudson.

"They're in the bedroom playing," Mrs Hillman replied, showing her into the one bedroom. Pat and Joyce were sitting on the floor in the corner of the room happily playing with a large dolls house.

"Look what we've got," said Pat, seeing Miss Hudson's familiar face, oblivious to any problems. "Do you want to play with us?" Miss Hudson glanced around the sparse bedroom as she slowly walked towards the children.

A double bed stood in the centre of the room, with a small single bed in the corner for the girls, and a small worn chest of drawers under the one window that looked out onto the cobbled yard below. Dark brown linoleum covered the floor. Miss Hudson sat on the floor beside the girls and played for a short time. Satisfied that they were happy and safe, she joined Mrs Hillman in the living room, where she had prepared a tray of tea and biscuits. It was still visibly clear that Mrs Hillman was very nervous at her unexpected arrival.

Slowly, she began to explain.

"We were too ashamed and embarrassed to let you know where we were," she began. "We feared you would take the girls back into care. My husband's employer wanted the cottage urgently for a member of his family, so he asked us to leave. We couldn't find anywhere else to live. We were at our wits end. We were offered employment as manager and manageress of this shop, with living accommodation, so we took it. Never thought we would come down to this level," she said, very humbly, shaking her head. "I feel very ashamed for not letting you know, I can't tell you how sorry I am. We've only had the girls seven months and we've grown very fond of them. We don't want to lose them, so please don't take them away from us. Hopefully in time we'll find somewhere better than this," pleaded Mrs Hillman, as she looked around the dingy room, and at the look on Miss Hudson's face.

"Well from what I can see, and looking around, it doesn't look promising," Miss Hudson replied. "You all sleep in one bedroom, there is no running hot water, only one cold water tap, no bath and the toilets are in the back yard, shared with other families. You must have to work all hours, so the children must be left on their own for long periods. There's a public house next door, and when I came, there were men sitting on a wall drinking pints of beer. I saw one man call into your shop, who was obviously drunk, not a good example to young children. However, it's not up to me," she concluded, "I'll have to talk to Mr Parnell, and then I'll be back to you see you."

Having heard that Pat and Joyce were safe, Mr Parnell was furious, but at the same time relieved.

"The accommodation is not acceptable," he declared, as he sat and read Miss Hudson's report. "It's in one of the poorest areas of Leeds. Therefore, for the time being, they'll have to be brought back into care. The problem is what to do with them. They're too old now for St Angela's Nursery, and if possible, I would rather not put them into another children's home just yet. However," he paused for a moment. "Let's not jump the gun. Why don't you visit Mr and Mrs Crampton and ask if the girls could stay with them until somewhere else can be found," he suggested. "It would be nice for them to stay with their older sister, and Tony doesn't live too far away, and it would only be for a short time."

"I think that's highly unlikely," Miss Hudson replied, "none of the family could take Tony before he was fostered, but I'll ask, and I suppose I could ask Mr and Mrs Hawkins. She always seems very obliging. If not, I'm sure Mr and Mrs Hillman would keep them until something turns up."

As expected, Mr and Mrs Crampton and the rest of the family were unable to take Pat and Joyce. Mr and Mrs Hawkins reluctantly said that they would take them as a last resort, but only on a temporary basis.

Miss Clark, Pat and Joyce's Children's Care Officer from Bradford, rang Mr Parnell saying that one of her colleagues from the Dewsbury office had heard, through the grapevine, about Pat and Joyce, and thought she might have the answer to their prayers. A Mr and Mrs O'Brien, who live in a quiet residential area of Dewsbury, had just been approved as foster parents and would like to see the children. If the girls could be taken to head office on a set date and time, she would arrange for them to be introduced to Pat and Joyce.

On a quick, unexpected return visit to the Hillmans, Miss Hudson heard the children screeching with laughter from the back of the fish shop. She walked down the side of the shop and into the small cobbled yard at the back. A scruffy middle-aged man, wearing an old worn dirty suit and a flat cap, was just leaving the outside toilet in one corner of the yard, lighting up a cigarette. Pat and Joyce were laughing and throwing wet mud at each other. On the ground beside them, stood a neat pile of mud pies that they had made previously. Miss Hudson was horrified. They were covered in mud, but were obviously enjoying themselves. Their clothes were dirty, their hair greasy, and they smelt of fish and chip fat. She hurriedly walked back to the shop. Mr Hillman was standing with his back towards her, frying fish. When Mrs Hillman saw her enter, she quickly served all the customers and ushered her upstairs to the flat. When they had sat down, Miss Hudson said.

"Before you say anything we may have found some new foster parents for the girls. It's quite clear you are not coping."

"No, we're not," Mrs Hillman, answered honestly, "in fact, the worry of taking care of them is making me ill. We have to work all hours that God sends. I know they have been neglected, so I'm glad someone else has been found to take care of them. It's not fair on them to be left as they are. I'll bring them to the head office on Saturday morning at ten o'clock," she announced, "so the other couple can take a look at them, if that suits everyone."

Mrs Hillman arrived outside the Children's Care Office in Woodhouse Lane, at ten o'clock sharp, as agreed. Pat and Joyce looked lovely and clean. They were wearing matching red gingham cotton dresses, red cardigans, with white socks and red sandals. Each was wearing a red and white slide in the side of their shiny, clean hair. On either side of her, Mrs Hillman held Pat and Joyce's hands as they climbed the steep wooden steps, then down a narrow wooden floored corridor, that led towards the waiting room. She had brought them here many times before on visiting days to see Shelagh and Tony.

In the waiting room, Mr and Mrs O'Brien were sat on wooden benches, patiently waiting for them to arrive. As they entered the room, Mrs O'Brien jumped up and ran towards Joyce, lifting her up and swinging her around high in the air.

"She's gorgeous," she said excitedly, sitting back down on the bench and cuddling Joyce on her knee. Eyes wide open and scowling, Joyce was staring at the woman, who she did not know, and curious as to who she was. Mr O'Brien reached out his hand towards Pat, now four and a half years old, who ran around the back of Mrs Hillman, holding tightly with both hands and burying her face in the bottom of her coat. Pat also wondered who they were, why she was there and why Tony and Shelagh were not there. Mr O'Brien kept leaning forward, elbows on his knees and bending his head to one side.

"I can see you," he said, catching her peeping at him. They began a game of peek-a-boo. Pat's giggling became loud laughter, and soon everyone was laughing at her. Eventually he coaxed her into letting go of the back of Mrs Hillman's coat and sitting beside him on the bench.

From the office across the corridor, Miss Hudson could hear them. She had purposely left them alone to get to know each other, and from the laughter she could hear, it sounded promising. Eventually she walked into the waiting room. She was pleased to see that Pat and Joyce had taken a liking to Mr and Mrs O'Brien. Mrs Hillman apologised on behalf of her husband for not being there, as he was busy in the shop.

"We'll take them," shouted Mrs O'Brien, not taking her eyes off Joyce. "We could take them now," she said excitedly, bouncing Joyce up and down on her knee. It was obvious to everyone she had taken a liking to the three year old who was still like a baby to her. Mrs Hillman looked at Mr and Mrs O'Brien from where she was sitting, and then at the children. She knew they would be happy and well taken care of. She turned towards Miss Hudson.

"I could have all their belongings ready next Saturday morning," she said, with a sad tone in her voice.

"It will take me a week to take care of the paperwork, and to exchange the children's boarding out and clothing allowances," Miss Hudson replied. "I'll collect the girls next Saturday morning and then take them to their new home."

Miss Hudson collected Pat and Joyce, as agreed, along with their ration books and identity cards. She sat them on the back seat of her car. Their clothes, wrapped in separate parcels, lay beside them.

"Please keep in touch and let me know how the girls are," shouted Mrs Hillman to Miss Hudson, as they drove away. Pat was waving, her face pressed against the side window.

After a long journey, they arrived at the Dewsbury Children's Care Office, where Miss Hudson's friend and colleague Miss Smith, who would be taking over the care of the girls, was waiting. As she climbed into the front seat of the car, Miss Smith leaned over and handed the girls a small white paper bag, each filled with dolly mixtures. They accepted them eagerly and, making themselves comfortable began to eat them.

Towards the end of the journey, Miss Hudson glanced at the girls through her rear view mirror. Joyce had eaten all her sweets and thrown the empty bag on the floor and was asleep in the corner of the back seat. Pat was happily looking out of the window, still eating sweets, one at a time.

Mr O'Brien was in the garden when they arrived, giving the finishing touches to a swing, he had made.

"They're here," he shouted to his wife through the open front door. Mrs O'Brien ran from the house down the path and grabbed Joyce from Miss Hudson as she lifted her out of the car, carrying her towards the house, shouting over her shoulder,

"I'll put the kettle on, and I've made us a lovely chocolate cake."

"Come and have a go on this swing I've made for you," shouted Mr O'Brien to Pat, as he squatted on the path, his arms open wide. Pat quickly let go of Miss Smith's hand and ran towards him. Within minutes, he was pushing her high in the air. She was holding on tight, the wind catching her breath and blowing her hair. She was laughing aloud and loving every minute.

Eventually, it was time for Miss Hudson and Miss Smith to leave. The girls were sitting at the table, Pat daintily eating her second piece of chocolate cake whilst Joyce was busily shovelling her second piece into her mouth with both hands. Her hands and face covered in chocolate.

I'll see you in a month's time, when you visit Shelagh and Tony," Miss Hudson said, though they weren't taking a bit of notice, as they were too busy eating cake. "I've known the children for a long time, any problems of any kind let me know, and I'll try and sort them out and I hope that, this time they're here for good," she said to Miss Smith, as they drove away.

Chapter 18

Miss Baker was well prepared for the questions and hostility she might receive on her next visit to see Shelagh. She was right.

"She's not in," snapped Mrs Crampton. "Every week straight from school she meets Tony and they play in Cross Flats Park, she's always back for tea, you can wait if you want," snapping again, "and seeing as she's not here, can I ask you a few things that's been bothering me," she said very abruptly.

"Here it comes," Miss Baker thought.

"On Sunday we visited Harry's mother and, as I have said before, that's when most of the family visit, and it's a good job we didn't take Shelagh, she spent the day with Tony, because Alice turned up with baby Robert and the new man in her life. His name's Jack seems a lovely man and thinks the world of Alice. She told us that she had applied for all her children to be discharged back into her care. You lot," Mrs Crampton, shouted angrily, "you lot, said she couldn't have her own children back. Can you explain why?" she said. "Because I tell you what, everybody's very angry. Me and Harry thought Shelagh would only be with us a few months, six months at the most, she's been here a year and a half and now you're saying she could be here a lot longer."

Miss Baker began to answer quietly and softly.

"When Mrs Gregson left her four children in Street Lane Children's Home and abandoned them, they then became the responsibility of the Leeds Authority under Section 1, of the Children's Act. We have a duty to make sure they are all fed, clothed and live in good conditions. As much as you all might be very angry, Mrs Gregson cannot give them what they have now. She lives in one room in a poor area of Harehills near the Gaiety Cinema, she has a small child, is co-habitating with a man who is not the children's father and she is expecting another child. We can't allow her to have them back under those conditions, but," she paused for a second, "we did tell her she can re-apply when she has suitable accommodation. Can I also say, she has never visited them, never rang to ask as to their welfare and has never sent any of the children birthday cards."

"It seems to me," still very angry and not listening to Miss Baker, "that once you get your hands on ANY child you don't give them back easily."

Shelagh came bounding into the kitchen.

"Tony's fallen off the see-saw and hurt himself, both his knees are bleeding and he's gone home crying."

That broke the atmosphere between the two women.

"Thank goodness for small mercies," thought Miss Baker. After assuring Shelagh that Tony would be all right, she headed towards her car, relieved that the visit was over.

Chapter 19

A little worried and concerned, and needing expert advice Miss Smith, Pat and Joyce's Children's Care Officer, asked Miss Hudson to accompany her on her next visit to Mr and Mrs O'Brien's, where Pat and Joyce had been boarded out only a few months earlier.

It was a warm sunny day as they drove to Dewsbury. When they arrived, Pat was pushing Joyce on the swing in the garden.

"Problem solved," Mrs O'Brien said, as they entered the house, "won't be a minute," she said, running out of the house up the garden path and down the street. She returned with a small round woman, wearing a grubby wrap-a-round overall, over a well-worn, long-sleeved jumper. Two metal curlers in her grey hair could be seen under the turban wrapped around her head. On her feet, she wore zip-up black ankle slipper boots.

"My name is Mrs Bell and I can take Pat," she said, looking at Miss Smith and then at Miss Hudson. A puzzled Miss Hudson looked at Miss Smith, then Mrs O'Brien, then back at Mrs Bell.

"I don't understand," said Miss Hudson, looking directly at Mrs O'Brien.

"They fight all the time and its wearing me down, Pat's always pushing and shoving Joyce about, I thought I could look after two but I can't, so Mrs

Bell has offered to take Pat, I think it's very good of her, don't you," she said, looking quite pleased with herself.

Miss Hudson held her face in her hands, closed her eyes and began to shake her head.

"I do not believe what I'm hearing, this can't be happening again."

"Don't worry," chipped in Mrs Bell, taking a packet of Woodbines and a box of matches from her overall pocket, lighting up a cigarette, and then folding her arms. "I'll look after her like my own. All mine are married and long gone, I have two bedrooms. Alf and me, that's my husband, have one and my father has the other, she can sleep in the same bedroom as him and I'll put a curtain down the middle."

Miss Hudson looked at Miss Smith with horror. No wonder she wanted a second opinion, for a moment she was lost for words.

"We don't allow girls to sleep in the same room as men," she found herself saying.

"Oh don't worry about that love," continued Mrs Bell, "he's eighty-seven, so he won't live that long, and then she can have that bedroom to herself, and I'll bring her every day to visit Joyce."

"I don't understand all this," began Miss Hudson, "the girls have always played together and I find it very hard to believe that Pat pushes Joyce, the only pushing I've seen is Pat pushing Joyce on the swing, they have always played happily together. There's never been any trouble between them before."

"Well you're not here all the time are you," said Mrs O'Brien, cocking her head to one side, "it's when you're not here that they fight," trying to sound convincing.

"You've only had the children three months," said Miss Hudson, "are you sure this is what you want?"

"Yes it is," she replied, "I'll keep Joyce, but Pat will have to go," she was adamant.

Miss Hudson had always feared this might happen. Mrs O'Brien had always given more affection and attention to Joyce. She wondered if she was subconsciously comparing Pat to her own daughter who had died two years earlier, she would have been the same age as Pat is now.

"You can come and see my house anytime," said Mrs Bell, lighting up another cigarette, "just let me know when you're coming and I'll make sure I'm in."

"Mr Parnell will go mad when I tell him," said Miss Hudson to Miss Smith as they walked down the path towards her car. She was right.

"WHAT," he shouted out loudly, throwing the papers, he had been reading, across the desk. As they landed on the floor, he started to bang on the desk with a clenched fist. "Enough is enough, how much more can these children take, I will not have them separated, it's bad enough the other two are separated, bring them back into care, find a place for them together, I don't care where it is just find one," he glared at Miss Hudson.

"I had a feeling that's what you would say. I have been making enquires; most of the Council orphanages are full. However, I did speak to Miss Ratcliffe, one of the matrons at Headingley Orphanage. It is a private children's home run by charities and local churches. They do occasionally take Council children, and she said she would willingly take the girls. Shall I make arrangements for them there?"

"YES," he replied.

Miss Hudson returned to her office to make the necessary arrangements.

"One more thing," he bellowed down the corridor, "take them off the foster register, indefinitely, it's time they had a few years of stability."

With sadness in her heart, Miss Hudson once more returned to Mr and Mrs O'Brien's for Pat and Joyce. Joyce was sitting on a chair ready with her hat and coat on. Mrs O'Brien began to put Pat's coat on as Miss Hudson entered the house.

"Time to go," she tried to say light heartedly, lifting Joyce's sturdy little frame from the chair onto the floor, then holding her hand.

"Where are we going?" asked Pat, looking up at Miss Hudson.

"To your new home," she answered, reaching out and holding her hand.

"Why?" Pat asked.

"Because Mrs O'Brien can't take care of you any more, so I've come to take you there."

"Don't want to go," shouted Pat quickly, pulling away her hand.

"You'll like it where I'm taking you, there are lots and lots of toys and other children for you both to play with," taking hold of her hand again.

As she walked down the path with both girls on either side, Pat was dragging her feet and then she began to cry. She sat them on the back seat of her car, one in each corner, where they had sat many times before. Their clothes wrapped in brown paper parcels beside them. Pat was now crying uncontrollably and wiping the streaming tears from her eyes with her coat sleeve. Joyce was sitting looking out of the window swinging her crossed legs backwards and forwards. As she drove towards Leeds, Miss Hudson's heart was breaking listening to Pat's loud sobs. She looked through her rear view window, Joyce was pressing her hands and face against the window, and drawing patterns with her fingers in the steam from her breath, she smiled to herself. Pat's small tiny frame was crumpled in the corner, her eyes swollen with crying. She wondered what the future held for these two little girls.

After a long journey, they arrived at Headingley Orphanage, Cliff Road. She drove down the side of the larger main house, past a large oak tree on the right, into a square open concrete yard. At the far side, boys of all ages were playing football. Two girls had tied a piece of washing line to the tree and were happily skipping. Opposite the main house, stood an impressive Tudor style building. She parked directly outside its front door. As usual, Joyce had fallen asleep. Miss Hudson lifted her out and carried her over her shoulder through the open front door, down the hall into the kitchen at the back of the house, and then handed her over to 'Auntie Jean' a young assistant. Then she returned for Pat.

"Go away," Pat, shouted. "Leave me alone," she screamed, now kicking her legs high in the air and throwing her arms around. Miss Hudson was shocked; she had never seen Pat behave this way.

"Come on now," she said leaning into the car and holding out her hand.

"No, go away and leave me alone," kicking and screaming louder. The children in the yard had now stopped playing and were listening to the screams and shouts coming from the car. Miss Ratcliffe, the Matron of the house, came walking towards the car.

"Whatever's going on?" she asked Miss Hudson, as Pat began to scream again.

"And you go away," Pat shouted directly at Miss Ratcliffe. Miss Ratcliffe peered into the car. Pat was sitting stiffly in the corner; as far back as she could get, glaring angrily at the two women.

"I've never seen a child so frightened in all my life, she's terrified and how old did you say she is?"

"Four and a half years old."

"And how many homes has she had since she was born?"

"This is her fifth."

"Fifth," Miss Ratcliffe shouted, "and were those homes all with different people?"

Miss Hudson nodded.

"Then I'm not surprised the child's frightened, I've got an idea." She began walking back towards the house and returned with rag doll in a cradle under her arm.

"You go back into the house, have a cup of tea and leave me with Pat."

Miss Ratcliffe climbed into the car and sat beside Pat, who stiffened even more and glared at her. She took the rag doll from the cradle and handed it to Pat who snatched it out of her hand and held it close to her chest with both arms. After promising Pat she could keep the doll and cradle, she managed to coax her out of the car.

They held hands and headed towards the kitchen. Joyce was now wide-awake and sat at the large wooden table eating jam and bread and drinking cocoa from a small white enamelled mug. Miss Ratcliffe sat Pat beside Joyce.

"Would you like some cocoa and jam and bread?" Auntie Jean asked Pat, she lifted up her eyes and nodded slowly.

"Can Rags have some as well?" Pat asked, turning the rag doll round to face the table and surprising everyone.

"Course she can," she said.

Auntie Jean cut a slice of jam and bread into soldiers then placed them on a small plate in front of Pat. Miss Ratcliffe looked across at Miss Hudson and gave her a wink, a nod and a satisfied smile.

"Don't worry about Pat," said Miss Ratcliffe to Miss Hudson as she was leaving, "I can assure you in a few days time she will be fine."

In the years that followed, everywhere Pat went, 'Rags' as she called her rag doll, was always tucked under one arm or inside her bed.

Pat, Joyce and Miss Ratcliffe

'The Little House'

Chapter 20

Mrs Crampton was very surprised at the unexpected arrival of Miss Baker.

"You were only here a few days ago," she said, looking very worried and concerned. "There must be something wrong. You only visit once a month. It's Janice Ward's birthday today and she's having a party. Shelagh's over there," she exclaimed, pointing towards the house opposite, "shall I go and get her?"

"No leave her there," Miss Baker replied, "it's a shame to spoil her fun."

"I'll have a chat with you and I'll leave you to tell her," she said mysteriously.

Mrs Crampton looked puzzled.

"I've just finished the ironing, as you can see," she explained, "so I'll just clear everything away and I'll make some tea, I could do with a break." She put the large iron kettle on top of the small gas cooker, which stood in the corner near the cellar steps.

She then put the freshly washed and ironed clothes onto the long wooden clothes airer, and with both arms, pulled the pulley up towards the ceiling, tying it to a double hook at the side of the wall in a figure of eight. Then, sitting down beside Miss Baker, with her elbows on the table and her arms crossed, she asked.

"Are the children alright?" she asked puzzled.

"Oh yes they're fine," Miss Baker answered. "All three are settled. We've been doing a check on all the children in care and it appears none of the Gregson's have been registered at the registry office when they were born, so I've been and got them all a birth certificate, and," she said, screwing up her face, "I'm afraid it was Shelagh's birthday two months ago."

"So are you saying she's been having the wrong birthday for nearly three years?" replied a shocked Mrs Crampton.

"Yes," answered Miss Baker, quietly.

"How can you get such a thing wrong, when you're so keen on so many forms and papers to fill in and sign," said Mrs Crampton, shaking her head.

"We don't always get everything right, and we're not perfect," Miss Baker replied, feeling hurt and solely to blame.

"Can I say," she carried on, "that if the parents had ever sent her a birthday card, which they haven't, they would have sent it on the correct date and we would have realised our paper work must have been wrong. Then we would have corrected it. So some of the fault lies with the parents, and it could have been worse. At least we got the right year! I have let the Medical Education Department in Great George Street know, and all our records are now up to date, so could you let her doctor and school know, and more importantly could you let Shelagh know when her birthday is and that she was seven two months ago, she concluded.

"I will, but I can't see the point of her having a birthday this year," Mrs Crampton answered angrily, "it's too late now, I'll just tell her that there's been a big mix up and we'll make it up to her next year."

Shelagh and Janice were racing each other on their scooters up and down the path in the cobbled back street.

"Miss Baker's at the top of the street with a new lady," shouted Janice. Shelagh threw her blue scooter, that she had received the previous Christmas, on the ground and ran towards them, grabbing Miss Baker's hand and looking up at the tall, new woman.

"This is Miss Hudson and she will be visiting you from now on," Miss Baker explained.

"Mr Parnell is a very busy man and he has asked me to help him in the office."

"I visit Tony, Pat and Joyce every month, so we thought it would be nice if I visited you and then I can tell you all about what they're doing," said Miss Hudson, leaning down with her hands on her knees. With a strange look on her face, Shelagh looked up at Miss Hudson, then Miss Baker, then again at Miss Hudson, then back again at Miss Baker,

"Won't you be coming to see me anymore?" she asked. "No, but don't worry, Miss Hudson will tell me every month how you are."

Shelagh quickly pulled her hand away and stood back. Then, turning her back towards them, she began walking away, slowly dragging her feet down the street, chin resting on her chest, towards Janice, who had picked up her scooter and was leaning against a wall.

"Well that went down like a lead weight," said Miss Hudson, "I didn't expect that."

"She's sulking," Miss Baker explained, "don't worry she'll come round in time. It's quite natural for her to feel hurt, and she'll feel as if I've let her down. I'll take you to meet Mrs Crampton."

They walked down the street and through the gate into the back yard.

"In time you'll know by Shelagh's face if something's on her mind," Miss Baker continued. "Between you and me, I find if you sit on the top step and get her to sit beside you; she'll tell you all her worries. Usually it's about her mother, father, brother and sisters. In fact, that is all she talks about and when they'll all be back together. If that will ever happen," she sighed, shrugging her shoulders. "What's in your favour and gives you a head start, is that you visit them every month. Be patient, and in time, I'm sure she will confide in you, as she has in me over the years."

The following month, Miss Hudson set off on her first visit to see Shelagh, not sure what sort of reception she would receive when she got there.

"She's upstairs getting ready for Brownies," Mrs Crampton explained to Miss Hudson. "She and Janice joined two weeks ago. Come in," Mrs Crampton shouted to a gentle knock at the door, "that'll be Janice now."

Shelagh ran down the stairs into the kitchen, muttered an hello as she passed Miss Hudson and headed towards Janice who was stood in the doorway waiting for her.

"My, my, don't you two look smart?" Miss Hudson remarked on their appearance.

They were wearing long-sleeved brown cotton dresses, yellow ties, white ankle socks and brown sandals. Around their waists both girls wore thin brown leather belts, and on their heads brown woolly hats. Janice stuck out her chest, held her shoulders back and lifted up her head showing off her new brownie uniform. Shelagh just wanted to leave as quickly as possible and get to the meeting as soon as she could.

"Why don't you walk to the end of the street with the girls?" suggested Mrs Crampton, tilting her head to one side and giving her a wink. Shelagh looked daggers at her auntie Ethel not wanting any part of Miss Hudson. She missed Miss Baker.

"I used to be a brownie when I was a little girl," said Miss Hudson, as they walked up the cobbled street.

"Did ya?" said Janice, "we love it, don't we?" elbowing Shelagh in the side. "We play games and sing campfire songs around pretend campfires, don't we?" she persisted, glaring at Shelagh. "Brown Owl's called Miss Shepherd and she's a Sunday school teacher at church, so we're going on Sunday aren't we?" she continued, elbowing Shelagh in the side again. "We're both pixies and are in the same team." Janice pointed towards a small pixie badge sewn neatly above her left breast pocket.

"Well that's very strange, what a coincidence," remarked Miss Hudson. "I used to be a pixie when I was a little girl and I used to go to Sunday school."

"Bet ya don't remember the brownies anthem," said Janice, with a twinkle in her eyes.

"Oh yes I do, shall we all sing it together?" Miss Hudson suggested. Then she and Janice began to sing the anthem.

"O Lord this week,

Help brownies seek," they sang cheerfully.

Shelagh could not keep quiet any longer and joined in the last two lines.

"Good deeds to do,

and to be true,

Ding-dong."

By the time they had finished singing, they had reached the top of the street.

"Can I come and see you next month?" Miss Hudson asked. Shelagh shrugged her shoulders. "Well a shrug was neither a yes nor a no," decided Miss Hudson, "it was a start, better luck next time." She stood and watched the girls both holding hands and skipping across the front of the 'brick field' shouting "ding-dong" loudly and laughing. She was pleased that they had developed a special kind of friendship.

One night, Pat, Shelagh's cousin, was laid in bed, propping up her head with her hand, watching Shelagh kneeling at the side of her bed. Her elbows were propped on top of her bed with her chin resting on her chest, and her nose touching her hands that pressed together.

"What are you doing?" Pat asked.

"I'm saying my prayers to God, I want to ask him something," replied Shelagh.

"What are you asking for?" Pat asked.

"Can't tell ya, it's a secret and it won't come true if I tell ya, so I cant," she cried, jumping into bed and hiding under the pillow and pulling the blankets over the top, so Pat could not see or hear her. With her knees bent up to her chest and her hands pressed together, she began to whisper quietly.

"Dear God, Miss Shepherd sez you can make things happen. Miss Baker has been trying to find my mother and father for ages and can't. So, can you find them please, and can you find them a big house and tell them where I am and then they can come and get me. I've been here a long time. I want to go home now. Can you tell them where Tony, Pat and Joyce are and they can get them too, and there won't have to be visiting days any more, cos we'll all be back together again. Just in case you're not in your office and you haven't heard me, I'm gonna say my prayers every night until you do. Thank you, Amen. Oh and if you find them God, I promise to be good and I'll never be naughty again. Thank you again. Amen."

Shelagh and Cousin Pat

Chapter 21

One warm, sunny day, Miss Ratcliffe was rocking backwards and forwards in her rocking chair on the veranda, watching all the children in the home playing in the yard.

"Come and sit beside me," she said to Miss Hudson, who was walking across the yard.

"I love watching them play," Miss Ratcliffe remarked, "it gives me a feeling of satisfaction listening to them laugh. They all come from different backgrounds and, all because of very different circumstances. Some still have parents. Eventually they'll be returned to them. Some are orphans, due to the war and illness. Many were abandoned and those are the ones I worry about," she said, with a worried look on her face and shaking her head. "One day they'll leave here to go to work and more foster parents will have to be found. We'll be sending them into the unknown. It won't be easy for any of them, but in the meantime, we'll try and give them as good a childhood as we can."

Miss Hudson's eyes searched round the yard and found Joyce's sturdy little body at the side of a group of girls playing hopscotch. She was pushing a tiny doll's pram, looking as pretty as a picture, dressed in long blue dungarees, turned up at the bottom several times, a white short-sleeved blouse, with a blue ribbon tied in a bow in the side of her short bobbed hair. Occasionally she would stop, throwing the doll's blankets on the ground, re-arrange the doll's position, then replace the blankets. With shoulders back, she would continue her journey pushing the pram proudly around the large, square concrete yard.

"If you're looking for Pat, she's over there," remarked Miss Ratcliffe, pointing to the far corner, "she's wearing blue shorts and a blue cotton blouse, with her back to us, skipping away. She prefers to play on her own. She's thinner than most and gets pushed about easily."

"Is that Rags under her arm?" enquired Miss Hudson.

"Yes it is," replied Miss Ratcliffe, "I don't know how she manages to skip like she does with that rag doll wedged under her arm but she does. Last visiting day, Shelagh brought Pat a skipping rope and spent most of the visit teaching her how to skip. When it was time to leave, she gave it to Pat as a present. She uses it every day, and when she's finished with it, she wraps the rope neatly round the handles, runs inside, then upstairs and hides it under her pillow, so the other children won't pinch it." They both laughed.

Suddenly there was a loud scream. A young boy had pushed little Robert to the ground from his tricycle and was riding on it around the yard. Within minutes Andrew Kelly, one of the older boys, ran across the yard and picked up Robert, dusted him down, grabbed George, and gave the two boys a good talking to. Within minutes, the two boys were taking it in turns to ride the tricycle.

"That's what I like to see," noted Miss Ratcliffe, "no need for me to interfere. Andrew Kelly is very good at that sort of thing. The older boys and girls are always there if any problems arise."

"That reminds me," butted in Miss Hudson, watching the boys. "I visited Tony yesterday and he's come on leaps and bounds. He's a changed little boy. It's amazing what a bit of tender loving care can do. It works wonders. I remember when he wouldn't look or talk to anyone," she went on. "He always looked so serious. All we ever got was a yes or a no if we were lucky, but now," she said, holding her hands in the air, "you wouldn't know it was the same little boy, he can even string a conversation along. Yesterday he was showing off doing cartwheels around the back garden and laughing. Mr and Mrs Hawkins and Mrs Schofield, Mrs Hawkins's mother, have worked miracles. All the family think the world of him. They won't want to give him up if the parents ever come back for him," she concluded.

"I can't see that happening for a long time, can you?" Miss Ratcliffe answered thoughtfully, looking at Pat and Joyce. "No one has ever been to see them on the mother or father's side, so I think that's highly unlikely don't you?"

Chapter 22

One Friday morning, Mrs Crampton, Shelagh's aunt, ran to the kitchen door and shouted to Pat and her cousin Shelagh, as they were racing each other down the yard steps on their way to school.

"Don't forget to run home as fast as you can at dinner time," she called. "Pat, it's your turn to go to the dairy for extra milk, and it's your turn Shelagh to go to the fish shop. Your Uncle Harry and Uncle Frank only get an hour for dinner. The quicker you get there the less you'll have to wait, and you know what the queues are like on a Friday if you don't get there early."

Uncle Frank was one of Mr Crampton's younger brothers and they both worked at the same tailoring firm not too far away. Fish and chips were for the adults, while Pat and Shelagh had a bag of chips with scraps accompanied with freshly buttered new oven cake that Mrs Crampton had baked that morning. Sitting in his high chair at the side of the table, Terry was playing with a bowl of cut chips occasionally taking a bite of buttered, new cake soldiers.

"Jesus shared two fish amongst thousands of people on a mountain," Shelagh said unexpectedly, looking at her uncle Frank who was sprinkling salt and then shaking vinegar over his fish.

"Who told you that?" asked her uncle Harry, slapping half of his fish and a few chips in between two pieces of new cake, making a sandwich.

"Miss Shepherd at Sunday school," she replied, "and Jesus shared five loaves of bread amongst millions and zillions of people as well, and that's what you call a miracle."

"Do you know any more miracles?" asked her uncle Frank. She nodded as an answer, having a mouthful of chips, scraps and new cake.

"Yes I do," she said, after swallowing the contents of her mouth. "There was once a very, very old man who had never been able to walk and Jesus laid his hands on his shoulders and said "get up and walk," and de ya know what?" she said confidently, "the old man got up out of his wheelchair and began to walk, and that's another miracle."

Her uncle Harry almost choked on the mug of tea he was drinking.

"A wheelchair!" he spluttered and shouted, and then they all began to laugh. "Tell her Ethel," he said.

Hurt and embarrassed Shelagh ran from the table and hurried upstairs.

"We shouldn't laugh," remarked Mrs Crampton, "she takes Sunday school very seriously. In fact, she's just been presented with a lovely green Bible with her name inscribed inside the front page. I'll go upstairs in a minute and explain to her wheelchairs hadn't been invented then, and it probably would have been a stretcher or a bed."

Miss Hudson felt uneasy and nervous as she walked down the cobbled back street. It was ghostly quiet, not a child to be seen or a noise to be heard.

"Where are all the children? You can hear a pin drop out there," she asked Mrs Crampton, as she was invited into the kitchen. Mrs Crampton beckoned her over to the cellar steps and held a finger to her closed lips. They tiptoed quietly down to the cellars. She couldn't believe her eyes when they reached the bottom. She held her face between her hands and gasped with amazement. The cellar underneath the front room had been converted into a small picture house. Children of all ages were sat on rows of seats, watching and laughing at cartoons on a large screen at the front. Behind the children, Mr Crampton was operating the large projector. He caught Miss Hudson's eye and gave her a knowing wink.

Back in the kitchen, Mrs Crampton explained that her husband had bought the seats, screen, projector and films from nearby Parklands Cinema that had closed down, and had converted the cellar into a small cinema.

Every week the children of the street would queue in the back yard. Mr Crampton would give each child two sweets and show them to a seat.

"They should be out soon," Mrs Crampton, said proudly, "would you like to wait? I know Shelagh wants to see you," she added, filling the kettle and placing it on the gas cooker. Miss Hudson smiled.

"I'll sit outside and wait for her on the step, and listen to the quietness."

A short time later, the children ran through the yard pushing and shoving each other. Within minutes, the street had come back to life with the noise of children laughing and shouting. Shelagh's small body sat on the top step beside Miss Hudson, leaning into her knees and proudly showing off the small green Bible that she had received from Sunday school. Proudly she pointed to the inside page where her name was inscribed.

It had taken Miss Hudson a long time to gain Shelagh's trust but eventually she had succeeded.

"Miss Shepherd sez I'll get a hymn book all of my own soon and it'll have all the hymns we sing at Sunday school in it, even my favourite. Shall I sing ya my favourite?" she asked, with a sparkle in her eye. Miss Hudson smiled and nodded. Shelagh began to sing.

"Jesus loves me this I know,
For the Bible tells me so,
Little ones to him belong,
They are weak,
But He is strong,
Yes, Jesus loves me,
Yes, Jesus loves me,
Yes, Jesus loves me,
The Bible tells me so."

Miss Hudson could see by the words in the hymn why it was her favourite. Suddenly, Janice came bounding through the gate shouting and jumping up and down.

"Quick, tell your Uncle Harry, Molly's at the bottom of the street," Janice cried.

"Molly, who's Molly?" asked Miss Hudson.

"Molly's the big horse that pulls the cart round the street that sells apples and oranges and loads of other things," explained Shelagh. "If Janice and me fill the bucket with manure for his allotment, we get threpunce each. So I'll have to go, cos if we don't get there quick it's all gone," she yelled, jumping up and running back into the house. Within minutes, she was back with a bucket and two shovels.

"See you next month," Miss Hudson shouted to Shelagh, as she ran down the steps and handed Janice a shovel. She could hear the sounds of the bucket and shovels clanging together as they ran down the street.

Chapter 23

Whitsuntide was a time when children wore new clothes, visited neighbours in the street and were given halfpennies and pennies for looking smart in their 'whitsy clothes', as they were called.

"Don't be long," shouted Mrs Crampton to Pat and Shelagh as they ran down the yard steps, eager to show off their new clothes to the neighbours. Pat wore a white and lemon cotton dress, a blue coat trimmed with a black velvet collar and black velvet buttons, with white socks and white sandals. On her head, she wore a peaked blue hat trimmed with black velvet that tied with straps under her chin. Shelagh wore a white pleated tennis dress, and a hat and coat identical to Pat's, only in red, with white socks and a pair of black patent shoes fastened at the front with a button.

"It's a long way to Grandma and Granddad Crampton's and we said we would be there before dinner," Mrs Crampton shouted to the girls as they ran through the gate.

When they arrived there later that morning, most of the family had arrived. Granddad Crampton was sitting in his armchair in the corner of the sitting room giving all his grandchildren a silver sixpence.

"Come and get your dinner children," shouted Grandma from the kitchen. She was standing at the end of a well-scrubbed wooden table, cutting Yorkshire pudding into small square pieces from a large black meat dish and placing them onto plates in the middle of the table. Then she began to ladle rabbit stew over the top of the Yorkshire pudding from a large stew pan that had been cooking on top of the fire for most of the morning.

"Don't want that, don't like it," shouted Shelagh, covering her plate with both hands.

"More for others," said Grandma, looking at her sternly. From where she was sitting, she could see through the open kitchen door into the sitting room, more aunts, uncles and cousins were arriving. Suddenly she froze. Staring into the sitting room, she couldn't believe her eyes. Her mother had just walked into the sitting room holding little Roberts's hand, and behind her, a tall dark man was carrying a baby girl. Shelagh dropped her knife and fork on the floor, quickly moved her chair away from the table with a scraping noise and ran towards her.

"Where've ya been? Where've ya been?" she cried again and again excitedly. "Everybody's been looking for you," she wailed, wrapping her arms around her mother's legs. "Where's my daddy?" Shelagh pleaded, her eyes wondering over to the strange man standing behind her mother. "I've been asking everybody to look for you, have you come to take me home?" she asked appealing. Alice looked round the room to see if anyone was watching or listening to Shelagh's non-stop questions.

"I don't know where your daddy is, nobody does," Alice muttered, leaning down and whispering to Shelagh, whose arms were still wrapped around her legs.

"Are you taking me home with you?" Shelagh begged again, jumping up and down excitedly.

"I can't take you home just yet," Alice said coldly. Shelagh pulled away and stepped back, puzzled.

"Why?" she pleaded.

"Where we live there's not enough room for all of us," exclaimed her mother "I'm trying to get a bigger house so we can all be back together again."

"You've been saying that for ages, when will that be?" said Shelagh, with tears in her eyes.

"I don't know," her mother replied.

Hurt and feeling rejected, Shelagh ran through the kitchen and out of the back door and sat on the grass in the middle of the garden.

Different thoughts were swimming around in her head. She did not know what to think. After a while, she walked back into the kitchen and began peeping from behind the door. From where she was standing, she could see her mother laughing and playing with her little brother. She looked across at the tall dark strange man who accompanied her mother and who looked very much like her father. However, it wasn't him.

"I wonder why she doesn't want to play with me," thought Shelagh, "I must have been naughty and done something really bad, and that's why she doesn't care about me, but I can't remember what it is. I can tell she doesn't love me any more." She brushed away a tear with her sleeve. She did not want anyone to see her cry. "I'm fed up of crying at night," she thought, "it's never got me anywhere before, so I'm not going to cry anymore."

Later that evening in the comfort of her bed, hidden under the pillow, Shelagh closed her eyes and held her hands together.

"Dear Jesus," she whispered, "I think I've been saying my prayers to the wrong person, I asked God to look for my mother and she's been there all the time. So can you help Jesus, can you help me? Please can I go live with Pat and Joyce at the Orphanage, cos my mother doesn't want me anymore, and I don't think my auntie and uncle like me anymore either, cos I'm always getting into trouble. My mother sez she doesn't know where my father is. I must have done something bad. That's why she doesn't love me anymore, and I can't remember what it is. She can't love Tony, Pat and Joyce anymore either. So can I live with Pat and Joyce cos it's my job now to look after them? So Jesus, if you let me go live with them, I promise never to be naughty ever again and I'll look after them all for ever and ever, thank you. Amen." She began to cry. Eventually, still crying, she fell asleep.

Chapter 24

Months later, Miss Hudson received a telephone call asking her to visit urgently, preferably while the children were at school. Mrs Crampton was pacing up and down the kitchen floor shaking her head and wringing her hands together. Miss Hudson put her coat on a kitchen chair and then sat down, not sure what to expect.

"I can't take much more of this," Mrs Crampton sighed, still pacing up and down and staring at the floor. "I don't know what to do."

"Just sit down and tell me what's wrong," invited Miss Hudson.

Mrs Crampton sat down at the opposite side of the table, and began.

"This has been going on for months, you must have noticed," she said, glaring at Miss Hudson "Shelagh's not the same little girl she used to be. She doesn't speak for days at a time. She sulks and she's moody. I have asked her repeatedly what's wrong. She just holds her hands together behind her back and stares down at the floor. She's turned into a very difficult child. I wondered if you would have a word with her, as she talks to you?" she added.

"Yes I have noticed." Miss Hudson replied. "She did tell me her best friend Janice, her brother and parents have gone to live in a corporation house in Seacroft. She misses Janice dreadfully. Just give her time to make new friends and I'm sure she'll be alright."

"There's more to it than that," Mrs Crampton snapped again. "It all started a few months ago when she saw her mother for the first time in over three years and probably realised she might not see her or be going back to live with her for a long time, if ever. She's worse after visiting days when she's been to see her brother and sisters. She doesn't speak for days. She's lost loads of weight and she's obviously not happy. She has a strange look in her face and a very faraway expression in her eyes. If she doesn't change her attitude, you'll have to take her back into care. After all, she was only supposed to be here six months. I know she misses Janice but she won't even attempt to make new friends. She comes in from school," Mrs Crampton continued to complain, "she doesn't speak, sulks, picks and pikes at her food, then either sits out there," tilting her head towards the outside door, "or sits on the flags outside feeling sorry for herself, until it's time for bed. You'll have to do something about it," she pleaded, her hands shaking. Nervously she lit up a cigarette from the mantelpiece, and then continued to reel off complaint after complaint. Miss Hudson sat very still, not saying a word, and feeling extremely uncomfortable.

"I'll have another talk with her," she suggested, when Mrs Crampton had finished, "and if I don't seem to be getting anywhere, I'll make an appointment for her to see Mrs Hughes the Child Psychiatrist. It's obvious something else is worrying her," said Miss Hudson, deeply concerned.

The Ringtons man, with his weekly delivery of tea, saved the day. Miss Hudson got up to leave, saying she would ask Mr Parnell and Miss Baker for advice first before she referred Shelagh to a psychiatrist. Then politely, she said goodbye and left.

Chapter 25

Mr Parnell pushed the chair he was sitting in away from his desk, stretched out his legs and crossed his feet, then with both hands, threaded his fingers through his hair holding his hands together at the back of his head. Miss Baker sat on a chair under the window with her legs crossed, and her gold-framed glasses perched on the end of her nose.

"We're listening," he barked, looking directly at Miss Hudson, who sat opposite them.

"I did explain when I asked you to see me," Miss Hudson began, "it's about young Shelagh Gregson, I've had a stream of complaints about her." She went on to tell them the problems Mrs Crampton had said that she was having with the girl. "But I think," she paused for a moment and continued. "There's more to it than meets the eye. I get a feeling that Shelagh has outstayed her welcome and she's not wanted any more. I think Mrs Crampton is missing her privacy and while ever she has Shelagh, she will not have any. From her point of view, I can see where she's coming from. It cannot be easy. I turn up at anytime, any day of the week, unannounced, and there is many a time I know I am in the way and not welcome. A few weeks ago, I went upstairs to check that the sheets and blankets were clean and she followed me and leant against the wall with her arms folded watching me, I could tell by her face she was angry. Then there's the trailing down to Great George Street, when her medical is due. I think it's all become too much," said a very worried Miss Hudson, not stopping for breath.

"I did notice when I read her case notes that she's missed a few visiting days to see her brother and sisters." Mr Parnell interrupted.

"Yes and when that happened I did ask why," agreed Miss Hudson. "Mrs Crampton just shrugged her shoulders and said she'd forgot. She also said something I found quite strange. She said that Shelagh never showed any affection toward them. However, I've never seen any given, and to my mind, it has to be given to be received. Overall, I do not think they are particularly fond of her and the social services system. I've come to ask for your advice as what to do next." She looked backwards and forwards at them both appealingly.

"Well you've known her for a long time now," explained Miss Baker, "and I think you should do what you think is the best for everybody all round, whatever that may be. When you've decided what that is, just let us know and it will be fine by us. What do you think?" she asked Mr Parnell, who was walking across the floor to answer the telephone that was ringing on his desk."

"I agree," he said, nodding.

Feeling sad and lonely, Shelagh sat on the flags in the cobbled back street, leaning against the wall, her chin resting on her bent knees. She jumped up and ran towards Miss Hudson when she saw her walking down from the top of the street, and grabbed her hand.

"Would you like to go and live with Pat and Joyce at the Orphanage," Miss Hudson asked to Shelagh's surprise. Shelagh could not believe her ears, and looked over both shoulders to see if anyone was listening or watching.

"Will I get into trouble if I say yes?" she said quietly.

"Of course you won't," Miss Hudson replied, dropping her briefcase on the ground and then kneeling down in front of her. "Because if you would, there is a place for you. If that's what you really want, I can take you there on Saturday. Would you like that?"

Shelagh nodded slowly, threw her arms around her, laid her head on her shoulder and began to cry, within seconds, she was crying uncontrollably. Miss Hudson wrapped her small body in her arms and with a lump in her throat and a tear in her eye, she wondered when was the last time Shelagh had been given a cuddle or told that she was loved. She suspected it had not been for a very long time.

Chapter 26

It was raining heavily as Miss Hudson began the long drive to Headingley Orphanage. She smiled pleasantly to herself, listening to Shelagh's non-stop chatter as she jumped up and down on the seat beside her.

"Couldn't sleep last night, couldn't wait for today, thought it would never come," Shelagh said, hardly stopping for breath. "I've been so excited and I've got some presents for them," she continued, leaning forward and reaching into the brown paper carrier bag wedged between her feet on the car floor. After rummaging in the bag, she pulled out a misshapen, multicoloured, hand made knitted scarf with different sized pompoms at either end.

"My cousin, Pat taught me how to knit a line, and pearl a line and I made this for meself," Shelagh said, proudly sticking her head in the air and wrapping the scarf around her neck. "So I'm going to give it to Joyce. Look what I've got for Pat," she carried on excitedly, reaching into the carrier bag again, and lifting out a small bobbin with four small nails nailed into the top. "I'm going to show her how to do cork wool."

She then emptied all the contents of the carrier bag onto the floor and grabbed another bobbin with a small ball of red wool wrapped around the four nails, lifting it high in the air. Protruding from the small hole underneath were yards and yards of different coloured cork wool.

"Are we nearly there?" she asked, eagerly leaning forward and shoving everything back into the carrier bag.

"Yes we are," replied Miss Hudson, "what are you doing with a small jar of Vaseline in your bag?"

"Oh that's what I clean my shoes with," Shelagh explained, "it makes them ever so shiny." She lifted both feet up together to show off her shiny patent shoes.

Miss Hudson was enjoying this journey. She had made so many unhappy trips ferrying children backwards and forwards, most of them heartbreaking. This one was different. She glanced at Shelagh, who was now sitting relaxed, her arms wrapped around the carrier bag, as she looked out of the window, enjoying the view.

It was raining when they arrived. Miss Hudson drove her car down the side of the house into the yard at the back. Some of the older children were playing table tennis on an old table under a wide, open fronted, corrugated shed at the side of the yard. Shelagh feeling a little frightened and nervous, got out of the car, ran and grabbed hold of Miss Hudson's hand. As they walked together towards the front door of the big house on the far side of the yard, they could see Pat's face pressed up against a window. They waved to each other.

As Miss Ratcliffe was inviting them in, the tall grandfather clock, in the hallway, was striking three. They followed her through the hall and into her sitting room on the left. Miss Ratcliffe invited them to sit down, pointing towards two smart armchairs under the bay window that looked out onto the square concrete playing yard. The room was filled with different shaped armchairs dotted around the guarded fire.

A small television sat on top of a cupboard at one end of the fireplace. Miss Ratcliffe's rocking chair was purposely positioned at the other end so that she could see and face everyone who spoke to her. Cluttered on the floor around her chair were piles of untidy newspapers and magazines. Behind the chair, piled against the wall were different size cardboard boxes. Placed beside her, a knitting basket full of different sized knitting needles and hanks of wool waiting to be wound into balls. On top of the basket lay a partially knitted garment wrapped around two needles. Within minutes, there was a gentle knock at the door.

"Come in Pat," Miss Ratcliffe called. "She's been waiting all morning for you to arrive," she remarked, looking across at Shelagh.

"Can I show her around?" Pat asked, grabbing Shelagh's hand.

"Yes you can," agreed Miss Ratcliffe, "it will give us time to have a chat and could you ask Auntie Ada to make some tea please." Auntie Ada was a voluntary worker, a middle-aged woman who had never married, who loved and cared for all the children in the 'little house', as it was affectionately called.

All the boys and girls in Miss Ratcliffe's care were usually under ten years old.

The two girls held hands as they left the sitting room and ran through the hall into the kitchen at the far end of the house.

"Hello," shouted Auntie Ada, leaning backwards from the big white pot sink in the scullery where she was washing dishes. After passing on the message, Pat led the way through the kitchen back into the hall, and into a glass fronted cloakroom under the sweeping staircase. At the far end of the cloakroom was a small toilet.

"That's your peg," said Pat, pointing towards an empty peg, and helping Shelagh take off her coat.

She then took Shelagh into the playroom/dining room at the far side of the staircase. Behind the door stood a small table and chairs for the staff. In the centre of the room, children were sitting on small wooden chairs around a long low table, dipping paint brushes into three small jam jars filled with water, painting colouring books using boxes of paints dotted around the table.

Auntie Jean was at the head of the table supervising. Pat ran across to the far side of the room and climbed onto the large grey and white rocking horse that stood in front of the bay window that looked out into the yard.

Shelagh stood motionless in front of the guarded hot fire, looking up at a large picture that hung on the wall above the fireplace.

"That's Jesus in the middle of the picture," said Auntie Jean, who had been watching her for the last few minutes.

"I know," Shelagh said, not taking her eyes from the picture.

"All the children that are standing around him are called the children of the world," explained Auntie Jean.

"I know," she said again, still staring at the picture. Then to Auntie Jean's surprise, she watched her put both hands together and say. "Thank you Jesus."

Not wanting to be left out, Pat shouted at the top of her voice from across the room.

"And your locker's next to mine," she shouted, jumping down from the rocking horse. She ran across the room pushing Shelagh towards a tall wooden cabinet in the corner behind the door and pointing towards one of the twelve small wooden lockers at the bottom. "That's yours next to mine. Look it's got your name on," she said excitedly. "Your bed is next to mine as well," she laughed, cockily, sticking her head in the air and showing off, grabbing Shelagh by the hand. Pat led the way up the winding staircase and into the six-bedded girl's room, opposite the top of the stairs, directly above Miss Ratcliffe's sitting room.

"That's yours," Pat shouted, running across the wooden floor and jumping on top of the bed in the corner under the bay window, forgetting that Joyce was asleep in her bed. "And that's mine," Pat carried on, swinging her legs backwards and forwards and nodding towards the rag doll that was neatly tucked inside the sheets on the next bed.

Behind a small sliding hatch door on one wall, was Miss Ratcliffe's bedroom. The sliding door was left open at night, so that she could keep an eye on all the children. On the far side of Miss Ratcliffe's bedroom, another sliding hatch overlooked into the six-bedded boy's room. Joyce sat up and rubbed her eyes. Her bed was directly under the hatch doors. Shelagh, pleased to see that she had woken up from her afternoon nap ran across and wrapped both arms around her, dragging her across the bedroom floor, and lifting her onto her bed. She sat in the middle between them both with her arms wrapped around their shoulders.

"Now," Shelagh announced very seriously, "I promised Jesus if he let me come to live with you both, I'd be good and I'd look after you for ever and ever and ever."

"Does that mean I won't get pushed and bossed about anymore?" asked Pat, looking up at her big sister with admiration.

"Yes," Shelagh replied. Joyce bored with the conversation that didn't mean anything to her, began to slide off the bed onto the floor.

"Want to go out to play," she cried. The three sisters skipped down the stairs holding hands through the hall, passing Miss Ratcliffe's room where she was still chatting to Miss Hudson, and out of the front door into the yard, and headed towards the climbing frame in the corner of the yard.

"I've had an idea," said Miss Ratcliffe to Miss Hudson as she was leaving. "Why don't you make arrangements for Tony to visit here next visiting day? Now that his sisters are all here together, I can't see the point of meeting in that dreary cold damp waiting room at head office. He might as well spend some time here, and he can play with his sisters outside."

"That's a good idea," Miss Hudson replied, "I'll make arrangements when I get back to the office."

Miss Hudson tried to catch the girl's eyes as she walked towards her car, but they were too busy playing and laughing. She felt pleasantly pleased with herself as she drove out of the yard into Cliff Road, heading towards her office.

Chapter 27

One month later, Miss Hudson parked her car on the road outside the main building of Headingley Orphanage.

It was a lovely, sunny, Saturday morning. She could hear loud shouting and laughing from the children in the yard and knew that there would be no room for her to park her car. She walked down the drive and into the yard. A rounders match was in progress, girls against the boys. She leant against the large oak tree at the entrance watching them play.

Suddenly the rounders ball came heading towards her at some speed. She dropped her briefcase caught it and shouted, "Out!" to the boy who was running towards first base.

"Not out, carry on," bellowed Andrew Kelly who was in charge of the boy's team. "She's not playing, so it doesn't count," he shouted out laughingly, encouraging the young boy to complete his round. Miss Hudson laughed and threw the ball to Andrew, picked up her briefcase and began walking around the yard, her eyes searching for the three sisters.

She could see Shelagh and Pat in the far corner of the yard, hanging upside down from the climbing frame, facing each other, sticking their tongues out, pulling faces and screeching with laughter. She smiled listening to them. They seemed so happy. Miss Ratcliffe was outside on the veranda rocking backwards and forwards in her rocking chair with Joyce wrapped in her arms.

Miss Ratcliffe beckoned to a chair beside her.

"Come and sit beside me," she invited.

"My, my, what have you been doing?" Miss Hudson asked Joyce, looking at her badly grazed knees and pointing towards her grazed forehead and nose.

"Fell in the river," Joyce replied, taking her thumb out of her mouth and then promptly putting it back.

"The river, what river?" Miss Hudson asked curiously.

Miss Ratcliffe began to explain how every year the taxi drivers of Leeds took all the children in children's homes on a day outing to Bolton Abbey and it was there that Joyce had fallen in the stream. Just then, Shelagh and Pat came skipping towards them, holding hands.

"We've been to the biggest party ever," said Shelagh, showing off. "We went in a big taxi with balloons tied to the side, and de ya know what. Everyone stopped at the side of the road and waved to us, and de ya know what?" she went on hardly stopping for breath, "all the cars stopped and stayed at the side of the road to let us through. It was wonderful, and when we got to Bolton Abbey, we all played games."

"And we got second prize for the three legged race, didn't we," butted in Pat, looking up at her big sister.

"And then we had the biggest and best party ever," carried on Shelagh excitedly.

"And we had jelly and ice cream, and we got a big bag of sweets when we left," said Joyce, not wanting to move from the comfort of Miss Ratcliffe's arms still wrapped around her.

"And we got an apple *and* an orange and a new two shilling piece," continued Shelagh, looking down at Joyce and still not stopping for breath.

"There was a piece in the evening paper and photographs were taken," said Miss Ratcliffe, tilting her head to one side towards the front door and looking at Shelagh and Pat. The girls ran inside and returned with a newspaper cutting and a photograph, and handed it to Miss Hudson.

"That's me at the front with the pointed hat on," said Shelagh, pointing her finger at the small girl on the right with a party hat on, "and that's Miss Ratcliffe, Auntie Ada, Mrs Young and Miss Lewis from the big house. I'll be going to live there when I'm ten. Now can we go back to play," she laughed, dropping the photo and newspaper cutting on Miss Ratcliffe's knee.

"She seems to have settled in very well," said Miss Hudson to Miss Ratcliffe.

"Yes she has," replied Miss Ratcliffe, "she's like a mother to Pat and Joyce, fusses about them all the time. Never leaves them alone, but she's right, in two years time, when she's ten, she'll be transferred to Miss Lewis' house." She nodded and pointed towards the right hand side of the back of the house opposite. "That's the big girls' house, as it's called, and that's the big boys' house," she went on, nodding towards the left side of the building.

"From there they will be sent to a normal secondary modern school and then at fifteen, they will hopefully have found a job. If they don't have parents or family to go to, they will be found foster parents. However, that's a long way away yet. Meantime we hope to give them the happiest childhood that we can, she concluded.

One Friday evening as the children lay asleep, Auntie Jean sat in the kitchen, wrapping string around the top of jam jars and making handles. She planned; weather permitting, to take the children fishing in the stream on Woodhouse Ridge nearby, the following morning.

"Who wants to go fishing?" she shouted the next morning as the children were finishing their breakfasts. A few children raised their hands.

"Me," they shouted back.

"Right," she shouted to Pat Gregson, who had not put up her hand and was looking down at the floor. "On the kitchen table," she said, still looking at Pat, "there are some jam jars and some small fishing nets. When everyone's ready, and make sure you're all wearing wellington boots," she carried on, looking at each child, "then Pat will give you one each. Then I want you all to line up in twos in the yard and I'll be with you shortly." Pat pushed her chair away from the table and across the floor, still looking down and now sulking, stamped and banged her feet towards the kitchen. Auntie Jean knew that she did not want to go without Shelagh, who had promised Auntie Ada that she would keep her company and pick some rhubarb in the field behind the house, to help bake a pie for after dinner.

As they began to walk across the yard, Miss Ratcliffe shouted from the front door.

"Be careful, I don't want any of the children falling into the water."

"You say that every time," shouted Auntie Jean over her shoulder, "you worry far too much."

The children loved Auntie Jean and she in turn loved them back. She loved listening to their non-stop chatter and laughter. They were so well behaved. She was so proud of them as she followed behind them through the winding cobbled streets and ginnels that took them to the top of the Ridge. They walked down a long path and down a steep embankment to the stream.

She helped all the children down and positioned them on either side of her.

"Right everyone," she ordered, "before we start there are some ground rules. We're fishing for tadpoles and sticklebacks only, not anything else. So you Paul Barlow can let go of that muddy, croaking frog in your hands," she said, looking sternly across at the young boy. He reluctantly put the frog down and watched it hop away.

"You're too near the water. Move back or you'll fall in and then I'll be in trouble," she shouted to Neil Kelly who was kneeling down on a large green slimy wet stone, his arm stretched out in front, as he lowered his fishing net into water. He looked at her sideways from under his peaked cap and slowly moved back.

"I've caught one with two legs," shouted Terry.

"And I've got one with three legs," boasted Ian, lifting up his jar for everyone to see.

"Oh my goodness," shouted Auntie Jean, looking at her watch a few hours later, "doesn't time fly when you're having fun. Time to go; don't want to be late for dinner or Auntie Ada will be cross." They all carried their jam jars now full of tadpoles back up the banking and stood in twos waiting to be counted.

"Where's your tadpoles?" Auntie Jean asked Pat, who was looking down at a bunch of bluebells and buttercups stuffed in her jam jar, which was filled with dirty water.

"I've got these for Miss Ratcliffe," Pat replied, with a long face and obviously still sulking.

"Don't like fishing and didn't want to come anyway."

"There's one missing," said Auntie Jean after counting, "where's Neil Kelly?"

"Oh, he's crying and still sat at the edge of the water, an he wont come back up, cos he's not caught anything," said Pat, pointing down towards Neil, who could just be seen at the waters edge, in front of a large oak tree. "There's always one," said Auntie Jean, lifting up her head towards the sky and tutting, "don't any of you move. I want you all to stay together; I'm going down to get him. I won't be long."

As she began to walk down the now muddy banking, she slipped onto her bottom with her legs out in front and landing waist deep in the middle of the stream. The children watched horrified with their mouths wide open, not knowing whether to laugh or cry. Stunned, her pride hurt for a moment, Auntie Jean propped her elbows on her knees and began to laugh. Now all the children joined in the laughter, including Pat.

"Throw me your jar," Auntie Jean shouted to Neil, who had jumped out of the way so as not to get wet and was now peeping at her from behind the tree.

"I'm in a perfect position where I can get the best and biggest tadpoles there are," she exclaimed.

After filling his jar, they walked hand in hand back up the embankment where the rest of the children were still howling with laughter, even more when they saw that she was up to her waist in mud.

"Can't walk home through the streets like this," Auntie Jean said, after checking all the children were still there. "I've got an idea. I want everyone to form a circle around me and help keep me covered until we get back home."

As they walked back through the cobbled streets and ginnels, people stopped and stared at the odd formation around her. Her pace became slower as the sun was drying her muddy clothes, making them heavy and uncomfortable to walk in. Eventually they arrived back at the Orphanage.

Miss Ratcliffe was pacing up and down the veranda her arms tightly crossed across her chest and constantly looking across the yard, worrying and wondering why they were late.

She breathed a sigh of relief when they appeared all huddled together. The children ran to put their jars on the veranda and began to take their wellington boots off. Miss Ratcliffe put her hands to her mouth and gasped when she saw Auntie Jean who was standing in front of her, hands on her hips.

"Well you did say not to let the children fall in the water, but you didn't say anything about me," she said grinning.

Miss Ratcliffe covered her face with both hands and they both began to laugh.

"I'm going for a long hot soapy bath," Auntie Jean said, as she walked past her into the hall and headed towards the stairs.

"And I'll have Auntie Ada make you a nice cup of tea when you're finished," replied Miss Ratcliffe, still laughing.

Taxi outing to Bolton Abbey

Chapter 28

Mr Hamilton-Forbes was away on a business conference in London. His wife had returned to see Miss Ratcliffe to inform her of what decision they had made. She was shown by Miss Ratcliffe into her warm, friendly, and as usual, cluttered sitting room, and invited to sit on one of the large, better armchairs in front of the window. Miss Ratcliffe sat opposite in her rocking chair with both hands clasped together resting on her open knees, eagerly waiting for the outcome.

It had been two weeks since the couple had been invited to spend the afternoon at the little house to watch and observe some of the younger boys. They had both been devastated when they were told that they could not have children of their own. After a lot of thought, they had decided to adopt, firstly a boy and then perhaps a girl, when the boy had settled into his new home.

It had been a warm, autumn, sunny, Saturday afternoon when they had visited. They sat on the veranda watching with wonder and amazement at the children playing.

"It's like looking into a picture, it's wonderful," Mrs Hamilton-Forbes remarked to her husband, looking around the yard. The sun was shining down from directly above, illuminating the red and orange leaves, which were falling slowly from the oak tree.

The yard was a hive of activity. Lively children of all ages from the big girls' house, the big boys' house and the little house were playing happily. A few children were playing on their own, some playing hopscotch with a piece of slate and some playing tig, chasing each other around the yard. The air was full of noise and laughter, safe from the outside world.

After much careful observation, two seven year olds caught the couple's eye. They were playing on a small see-saw with canvas seats near the climbing frame. David Haigh, an only child, had been placed into care when his mother had died of tuberculosis. His father had been fatally wounded on active service during the war a few years earlier. The other child was Frank Smith, whose mother had died in childbirth, and who had never known who his real father was. Frank had been placed unhappily with various foster parents before eventually being placed into a children's home.

Mrs Hamilton-Forbes was mesmerised with David, a thin little boy, and could not take her eyes from him. She followed his every move. Mr Hamilton-Forbes, on the other hand, took a shine to Frank, a rather meaty little boy with black hair and a loud infectious laugh. They decided it was too much to make a snap decision there and then, so Miss Ratcliffe suggested that they return home to discuss the matter in depth, and return two weeks later with a decision.

Two weeks later, Mrs Hamilton-Forbes returned on her own as her husband was away on business.

"Have you decided on which one of the boys you would like to adopt?" asked Miss Ratcliffe.

"Yes we have," answered Mrs Hamilton-Forbes, "after many sleepless nights and a great deal of thought, we would like to adopt little Frank. He looks a healthy young lad and my husband says he looks just like him when he was a boy. I'm sure someone will come along for little David," she added, lowering her head and looking uncomfortable at choosing one and not the other. "We would be grateful if you could get the wheels in motion," she continued, "the sooner the better. Christmas is not too far away and it would be wonderful to have him with us by then."

Bruce, the black and white pet Border collie, pushed the door open with his head, his lead still attached to his collar and dragging Pat who was still holding on. She quickly let go, almost falling forwards.

Pat loved Bruce and took him for a walk every day in the fields behind the house. She had run back to the home when it had begun to rain. Bruce shook his coat and ran to his basket with his lead still attached.

"What's your name?" Mrs Hamilton-Forbes asked Pat, now sitting up from a slouching position and taking Miss Ratcliffe by surprise.

"Patricia," Pat replied, staring and frowning at Mrs Hamilton-Forbes.

"You're honoured," said Miss Ratcliffe, "that's her Sunday name."

Mrs Hamilton-Forbes could not stop looking at Pat's tiny little frame. The rain was running off her short brown hair, down her neatly cut fringe and off the end of her nose.

"And how old are you?" Mrs Hamilton-Forbes asked.

"Six," Pat answered quickly, before running from the room towards the cloakroom under the stairs, to change her wet clothes.

"That's the little girl for me," Mrs Hamilton-Forbes blurted out. Miss Ratcliffe was speechless. "That's the little girl I want," the woman repeated. "We had planned to adopt a little girl in maybe a year's time, but looking at Patricia reminds me of when I was a little girl. She has my colouring, dimples, a cheeky little face and everything I would wish a daughter of mine to have."

"I'm not sure whether that will be possible," said Miss Ratcliffe still surprised at her sudden outburst, "she has a younger and older sister here and I don't think that any of them are on the foster register, never mind adoption. Mr Parnell, Head of the Children's Department, took them off when things didn't work out with various foster parents, but I'll ask Miss Hudson, their Care Officer, the next time she visits to investigate and I will let you know."

"If you give me Mr Parnell's address, I will write to him personally," said Mrs Hamilton- Forbes, now sounding a little angry. "My husband is a wealthy business man and we live very comfortably in the country. We both come from stable backgrounds, and we're very well financially secure and in a very good position to give her everything. She obviously loves animals and we have dogs and horses, so she would love it. Nevertheless, of course, we would have to change her name. Chances like this do not come around very often for children like these," Mrs Hamilton-Forbes concluded, trying to sound convincing.

"I will pass the message on to Miss Hudson," replied Miss Ratcliffe, "and I will ring and let you know if I hear anything, these things take time as you no doubt know, I will keep my fingers crossed and wish you good luck," she added calmly.

When Mrs Hamilton-Forbes left, Miss Ratcliffe watched her walk across the yard towards the side of the big girls' house and thought, "what a good opportunity this would be for Pat," but her stomach turned over at the thought of losing her. She knew that the Committee at Head Office would do what was best for her. "It would be in their hands," she thought, as she walked back into the hall and then into her room.

Miss Hudson rang to make an appointment to see Mr Parnell, briefly mentioning why.

A week later, she arrived and sat opposite Mr Parnell in his office. He pushed his chair away from his desk, stretched out his legs, crossed his feet, folded his arms and with a serious look on his face looked at Miss Hudson.

"This one has been a tricky one, for me and the Committee," he began. "A few days ago I received two letters, one from a Mrs Hamilton-Forbes, the other from a Mrs Jenkins, one of the Committee Members of Headingley Orphanage. Advising *me*," he said, raising his eyebrows, dropping his chin and looking over the top of his glasses, "that *she* and the rest of the Committee were of a view that Pat should be allowed to be adopted. Giving their reasons why," he added. Then looking at the letter, he quoted, "that at fifteen she would have to leave the home and have to be found foster parents anyway, and in their opinion it would be in Pat's best interest." He threw the letter back towards his desk, it landed on the floor.

"May I say," butted in Miss Hudson, who up to that moment had listened and had not said a word, "that it was only a few months ago that her older sister Shelagh has joined her and I dread to think what effect it would have on her. She would be devastated."

"Yes I know and I would be too," agreed Mr Parnell. "The thing is, none of the girls are up for adoption. It took me a long time to convince the mother and get her to give consent to allow them to be fostered, never mind adoption. I have written to Mrs Hamilton-Forbes, after speaking to our Committee, explaining that we are in no position to guarantee that Pat is available for adoption. The mother of these children, including their brother, who is already in foster care, can at any one-time claim them back, providing she has suitable accommodation. So the answer has to be *no*," he said, with a determined look on his face.

Miss Hudson breathed a huge sigh of relief.

"I am so pleased," she said, holding both hands together. "That is what I was hoping for, as it means the girls will still be together for a while. The home is not too far away from here, so I will make a quick visit and give Miss Ratcliffe the news. I'm sure she will be secretly relieved. She has had the two younger sisters for some years now and has grown to care for them."

Miss Hudson could now visualise the girls being together for a number of years and smiled to herself as she left the office.

Chapter 29

Every year, the students from Carnegie College in Headingley donated their large Christmas tree to the little house at Headingley Orphanage at the end of term. It was always delivered on a wagon a week before Christmas and every year the top had to be sawn off, as it was always too big for the playroom/dining room. The tree took pride of place in the bay window that looked out onto the yard.

After the children had gone to bed, Auntie Jean spent most of the evening decorating the tree with ornaments that had accumulated over the years, bells, different coloured baubles and other delights. Every year she took personal pride in trimming the tree.

In the days following, the children would add to the tree, silver milk bottle tops that had been collected over the last few weeks, washed, rinsed and pressed flat.

During the afternoons leading up to Christmas, Auntie Jean would supervise all the children, sitting them at the long, low dining table, looping and sticking coloured pieces of paper together to make long chains to hang from the ceiling across the room. The nearer Christmas got, the more excited the children became.

On Christmas Eve afternoon, the Salvation Army Band came to sing carols. It was an icy, bitterly cold day. They grouped themselves in the middle of the yard as the staff and children from all three houses stood around the yard ready to join in the singing. The atmosphere was wonderful. During the singing of 'Away in a Manger', always a favourite of the small children, it began to snow. By the end of the service, the snow was falling heavily. Some of the younger children stretched out their arms, holding their heads back with their eyes shut and mouths wide open to catch the snow. Joyce let go of Miss Ratcliffe's hand, and ran to the middle of the yard to a young woman who had been playing the tambourine, and began tugging the bottom of her skirt.

"My big sister's favourite carol is, 'See Amid the Winter's Snow', she cried, "can you sing it for her please?"

"Of course we can," the young woman replied, patting her on top of the head. Feeling very proud of herself, Joyce ran across the yard towards Shelagh who was leaning against the wall of the big girls' house with a crowd of other children. She shoved and pushed herself in, snuggling herself comfortably between Shelagh's legs and facing the Army in the middle of the yard. Shelagh affectionately wrapped her arms around Joyce's shoulders and held her close. Pat was sitting with her friend Valerie on top of the old table tennis table, under the corrugated roofed shed, joining in the singing. By the end of the carol singing, it was snowing heavily, so all the members of the band were invited back to the big girls' house for well-deserved mugs of cocoa and mince pies.

Back in the little house, after tea, Auntie Jean and Miss Ratcliffe were in the bathroom organising baths. Auntie Jean was kneeling down on both knees beside the high cast iron bath, threading her fingers through the warm soapy water. Twelve naked children stood in line at the other end; Joyce being the youngest was first. Miss Ratcliffe stood with a pile of towels waiting to dry the children as they were lifted out onto a wooden slatted board.

"It's the one and only night of the year when you all want to go to bed," she laughed, as she dried them one by one. Eventually all twelve children, six boys and six girls, were tucked into bed. "Now don't forget, Father Christmas will not come at all if you don't all go to sleep and those stockings at the end of your beds will not get filled," said Miss Ratcliffe, peering over the top of her glasses.

Later that evening, Miss Ratcliffe and Auntie Jean were sitting at the kitchen table enjoying a mug of cocoa. They could hear giggling and whispering upstairs for what seemed a long time. Eventually all went quiet.

"Time to put clean clothes at the end of their beds and collect their stockings," said Miss Ratcliffe later in the evening. She crept up the open staircase on her tiptoes, first entering the boys' room, where everyone was fast asleep. Miss Ratcliffe smiled as she gathered the six stockings and hung them over the banister, ready to collect after she had been into the girls' room. She shook her head and chuckled as she walked into the girls' room. Joyce was sitting at the bottom of her bed with her legs crossed, trying her best to keep awake. She was staring at her stocking and holding her eyes wide open with a finger and thumb.

"Why aren't you asleep?" Miss Ratcliffe whispered, holding her hands on her hips and tilting her head to one side.

"Want to see Father Christmas and want to see what he puts in my stocking and then I can tell everyone I've seen him for real," Joyce replied, opening her eyes even more.

"Well let me tell you, if you," continued Miss Ratcliffe, "if you don't get back into bed, Father Christmas won't come to you, or anyone else, if you're not asleep. He makes sure that everyone is fast asleep and they'll all blame you if there is nothing in their stockings. So come on, back into bed."

After she had tucked Joyce in, she gave her a peck on the cheek and looked at her sternly as she left the room. She filled the stockings much later when they were all well and truly fast asleep.

Christmas Day was no exception for Auntie Jean who seemed to be always on the go and never gave much time to herself. She worked tirelessly and was paid very little, earning five pounds every month, with one half day off every week and every alternative Sunday. She did not mind as she loved her job, and each child was special to her.

By the time she had lit the three coal fires, made a large pan of porridge and mixed a large enamelled jug of cocoa, the children had woken. She could hear them making a great deal of noise upstairs as they emptied their stockings and shouted to one another.

All the contents of the stockings were much the same; chocolate coins covered in silver and gold paper, an apple and orange, a small bag of sweets, a small toy and a feathered, paper roll-up whistle. The noise of everyone blowing their paper whistles woke Miss Ratcliffe. She quickly dressed and then helped all the children to dress, as no one was allowed downstairs wearing their pyjamas or nightdresses. When everyone was dressed, the children ran down the stairs, pushing and shoving each other out of the way in order to get to the dining room first. On each of their chairs was a parcel with their names on, each containing a new present. The parcels were quickly opened with shrieks of excitement and approval.

After breakfast, Miss Ratcliffe and Auntie Jean gave the children more presents, which were nearly new toys that had been given to the Orphanage. After careful selection, according to age and sex, the toys were divided amongst the three houses, wrapped and put under the Christmas tree.

The turkey had been slowly cooking in the small gas oven overnight. Auntie Jean and Auntie Ada, who had arrived earlier, to help Auntie Jean with the rest of the dinner, sat with Miss Ratcliffe watching the children sharing and playing with their new toys, squealing with delight and excitement as they did so.

"If only the parents and families could see these children right now at this moment," remarked Miss Ratcliffe, "they don't know what they're missing and what pleasure they give. Not a 'phone call, not a card, not even one small present for any one of these children. It's as though they don't exist anymore. It breaks your heart," observed Miss Ratcliffe, with sadness in her voice. She rocked backwards and forwards on her rocking chair with her arms folded and shaking her head. "I'm going to break one of my golden rules," Miss Ratcliffe smiled, winking at Auntie Jean and Auntie Ada, "after we all come back from the service at Wrangthorn Church and when everyone's eaten their dinner, I'm going to allow them to play in the yard as a special treat."

The yard was now a thick carpet of snow. Children were never allowed to play out on Sundays. Sundays and Christmas Day were classed as Holy Days.

"And I might join them," said Auntie Jean, with a twinkle in her eye.

After traditional Christmas dinner and Aunties Ada's home made Christmas pudding, laced with silver sixpences, all the children from the three houses played in the snow.

The older children helped the younger ones make snowmen, and after a few hours, snowmen of different shapes and sizes, appeared dotted around the yard. Then followed organised snow balling, girls against the boys. The yard was a hive of activity and fun, loud screaming and laughter from the red-nosed children filled the air.

Every Christmas Day, the children and staff from the little house were always invited to join the children that were left in the big girls' house for tea. Some of the older children were spending Christmas with parents or relatives.

Tea was always held in the long dining room at the back of the house that faced onto the yard. Everyone sang carols in the long committee room at the front of the house that faced the main road.

The younger children sat on the floor with their legs crossed, directly in front of the blazing guarded fire, while the older children and staff sat on chairs set out in rows at the back.

Mrs Harvey, a senior member of the Orphanage Committee, played carols on the piano, which stood at the side of the room. When the singing was finished, Mr Harvey, dressed as Father Christmas, came in and gave each child another present with their names on, again nearly new toys that had been handed in, again hand picked and wrapped according to age and sex. Mr and Mrs Harvey and all the staff sat back and watched with wonder and pleasure at the children's excitement as they ripped the paper off the parcels and screeched with delight at the contents.

"Where's Joyce?" Auntie Jean asked sometime later, looking around the room, "it's getting late. Time we were all going home."

Shelagh's ears always pricked up at any mention of Pat and Joyce's names.

"I'll go and find her," Shelagh shouted, jumping up and running from the room into the hall. She could hear Joyce's voice. It seemed to be coming from the dining room.

She was standing on a chair that she had dragged across the polished orange lino from the bottom of the room and was in a world of her own, playing inside the big doll's house that stood on a table at the side. She was talking to two tiny dolls, one held in each hand.

"I might have known where you were," laughed Shelagh, with her 'old head' on. She knew Joyce loved dolls houses. "Time to go home," she said to Joyce, taking the dolls from her hands and placing them back inside, then closing the front of the house. With a look of disappointment, Joyce dropped her head on her chest and pouted her lips, sulking. Shelagh wrapped her arms around Joyce's waist and lifted her down from the chair. "When I come to live here, I promise I'll let you come and play with the dolls house anytime you want," Shelagh said.

"Promise," asked Joyce, lifting up her head and smiling.

"Yes," she replied.

Chapter 30

It was Easter Saturday and Tony was due to visit his sisters at the little house. Now, being one of the eldest in the Orphanage, it was Shelagh's job to help clear the crockery from the dinner table, sweep the crumbs off the tablecloth onto a small dustpan and then quickly convert the dining room back into a playroom for those who wanted to stay indoors.

She ran to the corner of the yard and sat on top of a large concrete stump on the grass at the side of the climbing frame, a perfect view to sit and watch for Tony. She watched and waited, and waited and watched, and the hours passed until she realised that he was not coming. Eventually she ran inside, hysterical and in tears.

"Something's wrong," she cried, "he's never late. He's always here. I know something's wrong."

"Stop worrying," said Miss Ratcliffe, "he might not be very well. He may have a nasty cold. If I don't hear anything in the next few days, I'll make enquiries. There's probably some simple explanation. Now off you go back out to play and stop worrying," she encouraged, emphasising on the 'worrying'.

Shelagh walked away with her shoulders drooped, chin on her chest, and the worried look still on her face. Miss Ratcliffe shook her head as she watched her walk away.

A few days later Miss Hudson visited with an explanation. She began to describe the problems Mr and Mrs Hawkins's, Tony's foster parents, were having.

Over the last few months, Mr Hawkins had been taken ill. He was constantly having chest infections, and as his breathing had become so difficult, the single bed in the spare room that had used to belong to Mrs Hawkin's mother, had been brought downstairs into the dining room for him to use.

"He frequently misses work," Miss Hudson continued. "They are living on sick pay and are having financial difficulties. They've even had to sell the car, as they couldn't afford the upkeep. They really are struggling. Mrs Hawkins did ring me to apologise for not bringing Tony last Saturday, but she says she hasn't the time or the money for the bus fares and doesn't know if she can make it the next time. Her husband seems to need constant care and what with a small boy to take care of, she's not coping very well."

"Well that explains it," said Miss Ratcliffe. "For the last few days, Shelagh has nattered the life out of me, non stop natter, always sounding so sure something's wrong with Tony. Now I can put her mind at rest. She's very protective towards the others and worries far too much. When she first came here, she was always very serious and seemed to carry all the troubles of the world on her shoulders. She never talks about her background. I thought it best to leave her until she feels the need. There were times when I did my rounds in the bedroom at night, that I heard her muffled cries under the pillow. It breaks your heart. There's never been a birthday card, or Christmas cards, not a 'phone call or any interest for the children from the parents on either side of the family. It's as though they have been totally forgotten. If they only knew the damage that they may be causing in later years, *and* they come from such a big family. I really do not understand," she concluded, shaking and scratching her head.

"I could collect and bring Tony here for the day, what do you think?" said Miss Hudson suddenly.

"I think that's a wonderful idea," Miss Ratcliffe replied. "I know someone who will be very pleased to see him."

"What about Friday? The children are still on holiday from school. I'll tell Shelagh the good news when you're gone. That'll cheer her up no end."

The following Friday, Shelagh sat on top of the concrete stump eagerly waiting for her brother to appear. After what seemed a lifetime, Tony arrived, dragging his feet, with Miss Hudson holding his hand. In her other hand, she carried her briefcase and a small parcel. Tony was wearing the same clothes that he always wore when he visited, grey flannel and knee length trousers with blazer to match, knee length socks and black lace up ankle boots. His chin was touching his chest and he was staring down on the ground, his school peaked cap covered his face. Shelagh quickly jumped down, almost falling, and ran towards him. She grabbed his arm, and saying a quick hello to Miss Hudson, dragged him across the yard to her favourite corner.

As Miss Hudson walked towards the open front door, she could see Joyce, sitting on her hands on a medium height buffet at the side of the grandfather clock in the hall, hanging her head and swinging her legs.

"Hello," Miss Hudson called. Joyce lifted up her head. Miss Hudson began to laugh. "What have you done?" she asked. Joyce's face was covered in chocolate.

"Don't talk to her, and don't laugh at her," shouted Miss Ratcliffe, from her sitting room. "She's been a very naughty girl, haven't you? And when children don't do as they're told, they sit on the naughty buffet, don't they?" she insisted, appearing at the door and glaring down at Joyce. "I don't believe in smacking," she explained. "I find that," pointing to the buffet, "works a treat, now I'm going to shame you and tell Miss Hudson just what you've done," she pronounced, inviting Miss Hudson into the sitting room. Joyce's head shrank into her shoulders.

With a serious expression, Miss Ratcliffe began to explain.

"Every Sunday afternoon, after dinner, all the children are given a handful of sweets, and being Easter they are all given a small Easter egg. Pat is a bit of a saver, so she decided to save hers for another day and left it in the middle of the dresser in the kitchen. Several times today, Auntie Ada has caught Joyce standing on her tiptoes, glaring at the Easter egg. I heard her shout more than once. 'Don't you dare!' causing Joyce to run away and peep from behind the kitchen door. Auntie Ada had only been in the yard two minutes, hanging out washing, when she found that Joyce had dragged a chair across the floor and was shovelling all the Easter egg into her mouth with both hands. Weren't you Joyce?" she said pointedly, looking at her through the open door.

"Well, now there's a coincidence," said Miss Hudson, "I've bought all four of them a small Easter egg." She began to open the parcel on her knee, saying very deliberately, "I thought it would be nice for them to eat while they're playing."

Joyce's ears pricked up and she leant to one side, almost toppling over. "Chocolate," she thought licking her lips. She loved chocolate.

"Well seeing as Joyce has had two and Pat's not had one at all," Miss Ratcliffe said, raising her voice, "I think it would be only fair to give Pat Joyce's egg, What do you think Joyce?" she shouted, pulling a face at Miss Hudson. Joyce's face dropped. Her mouth drooped at the corners. Now she was sulking. "But this time *I'll* keep them in *my* sitting room," Miss Ratcliffe said loudly. "I think you can go out to play now, you've been sitting there for two hours and I've some catching up to do with Miss Hudson, so off you go." She went to the door and gestured to Joyce, waving her hand side to side. Joyce jumped down from the buffet and ran to find Pat to try to get on her good side.

Shelagh sat on the grass and pulled Tony down beside her.

"I've really missed you," she said, looking at him sideways on. Tony sat, not saying a word, his chin still on his chest. Suddenly Shelagh saw bruises on his knees below his trousers. "Are they bruises?" she asked. He quickly stretched out his arms and covered his knees with his hands. "And what have you done to your hands?" she insisted, noticing that his knuckles were grazed. She leant over, took off his cap and looked sideways into his face. Shocked at what she saw, she jolted back and demanded. "You've got a black eye and your nose is cut. How did that happen?" Tony quickly grabbed his cap off the grass and covered his face again. "I want to know," Shelagh said, with her bossy head on, "I want to know." She leaned down, took off his cap and threw it on the grass behind them. Holding his head between her hands, she turned his face towards her. "Tell me," she insisted.

"Can't," Tony said, quietly looking into her eyes.

"Please," Shelagh pleaded.

"Can't and don't want to."

"You have to tell me."

"Don't," he said, shaking his head again. "Can't," he kept saying repeatedly and shaking his head. "Yall tell."

120

"I won't," replied his sister. "If you tell me it will be our secret between me and you, and I promise I won't tell anybody else. Cross my heart and hope to die," she said, making the sign of a cross with a finger across her chest.

"Promise," he asked.

"Promise."

Once Tony began to talk, there was no stopping.

"Nobody wants to play with me," he began with sadness in his voice. "Nobody talks to me, nobody wants to be my friend and nobody likes me. They're always pushing and hitting me *and* they throw stones at me," he said rolling down his socks showing her his bruised shins and legs. "They punch me in face; an I haven't dun anything wrong. An when they hit me, I hit em back, and there's a lot of em and I always get the worst of it, and I don't know why." Shrugging his shoulders, he paused for a moment, and then carried on. "They're always shouting at me and calling me a bastard."

"What's a bastard?" Shelagh butted in.

"Mrs Hawkins sez it's kids that don't have a mother and father, and I tell em I've got a mother and father, so I can't be one, can I? An they ate me and I ate them. When can we go home? I don't like it there any more," he said, frowning and giving Shelagh a black look. "Why can't we all be together and then I won't have to come here any more."

"I've got an idea," said Shelagh suddenly, with a sparkle in her eye and a positive tone in her voice.

"When you go to bed tonight why don't you say your prayers and ask Jesus," she suggested. "Not God, cos he's not the right person. It must be Jesus. Ask him to find a great big house for our mam and dad. It might work if you ask, cos I think he's fed up of listening to me. So don't forget," she added.

"I will, cos I've had enough," Tony replied, now feeling the need to tell her everything and not stopping for breath. "There always laughing at me clothes," cos I get them from the Salvation Army, and they shout, "Mrs Hawkins gets paid a lot of money for me." Tears welled in Tony's eyes and he began to cry. Shelagh reached into the back pocket of her green flannelette knickers, pulled out a piece of rag and handed it to him. He wiped his eyes gave his nose a good blow then handed it back.

"Do you want to come and live with us?" she asked, putting her arm around his shoulder, "I'll ask Miss Ratcliffe if you want."

"No!" he shouted emphatically, sitting up straight and arching his back. "What if I come and live with you, and our mother and father never come back, I'll have to be found another foster home, so I'd rather stop where I am, even if I don't like it any more and you did promise not to tell," he added.

"Well if we don't ever get back to our mam and dad," Shelagh announced confidently.

"When I grow up, I promise, I'll get us a great big house, and we'll all live together, and I'll look after us all."

Just then, Miss Ratcliffe appeared on the veranda shaking and ringing a large brass bell.

"Its time for dinner," said Shelagh, standing up and giving Tony a pull up.

"You won't tell will ya," he pleaded, staring into her face.

"No," she said, "it will be our secret for ever and ever."

Chapter 31

When the older girls and boys from the big houses had completed their Saturday morning duties, weather permitting, they would join the younger children in the yard. Whenever fights or squabbles arose, the older children would intervene and encourage any new children to mix and share in with whatever they were playing.

One late Saturday morning, Sandra, one of the younger girls from the little house, stood at the side of the yard watching Kathleen playing whip and top. The top of the wooden cone, highly decorated with different coloured chalks, spun around on the concrete. Occasionally, Kathleen whipped the top with a short, wooden handled whip (more often than not made from a leather shoelace) with a quick flick of the wrist, making the top spin faster and faster. Sandra stood with her mouth wide open, her face filled with envy.

Kathleen was the seven-year-old daughter of Mrs Jones a newly appointed assistant in the big girls' house.

"Can I have a go?" Sandra muttered quietly. "Please, can I have a go?" she asked again, raising her voice a little louder, thinking Kathleen had not heard.

"No," Kathleen answered loudly with her back to her.

"I've never had a whip and top of my own. So please let me have a go. Only for a minute, please," Sandra, pleaded.

"I said no," Kathleen repeated, picking up the top and making a new pattern with the chalks in her pocket. Then wrapping the lash around the top again and with another flick of her wrist she sent the top spinning across the concrete. Sandra moved nearer and looked into her face. "Please," she asked pleadingly again, with deep feeling in her voice.

"Go play hopscotch with them over there," yelled Kathleen. "I've been told not to play with you lot," she answered, angrily pushing Sandra away.

Jane, one of the older girls who had been watching and listening from a distance, came running across in defence of Sandra.

"Don't be so mean and give her a go," she ordered.

"No," Kathleen shouted angrily, stamping her foot, "I won't."

"Everyone shares their toys here and one day you might want to play with theirs," Jane explained, "so don't be so mean and give her a go for a few minutes. It won't hurt you," looking down sternly at her.

"I've been told not to play with you lot and you can't make me," Kathleen insisted, with anger in her voice. She picked the top up from the concrete and ran inside the side door of the big girls' house.

"Ah, don't worry about her, come and play with us," invited Jane, shrugging her shoulders and grabbing Sandra's hand.

A few minutes later Mrs Jones came running from the house, across the yard, towards Jane, screaming at the top of her voice and brandishing the whip in her hand.

"How dare you ask Kathleen to share her toys," she screamed her face red with anger. "I've told her not to play with the likes of you lot," she screeched. Jane's face was white with fear. Mrs Jones grabbed Jane's long blonde hair and dragged her across the yard back into the house, up the stairs, across the landing and into the linen room, where she locked Jane and herself inside. Then she began to whip Jane hard and fast. Her screaming could be heard in the yard as her piercing cries of pain became louder and louder. All the children stopped and stood motionless, looking up towards the bedroom windows of the big girls' house where the screams seemed to be coming from. They stood frozen, fear in their faces. Eventually the screaming stopped. After what seemed a long time to the children, they returned to their playing, unusually quiet.

The following day, word was passed around in whispers. It was thought that when Miss Lewis, the Matron of the big girls' house, had returned from her day off the previous evening and was told of the incident, Mrs Jones and her daughter were asked to leave immediately. They were never seen again.

Jane bore the scar of her beating for a long time, and remembers the incident vividly to this day.

Chapter 32

Over the last few years, South Cliff Congregational Church in Scarborough, had offered Headingley Orphanage the use of the two schoolrooms attached to the back of the church, to be used as a base for a holiday during the summer school break. The largest of the wooden floored halls would be used for the big girls, the smallest for the children from the little house.

The big girls' house children and the younger children from the little house would stay the first few weeks, and then the older boys would stay the last few weeks of the school holiday. Plenty of long trestle tables would be supplied to be used as temporary dining tables and a make shift bathroom. At the end of a short narrow passage was a galley kitchen. Along one wall of the kitchen were two deep white pot sinks, and two small gas cookers. They would be used every day to make a hot meal for the children. Everything else that would be needed to run a home would have to be packed and sent on ahead of the coach on the morning of the holiday.

Every year, the night before the journey, Miss Ratcliffe would place new black pumps in rows down the hall floor.

"I want everyone to find a pair that fits," she would shout. "Make sure you write your names on the inside or they will get mixed up. As a lot of you take the same size, I'll write the names of those that can't, and then I want you all to put them in your pump bags for the coach in the morning, and make sure you all take your pillow for your camp bed."

Later that evening, the children stood in line waiting to be bathed. Frank Wilson, half way down the line, lifted his head and shouted.

"That's the last bath we'll be having for a few weeks."

Auntie Jean frowned at him and carried on dipping the children in and out of the bath, then passing them to Miss Ratcliffe to dry.

Once they were tucked in and lights out, the whispering began, Shelagh and Pat lay in bed, heads propped on their hands, facing each other.

"What's it like at the seaside?" Shelagh asked, quietly leaning forward.

"Oh it's wonderful," she replied.

"What do you do all day?"

"We play on the beach and make sandcastles, we paddle in the sea and on a morning, we sit on the sand and watch Punch and Judy," Pat answered excitedly.

"Punch and Judy, who's Punch and Judy?" asked Shelagh.

"They're puppets inside a long striped tent," explained Pat, "and they both have right long noses, and Punch is alus hitting Judy with a stick and shouting, that's the way to do it, that's the way to do it," she said in a squeaky voice. Then she began to giggle. "And when it rains we go down into Gala Land."

"Gala Land, what's that?" Shelagh asked curiously.

"It's underground, under Valley Bridge," Pat continued. "They have funny mirrors and a ghost train and loads of other things. There's a great big stage and every week they have a talent competition. If ya wear a nice dress and sing a song, and tell em ya live in an orphanage, ya nearly alus get a prize. Some days," she said, with a voice of authority, "if ya really, really, good Miss Ratcliffe buys ya an ice cream sandwich or an ice cream lolly, me favourite," she drooled, closing her eyes and licking her lips. Eventually, after much tossing and turning with thoughts of the following day, all the children fell asleep.

"Come on," shouted Pat, early the following morning and shaking Shelagh vigorously, "its time to get up. We're going to the seaside today."

It was a lovely summer's morning and the sun was beaming through the bay window. Children were running backwards and forwards, Joyce was sitting on the floor at the side of her bed already dressed and trying to fasten the buckles of her new brown sandals that were on the wrong feet. Shelagh ran across, changed the sandals to the right feet, fastened the buckles and sat her on top of her bed. Quickly she dressed herself with the clothes that had been neatly folded on the end of her bed that had been put there during the night. The sisters ran downstairs, holding hands, into the dining room. Bowls of hot steamy porridge had been placed around the table with mugs of hot cocoa.

"The coach has arrived," shouted Auntie Jean later that morning. It was music to the children's ears.

"Bags backseat," shouted Neil Kelly, as he ran across the yard, pillow under one arm, the string of his pump bag over his shoulder. The coach was parked on the road outside the big girls' house. In front of the coach, two burly men, wearing trousers held up with braces, the sleeves of their granddad shirts rolled up to their elbows, and both wearing flat caps, were lifting the last of the boxes onto a lorry. For the past few hours, the men had been loading boxes filled with crockery, knives, forks and spoons. Aluminium bowls and jugs to be used as washing bowls. Pans, provisions, large clothes horses, hampers full of towels, clothes, blankets and old sheets to drape around the clothes horses for a make shift bathroom, and dozens of camp beds.

Everything but the kitchen sink was on that lorry. When the entire luggage had been checked to ensure that it was safe and secure, the men waved at the children and shouted.

"See you when we get there."

Auntie Jean conducted a last minute check and Auntie Betty (Aunty Betty was the young assistant in the big girls' house) making sure that everyone had their pillow and pumps. Both young women walked up the aisle of the bus, giving everyone a brown paper sick bag and a stick of barley sugar, which was thought to prevent travel sickness. Auntie Jean laughed, as she stood back and looked at the back seat, where the children were squashed together, kneeling over the back seat looking out of the window.

Miss Ratcliffe and Miss Lewis always sat together behind the driver. Every year Joyce was instructed to sit behind them so they could keep an eye on her, as she was the only one that would probably need her sick bag.

Miss Ratcliffe and Miss Lewis had been close friends for years. Both had been engaged to soldiers who had been killed in the First World War, both were devout Christians. Both had been Sunday School Teachers. It was through their love of children that they had been asked by Mr and Mrs Harvey, founder members of the Orphanage many years ago, if they would act as matrons to unfortunate children, as they were called.

On the journey, both were happy to leave the entertainment to Auntie Jean, Auntie Betty and the older girls. As the coach pulled away, everyone shouted in unison, "three cheers for the driver." Then they began to sing.

"I love to go a wandering," and then, "I spy games," led by the older girls.

The atmosphere on the coach was electric. It was a beautiful summer's day as the coach travelled through the lush, green Yorkshire countryside. Some of the children, who had never seen cows, sheep or horses, were jumping up and down, their mouths wide open and pointing with wonder.

Halfway into the journey the coach parked outside a block of public conveniences. A penny each was given to those in need to slide in the slot above the brass handle on the door to release the catch and open the toilet door. After everyone had returned to their seats, and last minute checks had been made, the children were each given a packet of Smiths Crisps. Inside the packet was a tiny, dark blue, twisted bag of salt. During the second part of the journey, some of the children fell asleep in the comfort of their pillows. Joyce had crept round and climbed on Miss Ratcliffe's knee and was fast asleep in the warmth of her arms.

After what seemed a long time, they arrived at their destination.

"We're here," announced the driver, as he passed a Scarborough sign at the side of the road. Everyone began to sing.

"Oh I do like to be beside the seaside." As the last line was being sung, the driver had driven into the Crescent behind the church and parked the coach directly outside the back entrance, behind the lorry, which had arrived some time ago. The two lorry drivers were sitting on the church step in the sun, smoking cigarettes, waiting to be told where to put what.

When everyone had given three cheers for the driver, the children all charged to the front of the coach, all eager to be off first. Some, struggling with their pillows and pump bags, got wedged inside the door.

"I can smell the sea," cried Neil Kelly, screwing up his face, closing his eyes, breathing up his nose and holding his breath.

"And I can hear it," said young David, holding his head to one side.

The lorry drivers laughed at the two boys and the high-pitched voices of the excited children who were eager to start their holiday.

"Where's the toilet?" shouted one of the younger boys, jumping up and down on the pavement.

"Ugh," said Pat, wrinkling up her nose and running behind Shelagh.

"I'm not showing him where it is," she whispered from behind her older sister's back. "There's onny one and its alus full a flies," she explained, "and I hate flies."

One of the older girls grabbed the boy's hand and headed towards the side door of the church.

Around thirty-four children and four adults would share the one toilet for the next few weeks.

Those that had been before ran inside and led the way down a short corridor towards the small hall on the bottom right. The smell of musty wood filled the room. Four high arched, beautiful, stained glass windows decorated the two corner walls. In the middle of the room, the only furniture was two wooden benches placed on either side of a trestle table.

The little house children were instructed to sit around the table, where meat paste and cheese spread sandwiches, wrapped in Newboulds and Mothers Pride red and white striped grease proof bread paper, (they had been made before the journey) were shared out along with drinks of lemonade. While the children were busy chattering non-stop, excited about what they were going to do in the next few weeks, the lorry drivers were able to deliver safely the boxes and hampers to the appropriate halls.

Later, the older of the children would help empty the boxes and place cutlery into drawers, crockery into cupboards, and pans onto narrow galley shelves, and then assemble the camp beds at the bottom of the hall. One grey blanket, edged with red blanket stitch was placed on each bed. Every morning the camp beds, including Miss Ratcliffe's and Auntie Jean's would be folded and stacked away in a corner of the small room behind a large clothes horse and covered with old sheets, to give more room.

After tea on the first day, a good long walk was always in order for everyone. Down Valley Road, along the front of the South sands, past Jimmy Corrigan's, where all the big rides - Waltzers, Helter-Skelters, Bumper-cars, to name but a few, took place, then round the corner and along the long North Marine Drive.

The tide was in and the youngsters were in their element. Every time the high sprays from the waves, crashing against the wall, loomed high into the air over the railings, to the far side of the Drive under Castle Hill, the children would run underneath in order to get wet. They shrieked with laughter the wetter they became. Miss Ratcliffe and Auntie Jean dodged in and out, trying their best to keep dry. By the time they had returned to the church, everyone was soaking wet, including the grown ups.

On Sunday morning after breakfast, all the children, young and old, would walk through a wooden door at the end of the corridor that led directly into the front of the church where services would be held. The first few rows of pews were always reserved just for them. Sounds of "Ah!" could be heard from the large congregation, as the children walked to their seats. Some of the older girls held their heads down in embarrassment.

After dinner, everyone went on a long walk up the winding twisting road towards the top of Oliver's Mount. The Vicar of the church had asked if it would be possible for all the children to be occupied with outdoor activities on Sundays, as church services would be held throughout the day, and any noise would distract the congregation. Walks were usually planned for Sundays as playing on the beach was not allowed.

In the days that followed, everyone thoroughly enjoyed themselves, having done all that Pat said they would do. One morning, towards the end of breakfast, Auntie Jean shouted.

"Who wants to go on a boat trip, a *big* boat called the 'Coronia?'" emphasising the word *big*.

The local Scarborough newspaper had said that they would foot the bill. Hands of all shapes and sizes shot into the air.

"Not you, I'm afraid," said Auntie Jean, looking at Joyce and cocking her head to one side, everywhere you go you need a sick bag."

Joyce's happy round little face changed to disappointment. She dropped her chin on her chest and then reluctantly put her arm down.

"I'll stay with Joyce," volunteered Shelagh, also dropping her arm.

"Then I'll take you two on the beach with me and treat you both to a donkey ride and an ice cream sandwich," said Miss Ratcliffe smiling.

Pat looked at Miss Ratcliffe and frowned. "That sounds good to me," she thought. The thought of an ice cream sandwich, or even an ice cream lolly, sounded too good to miss. Half licking her lips, she began to lower her arm slowly. She looked back at Auntie Jean, but then again, a ride on a big boat also sounded too good to miss.

"What shall I do, she thought?" frowning and screwing up her face. "I might not get the chance to go on a big boat ride again." She glanced back again at Miss Ratcliffe. "If I'm really, really good in the next few days, chances are she might treat me to a donkey ride and an ice cream. No it had to be the boat ride." With that in mind, she shot her arm back into the air.

It was a warm sunny afternoon. The sun was shining and the sky was blue with the odd white cloud floating by. The children walked excitedly down towards the harbour, all dressed in smart tee shirts and shorts, white socks and sandals. They could see the two big passenger pleasure boats, the 'White Lady' and the 'Coronia', moored in the harbour. They began to run; frightened that it might leave without them.

A reporter was waiting to greet Auntie Jean and the children at the quayside. After he had taken photographs to be published in the newspaper, he helped to walk them across the narrow footbridge onto the 'Coronia', where they sat on wooden benches attached to the side.

A short time later, the reporter exchanged waves with the youngsters as they headed towards the open sea. As they approached the mouth of the harbour, the sun began to disappear behind the now grey clouds and the sea became a little choppy.

"Don't feel very well," remarked young Frank, his face changing colour, as they headed further out to the open sea. He then promptly began to be sick down his tee shirt, over his sandals and onto the deck.

"Neither do I," said Neil, the freckles quickly disappearing from his face. He then followed suit, then another child, and then another.

For a moment, Auntie Jean stood not knowing what to do. Then she had an idea. She ran and lowered one of the buckets; tied to the side of the boat with thick strong rope, into the sea, filling it with water, hoisting it back, beginning to swill the deck, bucket after bucket. After what seemed an endless journey, she breathed a sigh of relief when they finally returned to the harbour. Every one of the young children had been seasick. Eager passengers, wanting to help, gave the white faced, weak bodied and wobbly-legged youngsters, a hand across the narrow footbridge back onto the quayside.

It was a long, slow walk back, as they dragged their lifeless bodies uphill towards the church. Once they had arrived back at the church, Auntie Jean instructed them to undress and leave their stained clothes on the floor in one pile, while she disappeared and returned carrying a bowl of hot water and towels, which were thrown over her shoulders. One by one, she washed and dressed them into pyjamas and nightdresses. Then she sat them around the table and gave each child a hot mug of cocoa.

Some time later, Shelagh and Joyce ran down the corridor and barged into the hall, eager to hear of the afternoon's outing. Miss Ratcliffe stood in the doorway.

"My goodness," she sighed.

"Whatever happened?" she asked, peering at the long white faces around the table, all looking sorry for themselves.

"Don't ask, is all I can say," answered Auntie Jean, holding both hands in the air, "never again. Never thought for one minute they'd all be seasick, they've never needed a sick bag on the coach, I should have known, I should have known better. It's my fault, all my fault. But as I said, never again."

Miss Ratcliffe began to laugh, relieved that there was nothing more seriously wrong with the children.

"It could only happen to you," is all that she could say.

Eventually, Auntie Jean also saw the funny side and joined in the laughter. That night they all slept soundly.

Auntie Jean – Shelagh – Miss Ratcliffe – Pat - Joyce

Miss Lewis and Miss Ratcliffe

Church at Scarborough

Chapter 33

All too soon, the holiday was over. The return coach to Leeds was just as exciting as the journey to Scarborough had been a few weeks earlier. In between the singing and the playing of games, the children shouted noisily at one another, exchanging memories of what they had done and places they had visited. Not one of the younger children mentioned the dreaded boat trip.

"Can't wait to see Tony and tell him what a great time we've had," said Shelagh, nudging Pat, who was sitting beside her and not really listening. She was more interested in playing with a kaleidoscope that she had won in a talent competition in Gala Land a few days earlier. Her hands held tightly around the long tube, one end in the air and the other wedged around an eye. Sounds of "Oh," came from her puckered lips, as she twisted the kaleidoscope round and round, displaying the small brightly coloured glass fragments that formed the different shapes and patterns inside the tube.

"Tony's never been to the seaside," Shelagh said suddenly, "I'm gonna ask Miss Ratcliffe if he can come with us next year. That's if we're not all back home together with our mother and father," she added, with a ring of hope in her voice and shrugging her shoulders.

"He'd love it on the beach, making sandcastles and paddling in the sea. I've got something for him," she said excitedly, dipping her hand into a bag on her knee, which was filled with assorted seashells that she had lovingly collected on the beach. Carefully she lifted out the biggest, a long, twisted, patterned one.

"This one's my favourite," she said, still talking to herself and holding it close to her ear.

"He'll be able to listen to the sea inside the shell, I can't wait to see him," she continued, ignoring Pat's repeated 'Ohs.'

During the journey, Joyce waddled, as usual down the aisle, climbed on Miss Ratcliffe's knee and was asleep for most of the journey home, wrapped comfortably and securely in her arms.

All too soon, they arrived home and life quickly returned to normal in the daily routine of the Orphanage.

A few days after their arrival back from Scarborough, towards the end of dinner, Miss Ratcliffe walked across the dining room from the staff table and stood for a moment.

"When you've finished your dinner I would like to see you, Ernest Little and you Shelagh Gregson, in my sitting room," she announced, leaving them both looking at one another and scowling, trying to remember if they had done something wrong and wondering why she wanted to see only them. Pat looked across at her older sister and she too wondered.

When they had finished their dinner, Ernest and Shelagh walked slowly, with a worried look on their faces, towards the sitting room.

"Come in," Miss Ratcliffe shouted, through the open door. They sheepishly and nervously looked at one another and then stepped slowly inside. Pat tip toed quickly across the hall, arched her back, spread out her hands and leant against the wall directly outside the sitting room. Taking a deep breath, she tilted her head to one side, hoping to listen through the open door.

"Now," said Miss Ratcliffe, who was standing in front of the guarded coal fire, warming her hands behind her back.

"You two are the eldest here. We had planned to transfer you both to the big houses in the next few weeks before you start secondary modern school, but something has cropped up. I've had a 'phone call this morning from the Children's Care Head Office, asking me to take seven-year-old twins, a boy and a girl *today*." She emphasised on the word today.

137

Mr Parnell had telephoned earlier, asking if Miss Ratcliffe could find a place for the two children urgently. He explained that the parents of the twins were blind and were having great difficulty coping with the two boisterous children, and that they were at the end of their tether. The couple had an older son, who was also blind, but they were quite capable and happy to take care of him, as he was not as active as the two youngsters were.

"Auntie Ada will give you both a carrier bag to put your belongings in," she told Shelagh and Ernest, "and then I want you both to make your way over to the big house. You won't be the youngest over there," she assured, looking at Shelagh. "There are a few boys and girls younger than you, *only* because, when they came into care, I didn't have the room to take them. Miss Lewis and Mr Hughes are expecting you and will have a talk to you both when you get there.

Mr Hughes and his wife were in charge of the big boys' house.

Pat ran quickly across the hall and sat on the bottom stairs step, resting her elbows on her knees and holding her sad, little face in her hands.

"Where are you going?" she asked her older sister, pretending not to know, as Shelagh passed her slowly and quietly, carrying a brown paper carrier bag in her hand. Pat followed behind Shelagh to her locker in the dining room. After briefly explaining, Shelagh emptied her locker of comics, a pen and pencil case, and her beloved green Bible into the bag, and then holding Pat's hand, the sisters climbed up the open staircase towards their bedroom.

Pat sat on her hands on top of Shelagh's bed; swinging her legs and watching her sister shove a few clothes into the bag.

"Can I have Rosebud?" Pat asked suddenly, looking at the naked doll in the toy cot beside her bed.

"What for, what do you want her for?" Shelagh replied. "She's got an arm and a leg missing." She had become bored of the doll a long time ago.

"I want her cos she's yours," shouted Pat, jumping down from the bed and running down the stairs. Pat returned a few minutes later, carrying and struggling with a box almost as big as her, full of odd dolls heads, bodies, arms and legs.

"Will you mend her for me?" she asked, dropping the box on the floor. Between them, the girls rummaged through the box and found a suitable arm and leg. Shelagh fastened an elastic band to the spare arm, and then threaded it through the hollow doll's body, connecting it to the other arm, and the same with the leg.

"Good as new," she pronounced, handing the doll to her sister. Pat promptly dressed it in the well-washed, blue knitted outfit that had arrived with the doll when it was new, then laid it down in her own bed besides Rags. Rags was the name she had given to the rag doll Miss Ratcliffe had given to her when she had first arrived at the Children's Home. The sisters made their way down to the cloakroom under the stairs.

"Where are you going?" asked Joyce, who had appeared from nowhere and seeing her older sister lift her coat from a peg.

"I'm going to live in the big girls' house," replied Shelagh.

"What for?" Joyce asked, too young to understand, "don't want ya to go."

"Neither do I," said Pat, tears welling in her eyes.

"You mustn't worry about anything," Shelagh assured them. "I won't be far away, only over the yard and I'll see you everyday after school." She gave Joyce a big hug and kissed her on her cheek, then wrapped her arms around Pat, tears now streaming down her face.

"You must take care of Joyce now," said Shelagh solemnly, "cos I won't be here anymore, and ya must tell me if anything is worrying ya both." She gave Pat a kiss on her wet cheek, and then let go suddenly, holding her by the shoulders at arms length.

"Are ya worried that you'll start getting bossed about again if I'm not here?" she asked. Pat nodded slowly, her bottom lip quivering.

"Well let me tell ya," Shelagh insisted, with an angry tone in her voice,

"if anybody starts hitting ya again, you must tell me straight away and I'll hit'em back."

"Will ya?" Pat pleaded, looking sadly into her eyes.

"I will," Shelagh said adamantly, giving her another hug.

Looking slightly relieved, Pat wiped her eyes and face with her cardigan sleeve, and her nose with the other. Shelagh left her sisters holding hands on the veranda and could feel them watching her as she walked across the yard. Before she stepped into the back door of the big girls' house, she looked across and gave them a wave. They waved half heartedly back.

The back door of the house opened into a square hall, from which doors branched off to the dining room and kitchen. Turning a corner, Shelagh passed an open, sweeping staircase. Frightened and not knowing anyone, she walked down a short, cold, tiled floor corridor and gently knocked on Matron's partially opened door.

"Come in," Miss Lewis shouted. With butterflies in her stomach, Shelagh stepped timidly just inside the door, holding the carrier bag in front with both hands. Miss Lewis was sitting by the fire in a comfortable armchair.

"Come and sit beside me," she invited, looking over the top of her gold framed glasses and beckoning her to sit in an armchair beside her, "I've been expecting you."

The room was much the same as Miss Ratcliffe's sitting room with odd armchairs dotted around. An untidy pile of newspapers and magazines lay on top of a table under a bay window that looked directly onto a small garden under a wall. Beyond the wall was the main road. Beside the newspapers stood a large basket filled with newly darned socks, separated into pairs. Sensing the fright on the child's face, Miss Lewis leaned forward, sitting on the edge of the chair and reached out to hold her shaking hands.

"Has Miss Ratcliffe explained why you have had to be transferred today?" she asked in a gentle voice. Shelagh nodded slowly.

"And did she explain you won't be attending the same school as everyone else?" Shelagh lifted up her eyes with a puzzled look on her face and shook her head slowly.

"It's been decided by the Committee that you will attend a different school to the others." Miss Lewis explained. "The reason why, is that there are a few other children here, and in the boys' house, that are the same age as you, and if we send you all to the same school, not only will you live together, you will all be in the same class, and that's not a good idea. Brothers and sisters who live together are not placed in the same class. It's a mixed school, so it will be good experience for you to mix with other children from normal backgrounds. I want you to be on your best behaviour and make us very proud of you. Hopefully Pat will join you in a few years." She let go of her hands and sat back in her chair.

"I've asked Jane, one of the older girls, to watch out for you until you find your feet and get your bearings." She continued. You'll probably find her in the kitchen. She will show you around the rest of the home and explain the rules of the home. Don't look so worried; you've got two weeks to settle in before you start your new school. Now off you go," she ushered, picking up the partially darned sock beside her.

Shelagh found Jane in the kitchen with her back towards the door. She was draped over the end of the sideboard, swaying from side to side, listening and singing to a Johnnie Ray record that was playing on a small bakelite wireless on a narrow shelf attached to the back of the sideboard. Shelagh stood quietly, not daring to interrupt until the record had finished. Then she tapped Jane gingerly on the shoulder. The girls sauntered across the hall into the dining room that was positioned at the back of the house. Jane sat down on a long bench under a window at the other side of a long table. Propping her elbows on the top, she held her face between her hands frowning, her eyes scanning across a block of handbag size lockers behind the door.

"There's an empty one down there," she instructed, looking at an open door, which revealed an empty locker, "you might as well have that one."

Shelagh knelt down and began to put her belongings into the locker.

"Miss Lewis is very keen on manners," Jane pointed out, looking down the two long tables that filled the sidewall.

"If you ask for anything, always say please, and if you take anything from anyone, always say thank you and she's very strict on table manners. Always hold your knife and fork properly when you're eating. Eat with your mouth closed and never speak with your mouth full, and when you've eaten everything on your plate, put your knife and fork together on top. Only then can you have a pudding. Before you leave the table, make sure everyone has eaten everything on their plate, and then you can put your arm in the air and ask Miss Lewis if you may be excused from the table." Without pausing, she continued to relate the house rule to Shelagh.

"You will sit at the bottom of the table with the younger ones and move up to the top table according to age. By the time you get to the top table, I will have left, and you will have taken on some of the older girls' duties. Oh and you're not allowed to use the bathroom during meals."

Shelagh peered down the long tables that were laid out for tea, rows of small plates, each holding a triangle of cheese spread and a small apple had been carefully placed for the children.

"I love cheese," Shelagh sighed, licking her lips and looking sheepishly at Jane.

"But I hate meat," she mumbled lowering her chin.

"You're not allowed to 'not like', said Jane, with a serious look on her face, "you have to eat what you're given and all of it. But I wouldn't worry too much about that," she smiled, giving her a wink. A puzzled look appeared on Shelagh's face, not quite understanding what she meant.

"If we hurry upstairs," Jane urged, "I'll show you around and if we're quick, you might still have time to play in the yard with your sisters." The girls quickly ran up the open, sweeping staircase to the dormitory for the younger children, which was directly above the dining room. Rows of woodenheaded beds filled both sides of the room facing each other.

"This one's yours in the corner," Jane said peering behind the door to a neatly made bed.

"When Miss Lewis rings the bell on a morning, before you go to the bathroom, you strip your bed, put your pillow and blankets on the floor at the bottom and then turn your mattress. You must turn your mattress every morning, as it gives your mattress some fresh air and stops it from smelling. After you've dressed, you make your bed and it must be tidy or you will have to make it again. If you're not sure how to make a bed, don't worry, just watch and copy everyone else." They rushed across the landing to the bathroom. Behind the door, rows of hand made flannels hung above a long line of towels.

"Yours is number ten," Jane instructed, holding out a fresh towel on a hook displaying a red embroidered number in the corner. She stepped back and put her hands on the edge of the cast iron bath.

"Baths are once a week, on a Sunday after tea."

Shelagh smiled and replied, "the last time I was in a bath as big as that was with Tony in Street Lane Home." To Shelagh it seemed to have been years ago.

"Clean clothes and underclothes are once a week, on a Monday morning before school," Jane continued.

"Now if you run quickly, you'll still have time to play out with your sisters before tea."

Sometime later, Miss Lewis appeared at the back door, ringing a large, brass bell. Children of different shapes and sizes ran, shoving and pushing their way into the dining room. Shelagh found an empty space on the bench at the far side of the bottom table and sat in silence, watching and listening to their non-stop chatter and laughter. As Miss Lewis and Auntie Betty (Miss Lewis' young assistant, who had grown up in the home) walked into the room and made their way to the staff table in the corner, the children became deathly silent. Miss Lewis looked across the room directly at Shelagh.

"Has Jane explained table manners to you?" she enquired, Shelagh nodded.

"Then would you like to say Grace?" she ordered, holding both hands together, closing her eyes and lowering her head. Shelagh felt her face blush with embarrassment and looked up and down the tables. Everyone was holding their hands together. Some had their eyes tight shut and some were peeping at her and waiting. She began to mumble quietly and quickly not stopping for breath.

"For what we are about to receive," she could feel her heart pounding through her chest,

"May the Lord make us truly thankful. Amen."

No sooner had Shelagh said 'Amen', arms appeared, reaching for buttered bread on plates from the middle of the table. She watched the girl that was sitting beside her slide her cheese triangle onto her knee and give it to a boy sat next to her. He in turn slid his apple to her, all the while not taking their eyes off Miss Lewis who was busy talking to Auntie Betty. Now Shelagh understood what Jane meant. You could swap what you did not like as long as you weren't caught.

Hours later in the dormitory, in the last few hours of daylight, Shelagh lay in bed listening to the other children whispering across the room. Talking was not allowed at bedtime. As she lay motionless, drinking in the day's events, her eyes wandered around the dormitory. She caught sight of a small picture of Jesus sat on top of a chest of drawers at the bottom of the room. He was draped in white robes, and in his arms, he was carrying a small girl with short fair hair. She was wearing white socks, a grey skirt, an orange knitted jumper, and on her feet, a pair of black pumps. She reminded her of Pat. Three young teenagers stood around the feet of Jesus, two boys and a girl. One of the boys was wearing a peaked cap, knee length grey trousers and socks and on his feet, a pair of black, lace up ankle boots. Under his arm, he carried a pile of newspapers. The boy reminded her of Tony, although her brother was not quite old enough yet for a paper round. She wondered as she looked at Jesus if he could see her, and if there really was a real Jesus.

"Anyway," she thought, glaring angrily down at the picture, "I've fallen out with you. You've never answered my prayers or Tony's, so I'm not talking to you anymore." Sticking her chin in the air and moving her head further up the pillow, she promptly turned over to face the wall.

Her mind wandered to the new school that she would begin in two weeks time. It would be her fifth school and sixth home in six years. She hoped that this school would not be like the last one, where they were called 'home kids' and laughed at. She fell asleep dreaming that she would find a friend who did not care if she lived in a home or not.

As the time drew near, the prospect of a new school the following morning made Shelagh nervous. She lay, tossing and turning, not able to sleep; so much was going through her mind. She was nervous, frightened and excited at the thought of being the first person from the home to go to this school.

No sooner had she fallen asleep, than Miss Lewis appeared in the bedroom doorway, ringing the brass bell. By the time Shelagh had got out of bed, the room looked much like a bombsite. Mattresses were hanging over the edge of the wooden slatted beds, and blankets, sheets and pillows lay on the floor at the foot of every bed, which were waiting to be made.

A long queue formed across the landing after everyone had been to the bathroom. Miss Lewis was standing at the top of a stepladder with her arms and head inside the top cupboard of a large fitted wardrobe, sorting out and throwing down clean underclothes according to size. She threw Shelagh a white vest and a pair of green flannelette knickers.

"There's no elastic in one of the legs," Shelagh whispered sideways to Dorothy, who was standing behind her as Shelagh held them out.

"Stop complaining," Dorothy replied, "As long as you've got elastic in the top, that's all that matters," shoving Shelagh out of the way.

After the usual breakfast of porridge, bread and marmalade and cocoa, everyone formed a line across the hall waiting to be checked by Miss Lewis before school.

"Your shoe laces are not fastened," Matron remarked to one little boy, who promptly knelt down to fasten them. After she had checked that they had washed behind their ears, cleaned their teeth and their clothing was neat and tidy, they left by the side door, one by one.

Shelagh met Pat at the gate. They walked hand in hand down the long road. Behind them, Auntie Jean was escorting Joyce and the younger children to Quarry Mount School. At the bottom of the road, Shelagh and Pat separated.

It was almost a mile to Brudnell Secondary Modern School. When Shelagh arrived, she nervously reported to the teacher in the yard, who was carrying a clipboard in her hand and seemed to be in charge.

The teacher directed her to the cloakroom and then told her to report to the class that she would attend during the next year. The classroom door was wide open when she arrived. Some boys and girls were sitting together at the two-seater desks. A group of boys were standing in a circle, talking and laughing. Shelagh looked around the room, her heart was pounding and she did not know where to sit, as there seemed to be so many children. She caught the eye of a bonny, freckled faced girl with shiny, short brown hair. The girl was dressed neatly in a crisp, white, long-sleeved shirt, a green cardigan and a green pleated skirt. Her green and yellow school tie was neatly tied around her neck. She patted the seat next to her.

"Come and sit beside me," she beckoned to Shelagh, who gratefully accepted.

"My names Brenda, what's yours?" the girl asked.

"Shelagh," was the reply.

"My dads a policeman, what does your dad do?" the girl enquired.

"Oh, he's a foreman in a tailoring factory," Shelagh blurted, thinking of her uncle Harry, then suddenly realising what she had said.

"My mother doesn't work," Brenda persisted, "she stays at home to look after my older brother and me. His name's Tony. What does your mother do?" she asked.

"Oh she doesn't work either," Shelagh lied, thinking of her Auntie Ethel, "she stays at home to look after us. I've a brother called Tony as well. He's a year younger than me, and I have two younger sisters, Pat and Joyce."

"I live in a back to back house not too far away. Where do you live?" Brenda asked.

"Oh I live in a great big house, a long, long way away," Shelagh answered.

"There I've done it," she thought, "she doesn't know I'm telling fibs, she really believes me. How will she ever know? I'm the first from the Home, and there's no one to tell her the truth. If Brenda thinks I'm normal, she'll be nice to me, and everyone else will treat me the same as them."

Shelagh decided that seemed a good idea. She would pretend while she was at school that she came from the same kind of family as everyone else. "And there's another thing," she thought, while ever I pretend, they won't laugh at me and call me a 'home kid'. "Yes," she thought, "what a good idea."

Shelagh and Brenda became best friends, and while she was at school, she lived in another world, the world of normal people. Brenda had a talent for sewing, and helped Shelagh in the sewing class to hand sew and embroider a pink cookery apron and hat that would be used when they were to begin cookery lessons.

In the months that followed, Shelagh lived for school, always arriving early and often stopping late to help after class. Brenda asked her many times to visit her at home but she always declined, knowing that if she visited Brenda, she would have to ask her to visit her home. She couldn't have that, as it would blow her cover and she preferred just a school friendship. Shelagh lived in two worlds, one in a world of normal children, the other as an orphan in a children's home. She kept the pretence up for months.

Chapter 34

One late Saturday morning, when the usual chores had been done, all the children from the three houses were shouting, laughing and playing in the yard. Joyce was playing 'Happy Families' with her friend Maureen, and Pat was playing whip and top with her friend Valerie at the far side of the yard, on a large, smooth area of concrete. Shelagh was playing 'three balls' to rhymes against the wall in between the girls' and boys' houses. She was singing out loudly when in the background she heard someone shout, "Grego!" That was the nickname she was called at school and at home.

Finishing the rhyme and catching the three balls, she turned around to see who was shouting her. She stood frozen and horrified. Staring at her was Arthur Black, a boy in her class. He was straddled across a pushbike holding on to the handlebars with both hands and still shouting, "Grego!"

"What are you doing here?" she asked her face now crimson.

"I've got a Saturday job delivering bread," the boy replied.

Attached to the front of the bike was a large basket, filled with dozens of loaves of bread.

"No wonder you said you lived in a big house," he grinned, looking and nodding at the big house.

"Now I know where you live. You're an orphan aren't you? You don't have a mother and father de ya? You were lying weren't ya?" he jeered.

"Please don't tell anyone, please," Shelagh begged.

"What's it worth?" he asked.

"Anything, but please don't tell anyone, please," she pleaded

"What's it worth," Arthur said again, smugly tilting his head to one side.

"If I get you some cocoa and sugar, will that be alright?" Shelagh suggested. "I'll put it in a bag and mix it for you."

"That'll do nicely for now," he replied.

Shelagh ran inside the house, and luckily, no one was in the pantry. She returned with a mixed bag of cocoa and sugar.

"Now you won't tell will ya?" She begged, staring at his self-satisfied grin.

In the weeks that followed, she stole crab apples, oxos, more cocoa and sugar; and anything else she could to stop him from telling everyone at school where she lived.

"Why haven't you told me?" asked Brenda, some months later.

"Told you what," Shelagh answered, fearing the worst.

"You know what," replied Brenda, "why didn't you tell me you live in a children's home?" "How do you know?" Shelagh asked.

"Everybody knows," said Brenda, "Arthur Black told everyone weeks ago. You can tell by the clothes you wear. Your gymslip has a great big darn down the side. You keep the same clothes on all week. You're the only one in the class who wears second hand, lace-up shoes, and your socks always have big darns in the heels. Why didn't you tell me yourself? Why haven't you told me before now, I thought we were friends. You should have told me."

"I didn't think anyone would be my friend once they knew, and I didn't want to risk it," Shelagh replied.

"Well you're wrong," answered Brenda, warmly. "I'll always be your friend, and you'll find nobody cares if you live in a children's home or not, so there's no need to lie anymore."

Chapter 35

Several weeks later, on one of her monthly visits, Miss Hudson was pleased and delighted to hear that Miss Ratcliffe's niece had become the foster Aunt to Joyce and one of the older boys in the little house. She had taken both children to the cinema in Leeds city centre to see Walt Disney's 'Lady and the Tramp' the previous Saturday, and planned to spend every alternative Saturday with them. Pat had also acquired a foster Aunt and Uncle, a Mr and Mrs Wood, who had three children of their own, one a daughter called Patricia who was the same age as Pat. The two girls had built up an extraordinary friendship, so Miss Ratcliffe had said. Pat too planned to spend every alternative Saturday with Mr and Mrs Wood and their children at their house, which was near the Home. Joyce ran into the sitting room, climbed on Miss Hudson's knee, stared into her eyes and began excitedly to tell her the full story of 'The Lady and the Tramp'. Her eyes dancing around as she chatted non-stop. Miss Ratcliffe was sitting in her chair shaking her head and smiling at Joyce, who seemed to demand most of Miss Hudson's attention, and indeed took up most of her visit. Pat, who was most definitely the quieter of the two sisters, was standing to one side with a recorder in her hand, waiting to play a tune for Miss Hudson. Eventually, with great pride, she played 'Now the day is over,' then ran back outside into the yard to play with her friend Valerie.

Before Miss Hudson left, she handed over to Miss Ratcliffe, thirty-five pounds and fifteen shillings boarding out allowance, for the two girls, One pound seven shillings and sixpence, per week for each child. Then she threaded her way through noisy children, across the yard, towards the big girls' house, heading down the corridor towards Miss Lewis' sitting room. Shelagh was in the dining room playing 'snakes and ladders' with a few other children. She ran into the hall and grabbed Miss Hudson's hand from behind.

"I've got something to ask you?" Shelagh said hopefully. They stepped inside the sitting room. "Can I visit my auntie Ethel and uncle Harry?" she asked. For a moment, words failed Miss Hudson. She looked across at Miss Lewis who was sitting opposite in her chair.

"She's asked me a dozen times over the last week," said Miss Lewis wearily. "At eleven years old she's old enough to travel on her own, if permission is given. I will gladly give her the bus fare, but I did tell her the decision is not mine to make, she must ask you."

It had been over two years since Shelagh had seen or heard from her aunt and uncle, or indeed from any of her family on both sides. All kinds of things were going through Miss Hudson's head. This had totally taken her by surprise. For a moment, she did not know what to say. After a minute, she found herself saying.

"Why don't you write a letter asking if you can visit one Saturday afternoon, and I will pay them a call in the next few days?" She secretly thought that Shelagh was perhaps feeling a bit lonely and left out, knowing that Pat and Joyce would not be around every other week. She probably missed them terribly.

"When I've been to see your Aunt and Uncle, I will give Miss Lewis a ring and let her know," assured Miss Hudson, "meantime why don't you write a nice letter?" Shelagh thanked her and then ran back out of the sitting room to the dining room to continue her game of 'snakes and ladders'.

"I'm not sure what kind of reception I will get when I visit Mr and Mrs Crampton," said Miss Hudson to Miss Lewis. "I'm not sure what their reaction will be when they receive a letter out of the blue. It's best I call round first to see how the land lies."

Miss Hudson needn't to have worried. Mr Crampton was pleased to see her. He apologised for his wife's absence, who was out shopping. They had received Shelagh's letter a few days earlier and said they would be delighted to see her as long as she understood she would never be able to live with them again. Mrs Crampton was now working, and with two young children to take care of, that would never be possible. "There's no danger of that," thought Miss Hudson, "she would never leave her sisters now."

Pleased with the outcome, she rang Miss Lewis later that day to ask her to inform Shelagh that she could visit a week next Saturday, the same day Pat and Joyce would be out with their new foster Aunt and Uncle.

On the day of the visit, Shelagh helped clear and wash the breakfast pots and pans, ran upstairs and dressed in her Sunday best clothes. As soon as she was ready, she reported to Miss Lewis, who gave her enough bus fare for the journey there and back home.

"I want you back in the home by seven o'clock, no later," instructed Miss Lewis firmly, "now off you go and have a good time."

She caught a bus to City Square, then the number one bus to Beeston, with butterflies in her stomach all the way.

Her cousin Pat was sitting on the steps in the back yard. They nervously exchanged 'helloes' with each other.

"Come and say hello to my dad," invited Pat, "he's waiting to see you. Then we can go find Terry on the 'brick field'. Mr Crampton gave her a big hug, and said her Aunt Ethel was visiting her elderly sick mother but would be back in time for tea. The girls found Terry on the swings. All three children played on the roundabout, swings, and slid down the high slide, screeching and howling with laughter, they were having a wonderful time.

A few hours later Auntie Ethel appeared, peering over the 'brick field' wall.

"Tea, you three," she shouted.

"Is scrambled egg, beans and chips all right for you?" she asked Shelagh, as they were sitting around the kitchen table.

"I love chips," Shelagh replied, watching her uncle making a chip sandwich. "We don't often get chips. There are too many of us."

"How many children are there?" her uncle asked.

"About twenty four in the big house and about twelve in the little house," Shelagh calculated.

"Twenty four," exclaimed auntie Ethel, "I don't think I'd fancy making chips for all those children either."

"What kind of meals do you get?" her uncle asked.

"Breakfast and teas are alright, it's the dinners I don't like," Shelagh replied. "Roast meat on Sunday after church; cold meat, Monday; stewing meat, Tuesday and it's alus full of grizzle and lumps of fat; Wednesday, shepherd's pie; and Thursday, mince meat."

"I thought you were like me. You don't like meat, do you?" remarked her uncle.

"No I don't," replied Shelagh, "you have to eat what you're given and you're not allowed to not like anything. Sometimes I manage to swap with others, but sometimes I can't, so I swallow it down with water. Best day is Sunday, after dinner, when all the pots and pans are washed and put away. We line up outside Miss Lewis' sitting room and she gives us a handful of sweets and then we all go over to Miss Ratcliffe's house and watch 'Lassie' on the television. If you've been naughty in that week, you can't go, and you don't get any sweets either."

"Would you like me to make chips for you the next time you visit?" her aunt asked, watching as Shelagh also made a chip sandwich.

"Ooh, can I come again next month?" she pleaded.

"Course you can, and you don't have to write either," said her uncle.

"Yes I do," Shelagh answered, "Miss Hudson says its manners to write and ask first."

"Now, don't you be late home," said her aunt, "you've two buses to catch, and we don't want you getting into trouble or you won't be able to come again."

As Shelagh was about to leave, her uncle beckoned her over to where he was sitting. He slid a new shiny silver half crown out of his trouser pocket and handed it to her. She had never seen so much money.

Eventually, she got off the bus at Hyde Park and began to walk her way home through the cobbled street behind Cliff Road. She could see Pat in the distance, sitting on the flags outside the fish shop, leaning against the wall.

"What are you doing?" she asked her sister as she drew nearer. Pat was licking a piece of greaseproof paper held close to her face with both hands.

"Miss Ratcliffe sent me to get her a fish for her supper," Pat replied. The wrapped fish lay on the flags beside her. "And that lady in there," she continued, tilting her head over her shoulder towards the fish shop, "knows where I live and gave me a bag of scraps with bits of fish."

"Wait there and don't move," said Shelagh, disappearing into the empty fish shop.

"Fish and chips with scraps to eat now, with salt and vinegar, please," she asked hastily,

placing the half crown on top of the counter.

"One and six," said the assistant, taking the money then handing her the change. Shelagh sat down beside Pat on the flags.

"What are you doing?" Pat asked, watching her re-open the newspaper beside her, and then re- wrap the hottest fish for Miss Ratcliffe.

"Miss Ratcliffe can have the hottest and these are for us to share," Shelagh said generously.

Pat's face lit up. Shelagh tore the paper in half and placed half of the fish and chips on Pat's lap.

"Um! These are lovely," Pat kept saying, shovelling the fish, chips and scraps into her mouth with her greasy fingers. "I've never had fish before." It didn't take them long to finish. Shelagh screwed up the greasy newspaper and put it in the waste paper basket outside the shop. Pat wiped her hands and face on a piece of white rag that she had taken out of a pocket in the back of her green flannelette knickers before handing the rag to Shelagh.

Then the sisters ran as fast as they could up the long road, down the drive and into the yard.

"Here," gasped Shelagh, giving Pat two thru'penny bits, "one for you and one for Joyce, and I've still got sixpence left."

"Ooh thank you," said Pat, her eyes sparkling.

"You'd better hurry, Miss Ratcliffe will be wondering where you are. Go on, and I'll see you tomorrow."

Shelagh reported to Miss Lewis, just in time, one minute to seven.

Chapter 36

In the months that passed, Tony never arrived on visiting days. The girls were getting worried and began to ask questions.

"Why doesn't Tony visit anymore?" Pat asked Miss Ratcliffe.

"Has Tony forgotten us," wondered Joyce.

Shelagh, being Shelagh, constantly nattered Miss Lewis and Miss Hudson too, on her monthly visits.

"Can I have his address and I'll write to him?" Shelagh asked.

For some reason Miss Hudson did not give her Tony's address.

"We miss him. We want to see him. I need to know if he's alright, I have to see him," Shelagh constantly nattered.

"Mr and Mrs Hawkins have been having a lot of family problems." Miss Hudson explained. "I was hoping eventually they would be able to bring Tony. I know he hasn't been for a long time," she remarked, looking into Shelagh's concerned face. She took hold of both Shelagh's hands and sighed deeply.

"I know next Saturday is visiting day. I do have a very important meeting to attend to during the afternoon, but, if I have time, I could collect him for an hour or two early in the afternoon." Shelagh began to jump up and down, thrilled at the thought of seeing Tony.

"Thank you, thank you," she said excitedly.

"I can't promise, but I will try," smiled the kind-hearted Miss Hudson.

The following Saturday was a beautiful day. The sun was shining down on the children in the yard as they played. Not sure if Tony would visit, Shelagh and Pat played in the far corner of the yard, knowing that if he arrived he would know where to find them.

On Saturday afternoon, Miss Hudson collected Tony and dropped him at the Orphanage gates.

"I'll be back for you in an hour or so," she shouted, as she drove away.

Tony ran down the drive and stood under the tree at the entrance of the yard, his eyes searching for his sisters. Joyce was sitting behind Maureen, one of the twins, on a small tricycle, with her arms around her waist, using her feet as pedals as they circled the yard, screeching with laughter.

Tony ran over to Shelagh and Pat who were sitting on the grass. Pat was playing her recorder. Shelagh gave him a motherly hug.

From his pocket, he took a bar of chocolate, a packet of spangles and a packet of wine gums and handed them to Shelagh.

The three siblings sat crossed legged in a circle. Shelagh began to break the chocolate into six pieces. Joyce abruptly stopped pedalling, shoved her shoulders back and held her head into the air, her nose twitching. She could smell chocolate a mile away. She jumped up quickly from behind Maureen and ran over to her brother and sisters, leaving her friend straddled across the cycle a few yards away. Shelagh began to share out the pieces of chocolate. She caught sight of Maureen out of the corner of her eye, staring at them; so she beckoned her over and gave her a piece. The one remaining piece she gave to Joyce, who promptly shoved it into her mouth alongside the other. Shelagh then shared out the wine gums and the spangles, including Maureen in the sharing. As she was giving out the last of the sweets, a dark grey cloud hung above them and it began to rain. Pat grabbed Tony's hand and headed towards the large, open fronted, corrugated roofed shed at the far side of the yard. Shelagh wrapped her arms around Joyce's waist, picked her up and followed them. Maureen ran indoors.

When they were inside the hut, Pat climbed up and sat on top of an old table tennis table, with Tony sat beside her. Shelagh then lifted Joyce on top of the table alongside her sister and brother. All four of them sat beside each other in a row, watching the heavy rain. They looked a picture of contentment.

"Why haven't you been for a long time?" Shelagh asked Tony.

"We've missed you," added Pat, sitting on her hands and swinging her legs.

"Yes we have," said Joyce, nodding her head constantly so as not to be left out.

Tony dropped his chin on his chest, his mouth drooping at the edges.

"Mrs Hawkins has just had a baby boy," he said sadly. "He's only a few weeks old and Mr Hawkins is too poorly to bring me. I hate it there even more now. It's worse now there's a baby. All I ever do is trail to the shops after school, day after day after day, shop after shop after shop." His head tilting side to side as he spoke.

"First to the bread shop, then to the greengrocers, then to the dairy, then the butchers," he complained, "I'm sick of it, and it's a long way up that big hill, and I still have to go, even when it's raining. All the kids in the street call me a sissy."

"Why do you have to do all the shopping?" asked Shelagh.

"Mrs Hawkins sez she doesn't have the time to look after Mr Hawkins *and* a baby, and besides, she sez it's cheaper for her to buy food each day," he carried on. "Every time I complain, she grabs me by the ears, drags me upstairs and locks me in my room until the next day. I don't like being locked up, so I don't complain anymore. Is our mother and father dead?" suddenly he asked.

"Our mother is still alive, cos uncle Harry sez so," replied Shelagh. "She still has our brother with her and she has a new husband now, and they call him Jack, and they have three more little girls, and we still can't go live with them cos their house isn't big enough."

"What about our father?" Tony asked again.

"uncle Harry sez he's disappeared off the face of the earth," Shelagh explained, "that means no one knows where he is. Next time I visit, I'll ask uncle Harry for our mother's address and then I'll write to her and remind her that we're still here, just in case she's forgotten about us. Meantime, you must still say your prayers to Jesus even if you think he's not listening. He might hear you one night."

The rain had stopped and the sun came from behind the cloud, revealing a beautiful rainbow on the horizon.

"Piggy back ride," shouted Pat, jumping on Tony's back.

Joyce threw her arms around Shelagh's neck and wrapped her legs around her waist.

"Race ya," she shouted.

They began to race round the yard, laughing aloud. They were having a wonderful time.

Some time later, Miss Hudson made her way down the drive and stood under the large tree. The luscious green leaves on the heavy branches above her, hid her from sight. She watched with wonder as the children, of all ages, played happily together. She caught sight of the Gregsons at the far side of the yard. They were thoroughly enjoying themselves and their laughter was loud and infectious. Miss Hudson had not heard Tony laugh in a long time. She sighed heavily as she watched them.

She had been trained as a children's social worker to deal with all kinds of children from all different kinds of backgrounds, but nothing could have prepared her for the hurt and emotions that came with the job. She felt a big lump in her throat and butterflies in her stomach as she watched and listened.

First, she looked at Joyce, a strong little girl who loved life, and was quite capable of taking care of herself. Then her gaze turned to Pat, a tiny framed nervous little girl who was easily bullied. Then there was Tony, who over the months had become very quiet and distant. She had often asked him what was bothering him, but he always pursed his lips together, and looked down not answering her. In fact, he never shared a conversation with her anymore. She constantly worried about him. Then there was Shelagh, who at eleven years old was rapidly growing into a young woman. Shelagh was at her happiest when she was with her brother and sisters. Miss Ratcliffe had once remarked that from her being a very young child, she had taken on adult responsibility for her brother and sisters. It showed, as she loved them dearly.

It had been seven years since they had been put into care. The years had passed quickly and there was still no sign of any of the family taking an interest in them. It seemed as though they had been forgotten. Miss Hudson stepped out from under the tree and caught their attention, pointing to her watch and beckoning them over. Tony's face changed. By the expression on his face, it was clear he did not want to leave just yet. All four children held hands and followed

Miss Hudson to her car. As she drove away, Tony pressed his hands and face against the window and mouthed.

"Don't forget to find out where our mother lives."

"I won't," Shelagh mouthed back.

It was to be a few months later, that she would ask that very important question.

Chapter 37

The previous month Shelagh had written her usual monthly letter to her aunt and uncle asking permission to visit them. Her aunt had replied, saying that they would be on holiday that particular Saturday, but they would be pleased to see her the following month.

The days and weeks leading up to her next visit seemed to pass slowly. Eventually, after what felt like a long time, she made her usual journey to see her aunt and uncle. She spent the day, as she always did, playing on the 'brick field' with Pat and Terry.

Shelagh had thought about this day for a long time and had planned to ask that all-important question during teatime when they would all be sitting around the kitchen table. With butterflies in her stomach, she looked directly at her uncle.

"Do you know where my mother lives?" she asked.

He put his knife and fork down on his plate, propped his elbows on the table and held his head between his hands, then looked across at his wife with a frown on his face, and then back at Shelagh.

"Why do you want to know?" he replied, cautiously.

"Cos I think she might have forgotten about us and I want to remind her that we're still here," blurted Shelagh, "and besides, Tony is really unhappy. He sez he's had enough and wants to go back home. He wants us all to live together again and I thought if I wrote to her, I could go and see her and tell her we've been in that Orphanage a long time."

Her uncle looked at his wife and sighed. For a moment, he was stuck for words.

"Your Grandma Crampton is always asking how you are," her aunt butted in, breaking the silence.

"I could give you her address and I'm sure she would love to see you," said her relieved uncle. "Why don't you visit her next month?"

A disappointed look appeared on Shelagh's face. It was not the answer she had been expecting. She dared not ask again as he might think she was being cheeky and stop her from visiting. She could not have that, as her uncle was the only relative she knew, and if she wanted to find any more of her family, he was her only contact.

"Before you leave I'll give you grandma's address," he offered, sounding pleased that they had come up with an alternative solution.

On her journey home Shelagh kept on looking at the piece of paper with her grandmother's address written on. It was not the address she had been hoping for, but it was a start.

"One day I will find our mother," she thought. Then her attention turned again to her grandmother.

"First, I'll have to ask Miss Hudson if I can write," she decided, "and if she says I can, I'll save my pocket money and buy some posh writing paper and envelopes to match, and when I visit, I'll ask her if she knows where our mother is. I'm sure she'll know."

With that in mind, she felt more settled.

It seemed a long time before Miss Hudson made her monthly visit. After checking on Pat and Joyce's progress, she made her way across the yard to the big girls' house. Shelagh immediately pounced on her and followed her into Miss Lewis' sitting room.

"Can I visit my grammas, please?" she burst out. "uncle Harry sez she'd love to see me. Please can I write and ask?"

"Well I suppose so," replied Miss Hudson. "If that's what your Uncle says, then it's alright by me. However, before you write, I have a little surprise for you. Mrs Hawkins has invited you to spend the day with Tony at his house on your next monthly outing. Why don't you write to your Grandmother the following month?"

Shelagh began to jump up and down excitedly at the thought of visiting Tony. She had never been to his house, and she couldn't wait.

"I'll write the numbers of the buses on a piece of paper and give you the bus fare," added Miss Lewis, who was standing at the back of the room in the front of the bay window, listening to their conversation.

Once again, the days and weeks leading up to the visit seemed to drag, but eventually that all-important Saturday arrived.

During breakfast, Shelagh had butterflies and a strange feeling in her stomach that she put down to nerves. After helping wash and put away crockery and checking that the dining room tables were neat and tidy, she ran upstairs to change into her Sunday best. As she was dressing, she discovered she had started her periods. She knew what they were. In the school playground, she had heard many times the older girls talk about such things.

Suddenly, feeling very grown up, she knocked on Miss Lewis' bedroom door, hoping that she would be inside. Miss Lewis appeared holding a hairbrush in one hand, her grey and white speckled straight hair hanging down her back past her waist. Shelagh proudly told of her discovery. Miss Lewis reached into a cupboard behind her and gave her a small cardboard box, inside of which was a white Dr White's sanitary belt.

"This is for you and no one else," she instructed. "You won't get another so take good care of it. If you lose it, you'll have to make do with a bandage or safety pins."

Miss Lewis wrapped two thick sanitary towels in a piece of paper and handed them to Shelagh.

"I want you to try and make them last as long as possible, and as from today, you can call yourself a young lady," she said, stooping forward and laying her hands on her knees, her long hair falling forwards. "As from today you will grow into a young woman and it's very important that you listen to what I have to say. You must keep it a secret and tell no one, especially boys," she whispered.

"There are a few rules that you must remember." Miss Lewis continued. "You mustn't get a bath until your periods have completely finished, and you can't go swimming. Now you can move into the older girls' bedroom. Young ladies don't sleep in the same room as boys," she smiled knowingly, tilting her head to one side and giving her a wink.

"We'll sort a bed out for you later, after you've been to see your brother," Miss Lewis assured. Come and see me in my sitting room before you go and I will give you your bus fare and pocket money. I've written on a piece of paper which buses to catch from where and don't forget, I want you back in the home by seven o'clock."

Shelagh stood on the landing, taking all in that Miss Lewis had just said, not quite understanding why. Dorothy, one of the older girls, appeared at the bathroom door. Apparently, she had been listening to the conversation.

"Don't look so worried," she said, confirming that Miss Lewis was right. "It's very dangerous to have a bath or go swimming, and she forgot to mention you can't wash your hair either, cos if you do, the blood will go to your head and make you mad. So don't forget," she urged with a serious look on her face and shaking her head. Dorothy put her arm around Shelagh's shoulder and steered her towards the older girls' bedroom at the front of the house, directly above the committee room.

Twelve neatly made beds were arranged in two rows facing the windows.

"There's an empty bed in the far corner," instructed Dorothy, "you can have that one."

She then walked across the dormitory to a large chest of drawer, one for each bed. The drawers were standing underneath four high windows that looked out onto the main road. After opening nearly every drawer, Dorothy found one that was empty.

"You can have this one," she said. "Now you will be one of the big girls and soon you will be asked to do big girls jobs. You'd better hurry or you won't have much time with your brother. Oh and one more thing, you can sit with us at the top table from now on."

With her bus fare, pocket money and instructions in her pocket, Shelagh ran as fast as she could down the long road. Due to everything that had happened that morning, she was now late. She called at the cottage sweet shop at the bottom and bought Tony a bar of chocolate, some gobstoppers and aniseed balls out of her pocket money. She knew those were what he liked, and then she ran for the bus. As she approached the bus stop, a bus sailed by in front of her. When the next bus arrived, Shelagh climbed on the bus and sat on a seat near the door.

"Fares," the conductor shouted, jingling loose change in one hand and holding on to the ticket machine, strapped across his shoulder with the other. She handed him her fare in exchange for a ticket.

"Thank you," he replied, looking into her eyes and giving her a wink. Feeling very grown up, Shelagh pushed her shoulders back and held her head high in the air.

"I wonder if he can tell as from this morning," she thought, "I am now a young lady."

She looked up and down the bus at the rest of the passengers and wondered if they too could tell by looking at her that she was now a grown up.

A lot later than intended, Shelagh got off the bus in Elland Road and began to climb up the steep hill to where Tony lived.

Tony was sitting on the front door step bouncing a football up and down between his open knees.

"Where've ya been?" he shouted, as she appeared at the gate.

"Oh it's a long story," Shelagh replied, sounding far too old for her age.

She sat beside him catching her breath for a moment or two, then gasped and moved sideways.

"Have you been fighting again?" she asked, looking at his badly bruised forehead and nasty grazes on his nose and chin.

"Course I haven't," Tony answered indignantly.

"I fell off me bike."

Shelagh scowled and looked puzzled.

"I was sick a carrying shopping every day, so I saved me pocket money for weeks and bought meself a second hand bike for ten shillings," he exclaimed.

"Didn't know ya could ride a bike," Shelagh said, in a surprised tone.

"I couldn't when I bought it," replied Tony. "John, our lodger taught me. It took him ages up and down that hill. Last Saturday, after I'd been to the shops, I was riding up and down and I must have been going too fast, and fell off on the way back down and knocked meself out. John was walking up the hill and found me on the floor so he picked me up, threw me over his shoulder and carried me bike under his arm, then took me home and put me into his bed. He held me hand and stayed with me until I came round." Tony winced at the memory of previous incidents before continuing. "I like John," he carried on, smiling. "He makes me laugh and I know he likes me, I can tell. On a morning before school, I jump up and down on his bed and wake him up. He's always hanging me out of his bedroom window by me ankles and he swings me from side to side. I really really like him," he repeated.

Shelagh butted in, sounding a little jealous of his friendship.

"I still don't have our mothers address yet," she blurted, "but don't worry, I have a plan and I will find her."

"Don't care anymore, don't want to see her," replied Tony angrily. "She doesn't care about us, so why should I care about her? And anyway, I like it here now."

Shelagh was shocked, but pleased that his attitude had completely changed.

"Everyone wants to be my friend now," Tony observed. "I've never had so many friends since John came to live with us, and everybody likes him. He spoils me all the time. On a night, after tea, he plays football on the 'holler' and they come from all over to play with him, so," he said, staring into her face," You don't have to worry about me anymore cos I'm alright now." He paused for a moment. "He's playing football at Elland Road this afternoon," he beamed, "so ya might not see him today."

"I'm really glad you're happy now," Shelagh interrupted, "but I've still got to find our mother, cos in a few years time I'll have to leave the home and get a job and I'll have nowhere to live."

"Well if ya find her, don't tell her," said Tony, "were I live, cos I don't want her to know where I am. Come on let's go play on the swing and slides like we use to do," he laughed, throwing the football into the front garden. The day passed quickly and all too soon, it was time for Shelagh to return to the Orphanage. She never did see the young man that Tony was so fond of. He was the great John Charles, the legendary footballer, the immortal star of Leeds United and Juventus and also known as the 'Gentle Giant'.

Chapter 38

In the following weeks, Shelagh bought some posh paper and envelopes to match and wrote to her grandmother for permission to visit.

Miss Lewis received a 'phone call from a neighbour of her grandmother's saying that Shelagh could visit her on Easter Saturday during the following month.

In the days before she was to visit, Shelagh took Pat and Joyce by the hand, led them to the far corner of the yard, and sat them down beside her.

"I just thought I'd better tell you both I'm going to see our grandmother on Saturday," she confided.

"What's a grandmother?" Pat asked, frowning and looking puzzled.

Joyce, her eyes screwed up and her face in her hands, was watching Maureen her friend in the distance pedalling the small tricycle that they had shared so many times, around the yard.

"Want to play," Joyce said, sounding bored with the conversation, "can I go now?"

"Me too," said Pat.

"Off ya go then," Shelagh answered, after explaining what a grandmother was. She could tell that neither of them was remotely interested.

For days before her visit, Shelagh had knots in her stomach. Eventually the day of the visit arrived. Shelagh had not seen her Grandmother for years, the last time being when she had visited with her aunt and uncle, and that was years ago. Her mother had visited with her little brother and new baby that day, and she secretly hoped that her mother might visit again while she was there.

After two long bus journeys, she arrived at her grandmother's house. She had moved from Lupton Avenue many years ago to the Seacroft estate after her husband had died. Shelagh knocked nervously at the front door. She could feel her heart pounding in her chest. Her grandmother answered the door and invited her in. Her small neat round frame had not changed much over the years, although her hair was now much greyer.

"You sit down," her grandmother said, pointing to an armchair at the side of the fire.

"I'll make us some tea and then we can have a really good talk," she added, before disappearing into the kitchen.

A short time later Shelagh began to tell of her life in the Children's Home and how much she hated it.

"I have to find our mother," Shelagh insisted, "can you tell me where she lives?"

Before her grandmother could answer, there was a voice from the front door.

"Hello," someone shouted, "I'm back." A young woman in her early twenties walked into the room carrying shopping in both arms.

"You must be Shelagh," she smiled, "my names Iris, and I've heard such a lot about you."

"Iris lives next door," her grandmother explained, "and she's ever such a big help to me. She helps me do my cleaning and does all my shopping. Back to your question," she frowned.

"I don't know where your mother lives. I rarely visit any of my children as they always visit me, and if I did know, there would be no point in giving the address to you," she said, sounding a little angry that Shelagh had even asked.

She had always insisted that children should be seen and not heard.

"Your mother has a little boy and three more daughters now," her Grandmother explained gravely. "I do know they live in a back to back house,

166

and I know for a fact them there Children's Care Officers in them there offices wouldn't let you go live with her. There's no room for you or the others. It might be that you'll have to accept you'll never be able to live with her, or even see her again."

Shelagh's heart sank. She had not expected such cruel words. A feeling of emptiness and loneliness filled her. It seemed that no one wanted her, or her brother and sisters. No matter how she tried to be part of her family, no one seemed to care. It was as though they had never been born. All she ever wanted was for someone to acknowledge that they existed.

"Why hasn't she ever been to see us?" Shelagh asked bravely, "and why hasn't she ever sent us a birthday card? No one ever comes to see us." She put her face in her hands and began to cry. "Nobody seems to care about us or want us," she cried through her tears, her lips quivering. Her grandmother never answered. She seemed to be in deep thought.

"I have a spare room," she said unexpectedly, "you could come and live with me."

"I'm getting married next year," butted in Iris who was sitting on a chair near the sideboard at the back of the room.

"You'd be a great help to your Grandmother. You could help her with her shopping and cleaning instead of me. I'll still be around to help if need be."

"What about Pat and Joyce?" Shelagh asked, wiping the tears away. "I can't leave them." Her grandmother folded her arms and looked out of the window.

"I think I'm too old to take care of three young children," she said quietly.

"I'll help," offered Iris.

"I'll look after them meself," pleaded Shelagh, "and you won't have anything to do."

"I don't think for one minute those Children's Care Officers will let me have all three of you, but I'll give it a go," her grandmother said, with a very determined look on her face.

Shelagh could not believe what she had just heard. It was like a dream come true. At last a chance to be normal and live in a house of her own with real relatives.

"I hate that Orphanage," she thought, "we're still called 'home kids'. I can't wait to leave."

Later that afternoon her aunt Vera one of her mother's younger sisters arrived with her husband to visit her mother. She asked Shelagh about the Orphanage and seemed genuinely interested. She wrote her address down on a piece of paper and told her that she would be welcome to visit her any time, subject to Miss Lewis and Miss Hudson's approval.

On the way home Shelagh's head was exploding with excitement. No longer would she have to write and ask permission to visit her family. The three sisters would be with their real family, where they belonged. They would be there when everyone visited on a Sunday, and some day soon, they would see their real mother. She beamed with excitement. She could not wait to get back to the home. She was bursting to tell Miss Lewis.

"I will tell Pat and Joyce at church in the morning," she decided. "They will be so excited."

Shelagh got of the bus at Hyde Park and ran as fast as her legs would carry her home. When she arrived, she knocked hard on Miss Lewis' sitting room door, barged in, and blurted out the good news, not stopping for breath. Miss Lewis seemed pleased, but told her not to build her hopes up, as things were not always as simple as they looked. There were strict rules and guidelines to abide by, and it could take months before permission could be granted.

On a small table on the far side of the room, Shelagh noticed the biggest Easter egg she had ever seen. Thornton's of Leeds had sent the children at the Orphanage an enormous Easter egg. It was over three feet high and sat on a three-inch solid, chocolate base. The front was decorated with small, yellow, iced flowers. The delicious chocolate egg would be shared amongst the three houses the following day.

Chapter 39

Easter Sunday was always a happy day. All the children knew that if they behaved well during the week leading up to Easter, they were more likely to receive an Easter egg. This Easter began much the same as any other Sunday. When all the breakfast pots and pans had been washed and put away, and the dining room tables re-laid for dinner, it was time for the service at Wrangthorn Church.

As soon as you entered the old church, the aroma of freshly cut, colourful flowers, displayed around the interior, filled the air. The congregation always seemed full of smartly dressed worshippers. Bright Easter bonnets, of all shapes and sizes, were being worn by the women, and smartly dressed cubs, brownies, guides and scouts added to the colourful spectacle. One child from each pack would be chosen to be the flag bearer and sometime during the service, would proudly march down the aisle, reverently dipping their flags at the foot of the altar.

Before the sermon was read, the younger children would leave and race towards the hall at the side of the church for Sunday school. At the end of the service, groups of adults would gather together outside in the churchyard and catch up on the previous week's gossip. Eventually everybody would disperse to go there separate ways.

Shelagh, eager to talk to Pat and Joyce, caught up with them at the bottom of Cliff Road, and grabbed them by the hands.

"I've got something really important and exciting to tell you," she said excitedly. "Our grandmother is going to take all three of us out of the Orphanage, and we're going to live with her. What do you think to that?"

"Don't want to;" replied Joyce, screwing up her face, "want to stay with Miss Ratcliffe."

"Neither do I," chipped in Pat, "don't know her anyway. We don't want to live with someone we don't know, do we Joyce?" said Pat, leaning forward.

"No we don't," snapped Joyce.

"You can go if ya want to," Pat offered, leaning forward again and looking at her younger sister, "we don't mind, do we Joyce?"

"No we don't," snapped Joyce again, quickly pulling her hand away and running to Miss Ratcliffe who was walking a few yards in front with a group of young children. She pushed her way through the youngsters and slid her hand into Miss Ratcliffe's, looking over her shoulder at Shelagh in disgust.

"We don't mind," Pat carried on; "as long as ya still come to see us and don't forget us. Ya won't forget us, will ya?" she asked, looking up at her older sister. Shelagh was not prepared for that response. There was no question about her leaving them, "and anyway," she thought, "ya don't know it yet, but you'll be grateful in time. They'll soon get to know their real family," she thought again. With that in mind, Shelagh wasn't unduly concerned.

Shelagh and Pat parted company to return to their respective houses.

Sunday dinner was the usual; roast meat, potatoes, cauliflower or cabbage with rice or sago for pudding. One of the highlights of the week was listening to 'Two-way Family Favourites' on the wireless that was perched on a shelf above the dining room door. Cliff Mitchelmore and his wife Jean Metcalf would play records requested by soldiers in Germany for their loved ones and families in Britain, or those from families and friends over here for their loved ones in Germany. Favourite records included.

'Blue Suede Shoes' and 'Heartbreak Hotel,' by Elvis Presley,

'Lay Down Your Arms,' by Ann Shelton, and

'Singing the Blues,' by Tommy Steele, to name but a few.

During the meal, none of the children attempted to swap their disliked food. Instead, they would pull faces and swallow their unwanted food, helped down by plenty of water.

After dinner, everyone would form a single file and queue outside Miss Lewis' sitting room, hoping that an Easter egg would accompany the weekly handfuls of sweets. Pieces of the large Thornton's Easter egg would also be given to each child. Earlier that morning, the large egg had been divided, and placed onto three large meat dishes, one for each house.

Later in the afternoon, everyone ran across the yard to the little house to watch 'Lassie' on the black and white television in Miss Ratcliffe's sitting room. Yes, Easter Sunday was always a happy day.

One evening, a few months later, Miss Hudson made one of her usual visits. Firstly, she called at the little house where she found Joyce, who was in her usual high spirits. While Pat looked proud and dignified in her new school uniform. Happy with their progress, she made her way over to the big girls' house and headed towards Miss Lewis' sitting room to enquire about Shelagh's welfare.

"Unfortunately," greeted Miss Lewis, "you wont be able to see Shelagh today, as she's staying late at school for a recorder practice."

"I was really hoping to see her," Miss Hudson sighed, "I wanted to tell her we've received her grandmother's application for her and her sisters to be released into her care. A decision will be made at the next Committee meeting, but," she paused for a moment and sighed again, "I did want to tell her myself as this will be my last visit. I've been having health problems over the last few months, so I've decided to take early retirement. I was due to retire next year anyway," she concluded.

Miss Lewis looked shocked and disappointed.

"I'm really sorry," she said, with a look of sadness on her face and a regretful tone in her voice. "Shelagh and I will miss you."

"A Miss Foster, a young newly qualified Children's Care Officer, will be taking my place. She'll be taking over all the children who are in my care."

"Shelagh has known you for most of the years she has been in care," observed Miss Lewis, sounding a little disappointed herself. "She's not going to take too easily to a new officer. She can be a very difficult child at times, and she takes things far too seriously and very personally."

"I've asked Miss Foster to keep me informed on the progress of all the children that have been in my care," remarked Miss Hudson, and I've said to her that if she has any worries to let me know. I'm only a 'phone call away. I'm sure, in time Miss Foster and Shelagh will get to know each other, and besides, she won't be in care forever."

As Miss Hudson left, Miss Lewis wished her a long, healthy and happy retirement.

Chapter 40

One by one, Miss Foster began to sift through the papers of all the children that she had inherited from the care of Miss Hudson. She eventually paid a visit to Headingley Orphanage to meet the Gregson sisters. She introduced herself to Miss Ratcliffe, Pat and Joyce. She could see that the sisters were eager to join their friends in the yard and after a brief chat, allowed then back out to play. She complimented Miss Ratcliffe on the way she had brought up the two little girls and asked if there were any problems.

"There is one thing that is worrying me, but it's nothing I can't handle," said Miss Ratcliffe. "Joyce does like to get every possible attention to herself, as you will eventually find out. However, now she seems very muddled in her mind about the relationship between adults, possibly because her older sister Shelagh has been telling Pat and Joyce they'll soon be leaving to live with their grandmother. Joyce has never known her real family and does not understand who they are," she continued. "From nine months old she has spent all her short life in care and this is the only home she has ever known. She is only eight years old and does not know what a real mother and father is, let alone a grandmother. One day, when I think she's old enough to understand, I'll sit her down and explain to her."

Well satisfied with her findings, Miss Foster threaded her way through playing children in the yard to meet Shelagh. She was not sure what kind of reception she would receive. Taking a deep breath, Miss Foster was shown by one of the children in the hall to Miss Lewis' room. After a lengthy conversation, Miss Lewis stepped into the hallway and asked one of the children to find Shelagh and ask her to report to her room. Within minutes, Shelagh could be heard running towards the sitting room. She knocked hard and barged in.

Hoping to initiate friendship, Miss Foster asked Shelagh about school, her friends, and if she had any hobbies, Shelagh's replies were tentative and cautious.

Then Miss Foster's tone changed. "I've not been looking forward to this moment," she remarked, with anxiety in her voice, "I have some bad news for you. Your Grandmother's application, for you and your sisters to live with her, has been turned down."

For a moment, Shelagh couldn't breathe. She stood, stunned, with disbelief. She could not believe what Miss Foster had just said. She so desperately wanted to leave the Orphanage that she hated so much. A feeling of emptiness filled her body.

"Why?" she asked, tears beginning to well in her eyes, "I don't understand. We have to go live with her. It's our only chance." The tears were now rolling down her cheeks. With hatred in her eyes, Shelagh fixed her gaze on Miss Foster.

"Why?" she asked again.

"The Committee has decided that your Grandmother is too old to take care of three small children," Miss Foster explained. "It's not right to put that burden on an old lady."

"We're not a burden," Shelagh protested through her tears, "that's not fair," she continued through her tears. She could see out of the corner of her eye that Miss Lewis had moved to the front of her chair with her shoulders arched. She was shaking her head and glaring at her with a look of disapproval on her face.

Children were not allowed to question adult decisions.

Shelagh ran from the room into the hall, up the staircase and across the landing into the dormitory. Throwing herself onto her bed, she hid her head under the pillow, and began to cry again. She was heartbroken.

"I hate you Miss Foster," she shouted out loud, "and I hate you too Jesus." Pummelling her clenched fists into the mattress time and time again and kicking her legs in the air, she screamed, "it's your fault we're still here. Why couldn't you let us go live with our grandmother? We don't deserve to be here. We've never done anything wrong, I hate you," she screeched aloud. Shelagh heard someone walk into the bedroom.

"Are you alright?" a voice shouted.

"No I'm not, so go away and leave me alone," she screamed at the top of her voice. Whoever it was left her alone with her anger.

"Well, my first visit didn't go down very well, did it?" Miss Foster remarked to Miss Lewis, back in her sitting room, not really surprised at the outcome.

"I shouldn't worry too much," Miss Lewis replied, "I'm used to watching these unfortunate children handle rejection. If it's not the parents or relatives, it's the Children's Care Committee. Shelagh will be very angry over the next few days, but in time she will learn to accept their decision."

"Her grandmother has suggested it would be best if she didn't visit for a while," said Miss Foster, pausing for a moment before continuing. "She said," pausing again, "she will let her know when it will be convenient." As she spoke, she raised her eyebrows and shrugged her shoulders.

"That's a shame," replied Miss Lewis, "only a few weeks ago she received a letter from her aunt in Beeston saying the exact same thing. I'll leave her a few days to grieve and calm down, and then I'll give her something else to occupy her mind. Meantime you mustn't worry," she assured. Shelagh will come to terms with rejection, she'll have to," she insisted, shrugging her shoulders and peering over the top of her glasses.

Miss Foster left feeling very sad that she had had to be the bearer of bad news. She hoped that in time Shelagh would understand that she had nothing to do with decisions the Committee made.

For the next few days, Shelagh slouched around the Home with a constant look of anger on her face, a grudge against life, and feeling very sorry for herself.

In the early hours of Friday evening, as she was sitting at the dining room table doing her school homework, keeping herself to herself, Miss Lewis appeared from nowhere, sat beside her, and looked into her unhappy face.

Miss Lewis began to speak with a soft and gentle voice as she always did.

"In a few months time some of the older girls will have left, and at thirteen years old you will become one of the oldest. So for the next few weeks I want you to help Dorothy with her weekly duties. She will show you what you will be expected to do on your own in a few weeks time. Then your name will be put on the weekly roster."

Keeping her head down, Shelagh nodded and carried on with her homework.

When she finished, Shelagh put all her schoolbooks into her small locker in the corner of the dining room and looked through the window into the yard. Children from all three houses were laughing and playing together and thoroughly enjoying themselves. Pat and Joyce were playing with their respective groups of friends.

Shelagh knew that the following day, being Saturday, they would be going out for the day with their foster Aunts and Uncles. Staring into the yard, she knew that, as usual, she would miss them, but what was the point in sulking. No one seemed to care whether she was in a bad mood or not. Secretly Shelagh was planning another idea, although it would be better to wait for a few weeks before putting her plan into action. Deciding that there was nothing more she could do for the present, Shelagh gave a resigned shrug and decided to join the rest of the children in the yard.

The weekend passed quickly. Early Monday evening Dorothy shouted to her,

"Follow me," she called, with a broad grin on her face. Shelagh obediently followed her from the dining room, across the hall, through the kitchen and into the scullery at the back of the house. She watched as Dorothy filled a large white enamel bowl with potatoes, taken from a sack on top of the cellar steps, and covered them with warm water. She placed the bowl on top of a wooden table against the inside wall, then filled the biggest pan Shelagh had ever seen with cold water and put it beside the bowl of potatoes.

"Here," Dorothy instructed, putting a strange object with orange string wrapped around what appeared to be a handle into her hand. Shelagh had never seen a potato peeler before.

"Just watch and copy me peel the potatoes," laughed Dorothy.

The older girl was an expert. She began to peel the potatoes quickly and skilfully, before cutting into small pieces and dropping them into the pan of cold, clear water.

"My fingers are hurting," Shelagh remarked much later. "I'm getting blisters on me fingers," she said with a painful look on her face.

"Stop moaning. You'll soon get use to it!" Dorothy was not one for mincing her words. "And it's no good sulking, you'll have to learn. It's part of being one of the oldest. Think yourself lucky," she carried on, "we're only half ways down the sack. Wait until you get to the bottom and the potatoes are bad and soggy. You'll still have to peel them and get the best out of them you can."

Slowly Shelagh began to get the hang of using the potato peeler, though her fingers were now sporting large, pink-bubbled blisters.

"With a bit of luck your fingers will have hardened by the time new potatoes come out," her friend continued, "and let me tell you, they take forever to scrape."

"That's something to look forward to," thought Shelagh, looking at her painful fingers.

After what seemed an eternity, the two girls had peeled enough for around twenty-six children and the staff.

Dorothy carried the heavy pan, full of peeled potatoes, across to the large white pot sink, under the window, at the far side of the kitchen. Shelagh followed close behind.

"You must," Dorothy emphasised, make sure every bit of peel is peeled off and every eye is taken out, because if you don't, you'll be given an extra week of peeling to do on top of your other duties." She dipped her arm up to her elbow into the pan, rinsed the potatoes and covered them with fresh water.

"Now you can go ask Miss Lewis to come and inspect them," she ordered.

Shelagh disappeared and returned a few minutes later with Miss Lewis by her side. Miss Lewis threaded her fingers through the water and nodded with approval, then disappeared.

"Now," said Dorothy, looking at the two large cauliflowers at the far side of the table.

Cauliflowers were freshly cut, and brought to the three houses from the allotments at the back of the little house.

"You do one and I'll do the other," she instructed. Shelagh watched, and copied as Dorothy cut off the leaves, sliced the cauliflower into small pieces, placing them in the large white pot sink filled with water. Then Dorothy ran to the pantry at the far side of the kitchen, reappearing with a brown earthenware jar filled with salt. She took a handful and threw it into the water.

"What's that for?" Shelagh asked curiously.

"That's to kill all the caterpillars that might be hiding inside the cauliflowers," replied Dorothy. "You have a look in the morning and you'll see loads of dead ones floating about."

"Ugh," Shelagh replied, pulling a face.

Then with what little time there was left, Shelagh joined the rest of children in the yard.

The following day at school, Brenda, her best friend, noticed that she was holding her pen with her left hand and writing clumsily. The fingers on her right hand were wrapped in a piece of white rag.

"What's the matter with your fingers?" Brenda asked. Shelagh showed her the large blisters on her fingers and explained how she had acquired them. Brenda winced and kindly offered to do all her writing for her until she was able to write for herself.

By the end of the week, Shelagh had almost mastered the art of potato peeling, but she was dreading the time when she would have to do them on her own.

As she lay in bed on Sunday night, Shelagh wondered, with what she would be expected to help Dorothy with the next day. She could not begin to imagine, but knew that anything was better then peeling thousands and thousands of potatoes.

Early on Monday evening, as the youngest children ran out to play, Dorothy shouted to Shelagh again.

"Come on; follow me, the quicker we get done, the more time we'll have left to play out."

Shelagh tutted quietly and dragged herself slowly behind until they reached the shoe room. Behind a small, shaped door under the staircase, shoes from the youngest to the oldest were neatly laid on shelves. Placed in the far corner, a cardboard box, full of shoes of all different styles and sizes, which had been handed in by the Women's Voluntary Service, were waiting be given out, as and when they would be needed. The girls grabbed all the shoes from the shelf, together with a small cardboard box filled with small tins of different coloured shoe polish, old rags and shoe brushes, and carried them into the hall. They sat together on the long wooden bench just outside the shoe room.

"Now," said Dorothy, "this is called shoe week. You have to clean everybody's shoes. First, you take all the laces out and check them. If they need replacing, you pinch some from the shoes in that box in the corner, and replace them only after they have been polished and not before. Then you have to check the buckles on the others, and if they're loose, you will need to cut them off and sew them back on again. All white pumps need to be whitened and put out to dry on the windowsill outside." Shelagh listened carefully to the list of instructions.

"Right let's start," ordered Dorothy, handing her a tin of brown shoe polish. "You polish all the brown shoes and I'll polish all the black ones."

"This is a lot easier than last week," Shelagh thought. Dorothy showed her how to sew one buckle on with a bodkin needle, some strong cotton and a silver thimble.

"Now you have a go," she urged.

She watched Shelagh struggle, pushing the bodkin up and down and in and out through the tough leather, wincing with pain every time the needle pressed against the blisters, which were still on her fingers. Eventually, after all the shoes had been polished, laces replaced, buckles secured and re-sewn, and pumps whitened, Miss Lewis came to inspect them. She winked at Shelagh and praised both girls for a job well done.

"That wasn't so bad," Shelagh thought, running into the yard to play. "Anything has to be better than potato week." She began to put her family to the back of her mind and slowly began to accept that this would be her home for a short time only, especially if her next plan worked.

Shoe week passed quickly and again she wondered what she would be helping Dorothy with during the following week. Nothing could be worse than potato week she thought. She thought wrong.

Early in the evening of the following day, Shelagh followed Dorothy down the cellar steps into the two large cellars, one under the kitchen and the other under the scullery. Dorothy pointed to a broken chair.

"We have to chop chips for three fires," she explained, "the sitting room, the dining room and the kitchen range." She turned the chair onto its side and began to jump up and down on top of the broken chair breaking it into pieces. Then she began to chop the wood expertly into wooden chips with a large hatchet.

"Now you have a go," she instructed Shelagh, handing her the hatchet. Shelagh clumsily began to do the best she could.

"It looks as though we'll be alright for wood this week," remarked Dorothy, looking around the rest of the cellar at a few wooden objects dotted around.

"Sometimes there's not much wood," she explained, "so you have to try and chop hardboard, and that's not easy. In fact it's almost impossible."

Dorothy then began to show Shelagh how to make paper firelighters by rolling newspapers into long rolls and then tying them together at both ends.

"You'll need loads of these, they help to light a fire," she said knowledgeably.

Once the girls had finished, they divided all the wood and firelighters into three piles, carrying one portion into Miss Lewis' sitting room and placed them in the hearth, then another portion on the hearth in the dining room. Mrs Gibson the daily help would make and light those two fires the following morning.

"As soon as you've made your bed in the morning," Dorothy said, "I want you to help me in the kitchen, the earlier the better. It's our job first thing in the morning to light the kitchen fire."

The following morning, Shelagh joined Dorothy in the kitchen. Dorothy had already riddled the ashes in the fire grate and was layering newspaper with the wooden chips, paper firelighters and coal. She then twisted a piece of newspaper, ran to the small gas cooker in the scullery, to light the piece of paper from a gas ring, then ran back into the kitchen and lit the fire. She quickly grabbed a shovel and wedged it in front of the fire, and then wrapped a large piece of newspaper around the front of the shovel.

"That helps the fire to start," Dorothy explained, "it draws wind up the back of the chimney breast," she said, as they listened to the crackling of wood behind the shovel. Suddenly the newspaper caught fire, and bits of black burnt paper began to fly around the kitchen.

"That often happens," Dorothy shouted, throwing her arms around in the air in all directions trying to catch the floating bits of black, burnt paper.

"You have to keep your eye on it all the time or that happens."

"What if I'm late for school?" Shelagh asked.

"You can't leave the house no matter what time it is, until the fire's lit," said Dorothy firmly. "I tell you what you can do while I make the hearth clean and tidy. Go into the pantry and get the marmalade, and put one teaspoon on each plate. Then fill a small dish for the staff table."

Shelagh did as she was instructed before joining Dorothy back in the kitchen, who was now standing at the large, wooden table.

"Now we have to butter bread enough for four plates," Dorothy explained, "two for the bottom and two for the top, and then another small plate for the staff table." She then instructed Shelagh to fetch the leftover buttered bread from the previous evening, which had been wrapped in bread paper and placed inside the large, white, enamelled bread bin in the pantry.

"Always spread leftover bread on top of the plates," she continued, "that means it will get eaten first. If you're caught taking pieces from the bottom, you'll be in trouble. It's also our job to butter bread for tea."

By now, all the children were downstairs sitting at their appointed places.

Miss Lewis was standing at the serving table in the dining room, busy ladling porridge into small bowls. Standing beside her, one of the older girls was singing quietly to herself as she poured cocoa from a large, white, enamel jug into small mugs.

After breakfast, the younger children ran to the cloakroom, grabbed their school bags and coats and then lined up in single file in the hall, waiting to be inspected, before they left for school.

The older children helped carry all the used breakfast pots into the scullery.

"Follow me," Dorothy beckoned to Shelagh.

"Not something else," Shelagh thought, taking a deep sigh and dropping her shoulders. She trailed obediently behind Dorothy and followed her into the scullery.

"It's our job to wash up and clean the porridge pan," informed Dorothy.

Two other girls were already standing by the large, pot sink, holding tea towels, waiting to dry, and then put away the crockery and utensils into a cupboard at the side of the kitchen fire.

"You wash the pan," Dorothy instructed, moving to one side and handing Shelagh a piece of silver wire wool. After she had scrubbed the porridge pan, Dorothy ran her hand around the inside to make sure that it was clean.

"And that's something else," said Dorothy smugly, "make sure it's spotlessly clean, or you'll be called back to clean it again, no matter what time it is. By the way, your name has been put on the roster, so as from next week you will be expected to do duties on your own. Oh and another thing," she droned, "on a Saturday morning you might be asked to polish the dormitory floors, and sometimes the staircase. Don't look so worried; you will soon get use to it. Now off you go, I'll finish off here. My school is nearer than yours. You'd better run or you'll be late."

Shelagh ran all the way to school, her head exploding. "I'll never do all that work in a morning," she thought, "I might have to bring my next plan of action forward."

With only a few minutes to spare, she sat on the schoolyard wall gasping for breath and staring into space. Brenda sat beside her.

"Where've you been?" Brenda demanded, "I was beginning to think you weren't coming. I've been waiting ages for you. Where've you been," she repeated.

"Ya don't want to know," Shelagh replied, taking a deep sigh.
"Yes I do," insisted Brenda.
"I've been put on a job roster," explained Shelagh, "and when its fire week, I have to chop chips for three fires at night, and first thing in the morning, before breakfast, I have to light the kitchen fire, butter loads of bread, dish marmalade out and *then* I've to wash up, including that big, sticky porridge pan. I'll never do all that. I'm gonna be late for school every day."

"I'll come and help you if you want me to," Brenda offered, "I don't mind."

"No, it doesn't matter," Shelagh replied, still not wanting her friend to see where she lived, "I will have to get used to it."

The school bell rang, breaking their conversation. Brenda linked her arm into Shelagh's, and snuggled into her shoulder as they walked into school.

Chapter 41

A few months later Shelagh sensed the right day and time had arrived to put her next plan into action.

Early one evening around seven thirty, when the younger children from ten years old and under were safely tucked in their beds, and Miss Lewis had retired to her sitting room, Shelagh approached Dorothy, who was in the kitchen making Miss Lewis' supper. She was kneeling on the floor in front of the fire, toasting a slice of white bread, which was attached to a long toasting fork, inches away from the hot coals in the fire grate.

"Is Miss Lewis in a good mood?" Shelagh asked.

"What do you want to know that for," Dorothy enquired.

"Because," Shelagh paused before continuing. "Because I've got something really important to ask her, and I can't ask her if she's in a bad mood."

"She's in a very good mood, Dorothy replied, "give me five minutes to finish and take her supper into the sitting room, then you can go and ask her whatever it is you want to ask."

Dorothy slid the toast from the end of the toasting fork and began to spread the butter, making sure that every corner of the slice was covered.

Shelagh quietly crept up the winding staircase; tip toed passed the younger children's dormitory, crossed the landing and padded down a small passage to her bedroom. She took a piece of paper that had been folded into four, which she had hidden in the corner of her drawer in the dormitory. Clenching the paper tightly in her fist, she crept slowly back downstairs. As she headed towards Miss Lewis' sitting room, Shelagh could smell hot cocoa and freshly buttered toast wafting through the partially opened door.

"Come in," Miss Lewis shouted, in answer to her gentle knock on her door. Shelagh stepped cautiously inside, holding the folded piece of paper in both hands behind her back.

"Shouldn't you be in bed?" Miss Lewis remarked, looking at the clock on top of the fireplace, "it's almost eight o'clock," putting the cup of cocoa that she was drinking on a tray beside her.

"Yes, but I've got something really important to ask you," Shelagh said hopefully.

"Have you now?" Miss Lewis replied, beckoning to an armchair beside her, "well why don't you come and sit beside me."

"I know I can't visit my auntie and uncle or my grandma," Shelagh began, "so can I write to my auntie Vera instead? She gave me her address when I visited my grandma and said I was very welcome to visit her anytime, and she really did mean it." Shelagh tried to sound convincing, holding out her hand and showing her the paper. Miss Lewis took the piece of paper and, after reading it, looked over the top of her gold-framed glasses a little puzzled, she held her chin in her hand and shook her head.

"Please," Shelagh asked, with a desperate tone in her voice. "I'm not telling lies. I've got the proof haven't I? You've got to believe me. She wouldn't have given it to me if she didn't want me to visit, would she. Please," she pleaded.

Miss Lewis took a deep breath, sighed and stared at Shelagh. After a moment in silence, she said,

"If I give you permission to write to your Auntie Vera," she hesitated for a second, before carrying on, "I want you to promise me one thing." Shelagh began to nod her head up and down repeatedly.

"Anything," she pleaded.

"I want you to stop frowning all the time and start to smile, or you'll ruin that pretty little face of yours," Miss Lewis laughed, "Is that a deal?"

With a sparkle in her eye and a broad grin across her face, Shelagh nodded again.

"One more thing," added her kindly guardian, "I will have to let Miss Foster know. I'll keep this piece of paper until tomorrow, and then you can have it back. Now off you go. It's way past your bedtime."

"There I've done it," Shelagh thought, as she quietly climbed the stairs to bed. "Tomorrow I'll write to my auntie Vera in my best handwriting and when I see her I'm gonna ask her if she knows where our mother is."

This was part one of her plan.

The following day Miss Lewis telephoned and spoke to Miss Foster.

"Well that doesn't surprise me at all," Miss Foster remarked. "Shelagh is a girl who always turns to her own relatives and is old enough to remember being part of a family before she was taken into care. If you give me her Aunt's name and address, I would like to pay a call before I allow Shelagh to visit."

Early one evening during the following week, Miss Foster called to see Mrs Conner, Shelagh's Aunt Vera. She arrived at the old terraced house in the Burmantofts area of Leeds. As she waited for someone to answer the door, she looked around at the well-tended gardens on either side of the long path leading up to the front door. In the distance, St James's Hospital could be seen.

A tall, slim, young woman in her late thirties with ginger hair answered the door and politely invited her in. They chatted for several hours, discussing how and why the three sisters and their brother had been placed into care.

"There's no need to reply to Shelagh's letter," Miss Foster said, as she left, "I'll call and speak to her myself during the next week." She gave a big smile as she drove away, content in her findings.

A week later, Miss Foster made a visit to the home. As was her usual practice, she called first at the little house for a progress report on Pat and Joyce, and then made her way across the yard. She noticed that they were both playing happily, and gave them a wave as she passed.

She brought Miss Lewis up to date on her visit to Shelagh's Aunt and Uncle, and said that she would like to see and tell Shelagh of her findings. As Miss Lewis was about to leave the room to fetch Shelagh, the telephone rang from the corner of the room.

"You'll find her in the scullery," Miss Lewis said, as she walked over to answer the 'phone.

Miss Foster walked down the hall, through the kitchen and into the scullery. She found Shelagh standing at a table peeling potatoes; she went over and stood besides her, leaning on the edge of the table with her back towards the wall.

"I've got some exciting news for you," she said, with her arms folded and a pleased expression on her face. "I've been to see your Auntie Vera and Uncle Billy and I was very impressed. In fact, I'm delighted to tell you she wants all three of you to go and live with them. She has an empty spare bedroom that all three of you can use. I did tell her we will supply her with some beds and bedding."

Shelagh dropped both the large potato and the peeler that she was holding into the bowl of water, causing a large splash. She held on tightly to the edge of the table with her wet hands to steady herself. Never in her wildest dreams had she expected this. She was in a state of shock. She looked at Miss Foster disbelievingly, and was speechless.

"Isn't that what you have always wanted, to live with your own family?" Miss Foster asked, her face beaming.

"Oh yes," Shelagh answered, letting go of the table and throwing her arms into the air. In her excitement, she caught the edge of the bowl, causing it to tip over and spill its entire contents of water, potatoes and potato peelings onto the concrete floor. She ran through the spilt water to grab two floor cloths from under the sink, making Miss Foster chuckle.

"I'll give you a hand," Miss Foster said, with a twinkle in her eye, shaking her head and still laughing. They both began to scrape up the peelings and potatoes with their hands and mop up the floor with the floor cloths.

"How long do you think it will be before we can leave the Orphanage?" Shelagh asked, her eyes dancing about.

"Well this time it shouldn't take too long," replied Miss Foster. "Your Aunt and Uncle are young and healthy, and your Uncle has a good job. Their application to act as foster parents and take you and your sisters from the Orphanage has still to be discussed and approved by the Children's Care Committee. I would say it would be no more than a few months. There will be an awful lot of paper work to do, seeing as there are three of you, but this time you have nothing to worry about. If I were you, I would concentrate on having a good holiday, camping at Scarborough, in a few weeks time. I'll see you when you get back."

She left Shelagh as she found her, peeling potatoes. As she headed down the hall, she could hear her happily singing loudly the Doris Day song that was currently in the charts,

'Que Sera Sera,

Whatever will be will be,

The future's not ours to see,

Que Sera Sera.'

Miss Foster smiled to herself pleasurably.

It had seemed such a long time ago, since she had met Shelagh for the first time. On that occasion, she had brought bad news, telling Shelagh that Grandmother's application for the three girls had been refused due to her age. This time she had a good feeling that everything would fall into place. As she walked into Miss Lewis' sitting room, she could still hear Shelagh singing loudly in the distance.

That night just before she climbed into bed, Shelagh fell to her knees and held both her hands together.

"Thank you Jesus, thank you Jesus, thank you Jesus," she prayed, not being able to think of anything else to say. Her head was swimming with other thoughts. She did not care that some of the other girls were watching and listening, as she felt sure that she would not be there much longer. She jumped into bed hiding her head under the pillow and began to imagine life with her real family, and being normal. "A new school, new friends, although she would miss her best friend Brenda at school, but that was a small price to pay, and anyway," she thought, "I'll be leaving school in just over a years time when I'm fifteen." She decided that it was best not to mention this to Pat, who was eleven and Joyce who would be ten in a few months time. They would probably not want to go anyway. Shelagh knew that they would get used to their real family, and, she mused, "auntie Vera is one of our mother's youngest sisters, and sooner or later they were certain to see her, and when she sees us, she's bound to want us back." Shelagh's head was exploding with all these wonderful thoughts. Her plan had worked better than she had ever hoped.

She would make sure that Pat and Joyce had the best holiday ever at Scarborough, just in case they never visited the seaside again. Eventually, in the early hours of the morning, she fell soundly asleep.

Chapter 42

Early one Saturday morning, a few weeks later, the children set off on holiday to Scarborough.

Miss Lewis and Miss Ratcliffe, as usual, sat on the seat immediately behind the driver, busy chatting together and making plans for the next few weeks.

They had been given extra money by the Orphanage Committee that had been raised at coffee mornings and church bazaars during the previous year, and set aside especially to be used by the children on their camping holiday.

Auntie Jean, Miss Ratcliffe's assistant, and Auntie Betty, Miss Lewis' assistant were organising games and sing-a-longs. The coach was a hive of noisy, excited children, as always.

It would be Auntie Jean's and Auntie Betty's last time at Scarborough with the children, as both had planned to marry in the next few months. Eventually they arrived at the South Cliff Congregational Church. Two burly lorry drivers were sitting on the steps, having arrived much earlier with a full load of boxes and boxes packed with crockery, pots and pans, hampers full of clothes, blankets, food and dozens of pairs of shoes, everything but the kitchen sink was on that lorry. The men gave three cheers as the noisy, excited children began to climb off the coach.

The younger children made their way up the steps and down a short corridor, just inside the church to a small schoolroom, which would be their home for the next few weeks.

Shelagh and the older girls would occupy the large schoolroom at the top end of the corridor.

Once the lorry drivers had deposited the boxes and hampers to the appropriate rooms, the older girls were instructed to assemble the camp beds at the top end of the hall. In the top right hand corner, a make shift bathroom had been constructed. Behind two high clotheshorses, covered with old white sheets, were two long trestle tables. A large white enamelled jug, edged with blue, sat on top of one of the two trestle tables, waiting to be filled each morning from the kitchen tap, and emptied into four enamel bowls that were in the middle of the table. Numbered towels and flannels draped over another clotheshorse. Over on the right hand sidewall, two more trestle tables with benches on either side, would serve as the dining tables.

Miss Lewis and Auntie Betty would occupy a room adjacent to the large schoolroom.

As Shelagh had promised herself, she made the next few weeks the best holiday ever. She and Pat won prizes again in a talent competition in Gala Land, the underground amusement park under Valley Bridge.

After climbing Oliver's Mount and Castle Hill, they sat and drank in the spectacular views of the harbour and the sweeping bays. They swam in the sea, and sometimes Miss Lewis and Miss Ratcliffe would pay for them to swim and play in the open-air swimming pool at the South Bay.

The older children organised sandcastle competitions on the South Bay beach, brothers and sisters against other brothers and sisters.

Shelagh, Pat and Joyce made a spectacular sandcastle surrounded by a moat. Auntie Jean awarded them second place. Each child was rewarded with an ice cream or an ice cream lolly, whether or not they had won. The older girls often spent their daily pocket money on the jukeboxes in the amusement arcades on the sea front, listening to Elvis Presley, Tommy Steele, Bill Haley, the Platters, and many more.

Once a week, to give the adults a rest from preparing and cooking a hot dinner, all the children from both houses were treated to a bag of chips from the local fish and chip shop.

"It's your turn Shelagh to go to the fish shop," shouted Miss Lewis, handing over some money.

"Go and ask Miss Ratcliffe what she would like you to get for her children."

Shelagh held the money tightly in her hand and made her way down the short corridor to the small schoolroom.

"Can I go with you?" Pat asked, after Miss Ratcliffe had told Shelagh what she required. The sisters held hands as they walked the short distance to the nearby fish shop.

As they joined the long queue, they kept closing their eyes, taking in deep breaths, drinking in the smell, and 'fair tasting' the fish and chips.

Eventually they arrived at the front of the queue.

"Thirty six bags of chips and four fish," Shelagh asked politely.

"Thirty six," the assistant gasped.

"Yes please," Shelagh, replied calmly.

"And can we have some scraps please?" Pat asked. By now, she was standing on her tiptoes, peeping over the top and holding on to the edge of the counter with her fingers, her nose resting on the counter. A few 'tuts' could be heard from some of the customers, who were on their lunch break and in a hurry.

"My favourite meal of the week," said Pat, on their way back, "I love chips with scraps."

Once back inside the church, Shelagh began to share out the large parcel, fish for the adults and a bag of chips with plenty of scraps, accompanied with lots of bread and butter for the children. She rewrapped twelve bags of chips and two fish and gave them to Pat to take to Miss Ratcliffe.

One evening there was another treat. Miss Lewis had bought tickets for all her children to see a performance of 'The White Horse Inn'.

The open-air theatre, where the show was to be performed, was on the north side of Scarborough, in Peasholme Park.

Pat, now the oldest of Miss Ratcliffe's children, was allowed to join the rest of the big girls. She was so excited, she skipped and danced and sang happily all the way along the South Shore and then the long stretch across North Marine Drive.

Over the years, the open-air theatre had entertained audiences of thousands with spectacular shows such as 'Annie Get Your Gun', 'Oklahoma', 'Hiawatha' and many others. Pat sat with the rest of the children mesmerised at the colourful costumes, the loud music and the brightly lit decorated raft, that sailed down the lake.

They were nights to remember.

All too soon, the holiday was over. On the journey home, Shelagh snuggled into her pillow, reminiscing of what she thought would be her last holiday at the seaside. She knew that the Children's Care Committee sometimes took months to complete applications to foster children. She did not care anymore, as she knew that it would only be a matter of months before she left the Orphanage.

Chapter 43

The week before the new school term began in September, Miss Foster arrived with news of the Committee's decision. Shelagh was asked by one of the girls in the yard to report to Miss Lewis' sitting room.

"Come in," Miss Lewis called, in answer to her gentle knock on the door. Shelagh's face lit up as she stepped inside and saw Miss Foster sat in an armchair opposite Miss Lewis.

"I don't know how to tell you," Miss Foster began, with a sad look on her face, "your Aunty Vera's application to act as a foster mother to you and your sisters has been turned down."

Shelagh's face turned white. For a moment, she was stunned. She stepped backwards, leaning against the wall, and asked,

"why?" her lips quivering.

"Due to unforeseen circumstances," Miss Foster explained, "the tiles, on the roof above the bedroom that was to be yours, need repairing. Your Auntie and Uncle have been using buckets and pans to catch the water every time it rains. The property owner cannot afford to repair the roof, so we cannot let you sleep in a bedroom under those circumstances. She has put her name down for a corporation house but, sadly, that might take a long time. I'm so sorry," she said quietly, sounding genuinely concerned.

"You said not to worry," said Shelagh, sliding down the wall and falling into a heap on the floor, "you said everything would be alright. You said not to worry this time, and you did promise everything would be alright this time." Her voice was now beginning to break with grief.

"I'm so sorry," Miss Foster repeated, her face now red with embarrassment

"It's not your fault. It's one of those things that life throws at us," said Miss Lewis.

"Now get up off the floor and stop feeling sorry for yourself. There's nothing you can do about it, so please leave the room while I have a talk to Miss Foster."

"Do you know where my father is?" Shelagh asked, as she picked herself up from the floor.

"No, I'm afraid we haven't been able to trace him," answered a surprised Miss Foster, "but if we find him, you will be the first to know."

Shelagh could see through her clouded eyes that Miss Lewis was pressing a finger against her lips and shaking her head. Dropping her shoulders Shelagh pouted her lips, left the room and began walking slowly across the hall towards the side door. As she made her way across the hall, Miss Lewis shut the sitting room door so that no one could hear their conversation.

"There's a little bit more to it," Miss Foster began to say to Miss Lewis. "Mrs Conner, Shelagh's Aunt, works full time at Burtons as a tailoress and earns a lot of money. She was prepared to reduce her hours if the girls were allowed to live with her, but the rules are that a foster mother must not be in any kind of employment. She must be at home at all times to take care of the girls. That's something Mr Parnell is very strict about. She had calculated that the three girls boarding out allowances are not as much as she earns. She was beginning to worry that she would have less money to manage on, plus three healthy boisterous girls to take care of, so perhaps it's not meant to be. I always seem to be the bearer of bad news don't I?" said Miss Foster sadly.

"Don't worry," said Miss Lewis, she'll get over it, she doesn't need to know what we have been discussing, least said, best mended."

Angrily Shelagh crossed the yard winding her way through noisy children, and made her way to the grassed area in the far corner of the yard. She covered her face with her hands wondering what to do next. Over the years, she had tried so hard to be recognised by her family. Every plan had failed. She felt someone sitting down beside her.

"What's wrong now?" a concerned voice asked.

Bernard Kelly, Andrew Kelly's younger brother, now one of the older boys, never missed a trick. He knew instinctively by looking at any of the children if there was anything troubling them. Putting his arm around Shelagh's shoulder, Bernard pulled her towards him, resting his chin on top of her head. She relaxed in the comfort of his arm and began to cry silent tears. Eventually she told him her story. He did not seem at all surprised.

"Now," he said, pausing for a moment, "you have to forget about your family. Like it or not, you might have to accept they don't want you or your sisters. Nobody has ever been to see you, have they?" Shelagh looked down and shook her head slowly.

"Then start thinking what's best for you and your sisters," he said emphatically. "Even, if you get separated in the next few years. *You* will have to make sure that you'll always be together. No good making yourself poorly. What good will that do? At the end of the day, nobody cares. It's up to you to be strong. As long as you care about your sisters, that's all that matters."

Shelagh listened silently to his understanding voice. Then, jumping up and pulling her up with his hand, he said.

"Now come on dry your eyes. I'm organising a game of rounders and I know you're very good, so come on." Then turning his attention back to the home, he said, "who's that girl over there, sitting on her own on the back steps?" he asked, frowning and looking puzzled.

"I don't know," Shelagh answered, staring across at the young girl. She looked to be around ten years old, had short, shiny, brown hair with a neatly cut fringe; her face was full of freckles. She was wearing a white cotton print dress with small yellow daisies, a smart navy cardigan, navy sandals and white socks.

"She looks like a new girl," Bernard remarked, "why don't you go and talk to her and ask her if she would like to play rounders with us."

Shelagh went over to where she was sitting and asked.

"What's your name and how old are you?"

"My names Carole Green and I'm nearly eleven," the girl replied.

"My name's Shelagh, and why are you here?"

"My mothers very poorly," Carole answered. "She's always in and out of hospital. My dad's in the navy and away at sea a lot, so there's no one to take care of me. So, I've had to come and live here. But I won't be here for long," she said indignantly, "I'll be going home when my dad's on leave, and one day he'll be home for good. Will you be my friend?" she added.

"Only if you come and play rounders with us," teased Shelagh.

Carole fitted in with the others immediately. That day she got more rounders than anyone else did, and although there was an age difference, Shelagh and Carole became great friends.

Chapter 44

In the months that followed, Auntie Betty married her fiancé Jack at Wrangthorn Church in Hyde Park. Auntie Betty looked stunning in a long white shimmering dress, her head covered with a white veil that ran down the back and trailed down the church aisle. One of the younger children gasped when she saw her and whispered that she looked like an angel. Jack looked extremely smart in his blue Royal Air Force uniform. All the children from the big house were invited to the church service and afterwards to a wonderful reception in the hall beside the church.

A Mrs Jones was employed as deputy matron to Miss Lewis. She was of medium height, stiffly built and in her early forties. Her short blonde hair turned up around the edge, and she always wore a v-necked cardigan over a silk blouse and knee length, box pleated skirts. She always wore different coloured sandals on her feet. Behind her rimless glasses, her eyes were cold, and her face looked as though it rarely smiled. Her voice was hard and commanding and her large hands were strong and powerful.

Within days of her arrival, things began to change. The crockery that Miss Lewis shared with the children suddenly changed to a delicate china tea set, a matching teapot, a milk jug and sugar basin. There was even a matching bread and butter plate. The stronger character of Mrs Jones quickly overruled the few softly spoken words Miss Lewis voiced about the change. Some days she was pleasant, caring and very amusing. On other days, she ruled with a rod of iron. Strict rules were adhered to and she never tolerated naughty, disobedient children. Slowly she began to take on the role of matron, leaving Miss Lewis in the background. Gradually Miss Lewis began to take a back seat.

One day, a young Chinese boy, around eight years old arrived at the Orphanage. There was no place for him in the little house or the big boys' house, so he was placed in the big girls' house. His name was Sam Ling Wong and his Chinese father had met his English mother in Hong Kong. Both were professors and both had been offered employment at Leeds University as lecturers. They had recently arrived in England, and had approached the Children's Care Office in Woodhouse Lane to ask advice on who could possibly take care of their son Sam, until they could find a suitable nanny and accommodation. They were willing to pay, however much the cost.

As the Headingley Orphanage, which was not too far away from the University, was beginning to have financial difficulties, paying parents were gratefully welcomed. A few days after Sam arrived; he was given the usual medical. He was found to be suffering from scabies, a highly contagious skin disease caused by the itch mite. All the children and staff, including the daily helps, were asked to present themselves to the Cleansing Department near St James's Hospital. The little house and big girls' house were asked to attend first. They arrived at the Cleansing Department in Beckett Street, where a strong smell of disinfectant filled the air inside the small, square, clinical building. Large shiny white tiles covered the walls. A small, very round nurse, was sitting on a low bench just inside the door. On her head, she wore a white stiffly starched hat, and her long sleeved grey dress, trimmed with white collar and cuffs, was hanging between her open knees touching the floor. In her hand, she was brandishing a wide paste brush and on the floor, by her side, stood a large enamelled bucket filled with an odourless liquid

"Everybody take their clothes off," she bellowed, pointing the brush to the far side of the room to where there was a row of benches. "Then I want you all to form a single line in front of me," she continued. The staff were instructed to stand to one side until all the children had been treated. Carole looked behind her, frowned and glared at Shelagh.

"Everything off," the nurse shouted, looking at Carole. The older girls began to blush with embarrassment.

"Hurry up," she yelled, "I haven't got all day."

They lined up in single file, the youngest at the front. Every child was completely naked. The older girls at the back of the queue covered what bits they could with their hands.

"Wait till I tell my mother," said Carole, "she won't believe this."

"I've never been so embarrassed in all my life," said Shelagh, trying to hide herself behind Carole, her face now crimson.

After the nurse had whitewashed the younger children, they ran back to the bench and dressed themselves. Soon Carole was facing the inconsiderate, uncaring nurse.

"Legs open, arms stretched," the nurse instructed, and then promptly began to whitewash the front of Carole's body, taking care not to miss an inch.

"Turn around," she instructed again. Quiet tears were slowly falling down Carole's cheeks as the nurse continued to whitewash from behind. Finally, after what seemed to take an eternity, the nurse had finished treating every single child.

"I've never been so embarrassed in all my life," said Shelagh to Carole again, as they very quickly began to dress themselves, "I'll never forget this day as long as I live."

"Neither will I," replied Carole, throwing on her clothes as fast as she could.

"Before you all go," yelled the bossy nurse, "no one has to wash for the next two days. Did you all hear me? You mustn't get washed for the next two days," she repeated.

"Hooray!" shouted some of the younger children. Everyone was instructed to wait and form a queue outside while the adults were treated.

Mrs Jones genuinely felt sorry for the older girls. Back at the home, to cheer them up, she allowed them to occupy the committee room at the front of the house for the afternoon, where they were given permission to play records on the wind up 'His Master's Voice' gramophone in the bottom corner of the room. They danced around to the tunes of Glen Miller and tried to put the morning's episode far behind them.

Chapter 45

One teatime, a small piece of finny haddock was served on small plates. Carole, who was now eleven years old, was now allowed to sit with the older girls on the top table. She chose to sit beside her friend Shelagh. During the meal, Carole sat twiddling her hands together on her lap under the table, staring at the piece of finny on her plate.

"What's wrong?" whispered Shelagh.

"Don't like finny haddock," Carole replied, the corners of her mouth turned down and a look of disgust on her face.

"You have to eat it whether you like it or not," Shelagh whispered, lowering her head, "I don't like it either. Just put some in your mouth and swallow it down with water. You can't leave it. The last time I left a piece, I was given it to eat for the next four days, and eventually I had no choice but to eat it."

"Can't," Carole replied, pulling a face.

"Someone's ringing the bell at the front door," shouted one of the younger boys, sticking his hand up in the air and looking towards the staff table. It was Miss Lewis' day off, and as she would not be back until around eight that evening, Mrs Jones rose from her chair and strutted across the dining room, down the hall, towards the front door, tutting at the inconvenience. She could be heard talking to someone.

"Give us it here," Sue Oakes said to Carole, "quickly, before she comes back."

Carole lifted her plate and quickly scraped the finny haddock onto Sue's plate, wiped the edge of the plate with a finger and then wiped it on her skirt.

"Will you have mine?" Shelagh asked.

"Yes, but you had better be quick," replied Sue. Shelagh shoved her piece across onto Sue's plate, also wiping the edge of her plate with a piece of white rag and placing her knife and fork neatly together on her plate and pretended to chew. She kicked Carole under the table, beckoning her to do the same. On her way back, Mrs Jones looked out of the corner of her eye at the plates as she passed by.

Sue Oakes was twelve years old and had been in the Home for several years. Her mother was having great difficulty coping with eight children after her husband had deserted her. The Children's Care Committee had decided to take a few of her children into care, until she was strong enough to cope. Sue often spent the weekends at home with her mother.

Later, outside in the yard, Shelagh began to reiterate to Carole the importance of eating everything on her plate at meal times.

"Once," she began to tell her, "I left a lump of meat on the side of my plate which was covered in thick fat and grizzle. I was dragged by my hair into the scullery and pinned against the wall. That piece of grizzle was shoved and forced into my mouth, and I was made to swallow it. I was sick all over the scullery floor. So, however much you don't like anything you either have to eat it or get rid of it discreetly."

Carole just held her head back, pulled a face, and made no comment.

A few months later, Miss Lewis retired, leaving the children in the hands of Mrs Jones. Kathleen, Miss Lewis' sister, had asked her time and time again to finish, reminding her that she was getting old and that she tired very easily. She had spent all her life taking care of unfortunate children as she had always called them. She knew she would miss them.

After she had left, she decided that, as a leaving present from her, she would take four of the children to York for the day as her treat. She chose Janice Wilson, Shelagh, Wendy Spivey and Catherine Ideson. Early one sunny warm Saturday morning, she met the girls in Vicar Lane, in the centre of Leeds, where they boarded a red bus bound for York. In their hands, they carried bottles of pop, and pre-packed sandwiches of meat paste, cheese spread and marmite, wrapped in Mother's Pride red and white striped bread wrapper.

When they arrived in York, they walked on the medieval wall that surrounds part of the city, taking in the views of the ancient Roman town, now the proud capital of Yorkshire.

Then, as a special treat, they rode on a pleasure boat along the River Ouse, drinking in the wonderful countryside. The sun was shining down on them with not a cloud in the sky. Miss Lewis felt a warm, grateful feeling in her stomach, as she smiled and watched them enjoying themselves. As usual, their manners and behaviour were impeccable and she was so proud of them.

After the boat trip, the party sat on the grass verge beside the river and ate their sandwiches, sharing them with Miss Lewis as they watched the boats sailing up and down the river. After dinner, they made their way to York Museum, heading towards the famous 'Shambles', a cobbled street depicting the Victorian age. On either side of the street were mock shops, identical to Victorian times, and in the centre of the cobbles stood a huge, statue of a black horse attached to a magnificent, polished hansom cab, which was manned by a striking uniformed figure. All too soon, however, it was time to travel back to Leeds.

When they arrived back at the 'red bus station', as it was called, it was a little after five o'clock in the afternoon.

Miss Lewis then invited them back to her brother and sister's house, where she now lived, situated in a street near the Leeds General Infirmary. Her sister Kathleen had one of the kindest faces Shelagh had ever seen. Her black hair shone and her eyes sparkled. She made them tea, served in china cups and saucers and placed large pieces of Victoria sandwich cake on matching plates.

"I think you ought to be making tracks home," said Miss Lewis, after they had finished eating, "I don't want you getting into trouble. I did promise you would be home by seven o'clock, in time to do your chores." Wendy pulled a face and promised that they would go straight home.

"You can call and see me anytime," said Miss Lewis, as they were leaving.

"And I know you swim a lot at Cookridge Street baths," she added, looking at Shelagh, "it's only round the corner from us, so don't forget to call."

They all thanked her for a wonderful day, a day none of the four girls would ever forget.

In the months that followed, whenever Shelagh went swimming, she called in to say hello.

One Friday night, Carole returned to the Home, having spent the last few weeks at home with her mother and father. Her father had been on leave from the Navy and was required back at Plymouth Docks ready to sail to the Far East in the next few days. She talked non-stop during breakfast, of stories about the countries her father had visited and of the presents he had brought her back, colourful sequined shoes, jewellery boxes and a gold bracelet from India.

"I won't be here for much longer," she bragged, smirking and not stopping for breath, "next time my father comes home, he's stopping for good." Her face beamed with happiness.

"Can I interrupt a moment," shouted Mrs Jones sarcastically from the staff table, "there's work to be done. You can chatter all you want Carole when jobs are finished. Now you, Susan Oakes, can polish the staircase. You Shelagh Gregson can polish your dormitory floor, and you Wendy Spivey, can polish the younger children's floor. I've torn up an old sheet into dusters and they're in a skip bag just inside the linen room. Now it's time these breakfast pots were cleared away." She clapped her hands together and shouted 'chop chop' as she left the dining room. Sue shrugged her shoulders and gave a big sigh.

"I'll help you if you want," whispered Carole to Shelagh.

"You know no one's allowed to help us," Shelagh replied.

"No one will know if no one sees me," she grinned, "you'll get done twice as quick."

"O K," agreed Shelagh, "but you'd better make sure no one sees you."

When all the breakfast pots had been cleared away, Shelagh made her way up the winding staircase to the large dormitory at the front of the house, carrying in her hand, a large tin of mansion polish. On the way, she helped herself to a few of the pieces of sheets which were to be used as dusters, then began to move all the beds on the back wall to the front alongside the beds already there.

"I'm here," whispered Carole from behind her.

Side by side, they both knelt down and began to smear the mansion polish across the orange lino. Then, with clean dusters, they polished vigorously until the lino shone.

They looked a picture from behind, kneeling on all fours, swinging their hips from side to side in unison and singing and polishing to 'Jailhouse Rock.' Suddenly Carole stopped and pressed her finger to her closed lips.

"Someone's coming," she whispered.

"Quick hide," Shelagh urged.

Carole grabbed the dusters that she had been using and crawled under the beds hiding herself in the far corner.

Mrs Jones appeared in the doorway.

"Who were you talking to?" she asked.

"No one," answered Shelagh nervously, "I was just singing to myself out loud."

Mrs Jones screwed up her face, not quite sure whether to believe her or not, and then left. After what seemed a long time, Carole crawled from under the bed.

"Phew," Carole exclaimed running her fingers across her forehead. She tiptoed towards the stairs and watched through the rails as Mrs Jones disappeared down the hall into the sitting room, then tiptoed back to help her friend finish polishing the floor. To make the floor even shinier, they tied dusters over their shoes and began to skate up and down the floor, quietly giggling to themselves. When the entire floor was sparkling, Carole made her way discreetly down stairs into the yard, making sure that no one saw her.

Later, Mrs Jones sauntered up the stairs to check on the work the girls had been given. When she entered the large dormitory, Shelagh was waiting for her, standing proudly and confidently just inside the door. Mrs Jones knelt down on the floor on her hands and knees, scanning the whole floor, even under the beds, expecting to see some patches that had been missed. She was pleasantly surprised to see that the entire floor was gleaming.

"I'm very impressed," she remarked, raising her eyebrows, and then added. "There's one more thing I would like you to do for me."

Shelagh sighed and dropped her shoulders. "Not something else," she thought.

"After tea I want you to take a bus to town," instructed Mrs Jones. "The manager of Marks and Spencer will meet you at the back door at seven. You can take a friend with you if you want to help carry the boxes."

For the past few months, Marks and Spencer had been taking an interest in the children, and when any sandwiches or cakes were left over on Saturday evening from the snack bar on the ground floor, they would donate them to the Orphanage.

Shelagh asked Carole to accompany her. Sure enough, a smart young man met them at the rear door entrance of the Store. Just inside the doorway were a number of boxes, some containing ham and egg and cheese salad sandwiches. Others full of blocks of angel and Battenberg cakes, and packets of jam sponge drops. The manager had booked a taxi to take them back to the Home, so the driver put what boxes he could in the boot of the car, and one in between the two girls on the back seat.

"This is exciting," said Carole, "I've never been in a taxi before." Her fingers slowly and slyly began to open the box that was beside her.

"Have you seen what's in this box," she whispered, licking her lips and kicking Shelagh's foot. They both looked at the driver who was watching them through the rear view mirror.

"What's in the box?" he enquired smirking.

"Packets of jam sponge drops," Shelagh answered.

"Why don't you have one each and treat yourselves," he urged.

"Not allowed," answered Shelagh indignantly.

"I won't tell if you don't," he said grinning. "Just leave the wrapping on the floor and I'll clear it away later, go on," he encouraged.

The girls did not need asking twice. They opened the box gently, so as not to damage the carton, and devoured two jam sponge drops each, all the time watching the driver, who was laughing at them.

After they arrived back home, the driver carried all the boxes into the big girls' house and deposited them in the hall. He gave the girls a wave, a wink and a cheeky smile as he left. The sandwiches and cakes were then shared amongst the three houses.

Chapter 46

A few weeks after Miss Lewis retired, a Mrs Phillips was employed as an assistant to Mrs Jones. She was a tall, well-built woman in her late thirties with light brown hair that was straight and turned up around the bottom. She always wore paisley short-sleeved, v-necked, knee length overalls. Behind her square, red-rimmed glasses were bright blue mischievous eyes and her voice was soft and gentle. She rarely shouted at the children, she didn't have to, and could get them to do anything. Often, impulsively, she would play with them in the yard, her favourite games being skipping, and rounders. She loved all the children and they in turn loved and respected her. Mrs Phillips was always laughing and singing aloud, and smoked Craven 'A' cigarettes. She would occupy Miss Lewis' bedroom.

Early one dark and rainy morning, a scared and frightened Shelagh ran as fast as she could out of the side door, at the same time as the others were leaving for school. She ran as fast as she could down the road, without a backward glance, until she knew the home was out of sight.

The hard slaps that she had received had caused her now painful lip to swell so much it was now touching the bottom of her nose, and her eyes were puffy with crying.

"I can't go to school looking like this," Shelagh thought, "and I daren't go back to the Home." She did not know where to go. She wanted to run away as far away as possible, but there was nowhere to go. She found herself heading towards the Children's Care Office in Woodhouse Lane.

Stumbling up the narrow wooden steps, she knocked on one of the closed doors that branched off the narrow wooden floored landing. Within minutes Miss Baker, her old Children's Care Officer from many years ago, answered the door. She was shocked and horrified to see Shelagh in such a distressed state. She ushered her to a chair under the window at the side of her office and gave her a white lace handkerchief from her handbag.

"When you have stopped crying, I want you to tell me what all this is about," she said kindly.

When Shelagh eventually stopped crying, she wiped her eyes, face, and then blew her nose on the handkerchief before offering it back.

"I'm ready to listen," said Miss Baker, now sitting back at her desk, with her elbows and hands propping up her face. Shelagh began to tell her what had brought her to the office that morning. Miss Baker listened patiently not once interrupting. When she had finished relating her story, Miss Baker dialled a number on a telephone at the side of her desk and asked whoever she was talking to if they would join her in her office.

Moments later, huge strides could be heard on the narrow wooden landing. A Mr Waters appeared in the doorway. He looked puzzled at Shelagh crumpled in a chair.

"You look as though you've been in a fight," he remarked.

"She has, haven't you?" Miss Baker remarked.

He introduced himself to Shelagh and said he was a senior member of the Committee.

Mr Waters was a very tall smart man in his mid forties with Brylcreemed black hair swept across his head. He wore a white, crisp, long sleeved, open necked shirt, and black trousers held up with black braces. A pen could be seen tucked behind his ear. He sat in a chair that he had pulled from the other side of the room and bent forward, leaning his arms on his knees.

"I think you had better tell Mr Waters the reason why you were in a fight this morning," said Miss Baker.

"I'm all ears," Mr Waters said, leaning forward and staring at her.

"Well it all started early this morning," Shelagh began, her voice beginning to break.

"By the time I got the kitchen fire going and washed the porridge pan, I was the last to get ready for school, and if it's raining you have to wear Wellington boots. They're kept on a shelf in the cloakroom and its first come, first served, so when I got there, there was only one pair left. They were mens grey ones," Shelagh explained, "and they were miles too big for me. They must have just been handed in, because I haven't seen them before. I put one foot inside and it buried me. The top came up to here," she indicated, placing her hand half way up her thigh. "Nobody wears wellington boots in my class. They would have laughed at me. They laugh at me enough, so I pleaded with the person in front of me, who was checking us, not to make me wear them, she kept slapping me really hard across my face, so I hit her back and then ran out of the door as fast as I could."

Mr Waters held his chin in his hand and shook his head even more.

"You're telling me you've been in a fight with a member of staff over a pair of boots?" he said.

"I can't go back; I'm too scared to go back. You don't know what she's like," Shelagh said, with fear in her voice, "can't you find somewhere else for me to live?" she pleaded. "I can't go back there. Please don't make me," she begged, biting her bottom lip and causing the tears to flow down her cheeks again.

"There's no question about it," he replied. "You have to go back. There is nowhere else to put you. The Homes in Leeds are full of unwanted children, and besides, you'll be leaving in six months time. I suggest, Miss Baker takes you back, talks to the member of staff in question, and try and make some sense of the matter."

Shelagh was petrified, as she did not know what kind of reception she would receive when she returned to the Home.

"You don't know what it's like to live in an orphanage," chuntered Shelagh to Miss Baker as she drove back to the Home.

"Why does no one believe us?" she continued. "A few weeks ago a few of us decided to tell the Home Committee, after one of their meetings. We met them outside in the road, Carole said she was leaving soon and wasn't frightened to tell, so she told a few of the women how awful it was and that all the children are frightened of her. But no one seemed bothered."

Miss Baker listened, but never said a word. When they arrived at the Orphanage, Miss Baker asked Shelagh to wait for her in the dining room.

After what seemed a long time, she returned and sat on a bench beside Shelagh, with a very serious look on her face.

"I have been hearing you are not the easiest of girls to please," she began, "I've been told you are rude, insolent and disobedient to the point of hysteria. What happened this morning cannot and will not be tolerated. You cannot hit a member of staff. You are a young woman and must learn to hold your tongue and keep your hands to yourself, no matter what, and show a good example to the rest of the children. You are typical of hundreds of deprived children. You have to stop acting like little 'orphan Annie' and move on. Mrs Jones has shown me those boots in question and, apart from them needing a good clean, they are in good condition and, in my opinion, are the most sensible kind of footwear to wear when it's raining. It is up to you, when it's raining, to get your chores done as quickly as possible. The quicker you are done the better the choice of wellington boots. Now, what is done is done and the past is the past. I want you to put all this behind you and behave and act like a young lady."

Miss Baker left Shelagh in the dining room, hanging her head, deep in thought. Shelagh was not proud of her conduct that morning, but she judged that she had been provoked.

The following day Shelagh told Pat and Joyce, that she would not be getting any sweets or be joining them to watch television for the next few Sundays as punishment.

On the Sundays that followed, she quite liked being on her own in the dining room. Each Sunday she took her writing pad, from her small locker, and began to calculate how many more months she would have to spend at the Orphanage. Then she counted how many weeks, then days, then minutes, then seconds that she had left up to her fifteenth birthday.

She also found a disused garage not too far away from the home and when it rained, she wore wellington boots, and never said a word. She would change into her black pumps and hide the boots until she returned from school. No one was the wiser.

Carole's father was de-mobbed from the Navy, as she had hoped, and she returned home for good. Sue's mother made a good recovery and she too returned home with her sisters. Shelagh, still resentful towards life, did try to improve her behaviour. She also looked forward to finding employment in the next few months and hoped that Miss Foster could find her suitable foster parents.

All the children from the three houses had now been told that the Home was closing in the next few months. For a long time now, the Orphanage had been having financial difficulties. All the children would have to be found foster homes or be placed into other homes. For those it concerned, it would prove to be a mammoth task.

One morning, Shelagh received a letter. From the handwriting, she knew it was from her aunt in Beeston. She ripped open the envelope, discovering a letter and an invitation to her cousin Pat's wedding. She read the letter over and over again. She could not believe it as she had not seen or heard from them for such a long time. Her stomach churned with excitement. Shelagh quickly took the letter to Mrs Jones, who was in her sitting room, and showed her the wedding invitation and the letter stating that her aunt had asked her if she would like to stay over, on the night of the wedding.

"You know the rules," said Mrs Jones, with a serious tone in her voice, "you can only stay overnight if your Aunt makes an application in writing to the Children's Care Office, and then it will have to be approved."

With a heavy heart, Shelagh wanted to scream.

"You'd better write to your Aunt quickly and explain, or it will be too late," added Mrs Jones.

Shelagh ran into the dining room, took her writing pad and an envelope from her locker and began to write to her aunt and uncle. She was not sure if her aunt would write to the authorities. Her aunt did not much like the 'powers that be', as she called them, and she said that there were too many rules and regulations for her liking. After she had hurriedly written the letter, Shelagh ran down the long road and posted it in the letterbox on the Post Office wall. She crossed her fingers all the way back, hoping that her aunt could be bothered to write to head office. All she could do was wait.

A month later, a new Children's Care Officer came to visit the girls. Miss Foster had taken up a new post in Manchester, after she had moved some weeks ago.

Miss Porter was in her late twenties, slim, of medium height and very attractive. Not a hair was out of place amongst her short brown curly hair. She was wearing a smart, tweed suit, a peach blouse with matching lipstick. Firstly, she met Joyce, now a chubby, healthy ten year old, full of the joys of spring, a friendly chatty little girl. Joyce talked non-stop about her foster Aunt who had taken her to the cinema on the previous Saturday. Pat now a slim twelve year old, entered the room. It was plain to see that she was the quieter of the two. She was dressed in a Guide uniform, a long sleeved, blue dress with two breast pockets. Pat told Miss Porter that she was meeting Shelagh later at the main gates and that they were going to a Guide meeting at Wrangthorn Church. She was full of praise for her older sister. On the previous Saturday, all the Guides of Leeds held a swimming gala at Cookridge Street Baths. From the balcony, she had watched Shelagh come third after swimming on her back, wearing a flannelette nightdress and holding a lit candle in her hand. "And then," Pat said excitedly and not stopping for breath, "she won First Prize in the surface diving, giving Wrangthorn Church enough points to be second place in Leeds."

Miss Porter smiled as she listened to both girls. They seemed to be two normal healthy children, and she was very impressed by them. She then made her way across the yard to meet Shelagh, as there was something of great importance to tell her.

Shelagh, also dressed in her Guide's uniform, was coming down the stairs as Miss Porter knocked and walked in the side door. Miss Porter knew instinctively that it was Shelagh, as she looked so much like her younger sisters. She introduced herself to Shelagh, congratulating her on her swimming achievement, and then she told her that she had some important news for her. Shelagh had been waiting for this moment.

"I've been to see your Aunt in Beeston after we received a letter asking if you can stay overnight on the day of your cousins wedding," Miss Porter began.

Shelagh impatiently wished that she would get to the point.

"I'm pleased to say, you can," she pronounced, "and I hope you have a wonderful time."

Shelagh stood with her mouth wide open and then began to jump up and down excitedly.

"Oh thank you, oh thank you," is all she could say. Instinctively she decided that she liked Miss Porter.

"I won't keep you any longer than necessary," said Miss Porter, "I know you are meeting Pat soon. Before my next visit, I want you to think of what employment you would like to do and we'll talk about it when I next visit. Now off you go. Pat will be waiting for you," she remarked, as she looked at the watch on her slim wrist, "and I'd better go and introduce myself to Mrs Jones."

On the morning of her cousin's wedding, Shelagh hurriedly ran upstairs after breakfast. She wore a crisp, white cotton blouse, a white button-up cardigan and a paisley print, full flared skirt. At the request of Miss Porter, Mrs Jones had bought her, out of next month's clothing allowance, a pretty, white, broderie anglaise top, her first suspender belt, a pair of seamed nylons and her first pair of slip-on brown shoes.

Shelagh walked proudly down the road showing off her new clothes. She was carrying a small suitcase that she had found in the linen room. Inside the case, she had put a change of clothes, and a handmade, embroidered tablecloth, wrapped up in pretty paper, that Mrs Jones had given her to give as a wedding present for her cousin.

When Shelagh arrived at the house, her auntie Ethel and a few neighbours had just finished making sandwiches for the reception that was to be held in the large kitchen.

Shelagh ran upstairs to see Pat, who was just putting on her wedding dress. She stood back in amazement. Her cousin looked beautiful, just like a princess. Her dress was three-quarter length, white lace over satin, and on her head a short veil. Shelagh was so envious of her.

A short time later, everyone made their way to St Peter's Church in Dewsbury Road.

Malcolm, Pat's future husband was a handsome young man, who reminded Shelagh of Tony Curtis. He was standing just inside the doorway with his brothers, who all looked extremely smart in their new suits. During the Service, Shelagh sat with her auntie Vera and uncle Billy.

As Pat and Malcolm walked back down the aisle, Shelagh wondered if, one day, someone would marry her, and would she look as beautiful as Pat. She lived in hope.

Back at her auntie and uncle's house, family and friends mingled together. Shelagh spoke to as many of her aunts and uncles as possible, telling them that the Orphanage was closing in a few months time and that their Care Officers were looking for foster homes for her and her sisters. Sadly, no one appeared to be interested. Shelagh sat on the top step outside the kitchen door; where she had sat such a long time ago, thinking of the years that had passed. She had noticed that her mother, her new husband and their four children, were not there among the guests. Shelagh had long since past caring about her mother. Her mother did not care about them. "Why should she care about her," she thought, "too many years had passed. Not a birthday card, Christmas card. Not even a `phone call. Nothing. Her mother was not worth caring about."

Pat, her newly married cousin, came and sat down beside her. Shelagh thanked her for inviting her to the wedding.

Pat asked how she was, and how life was treating her.

"I'm fine," Shelagh replied, "I have to be, don't I? I'll have to start looking for a job soon, and one that pays good wages. I'll need enough to pay board money, tram fares, pocket money and some extra to put by for clothing. I used to want to be a secretary, but Miss Lewis always said I didn't speak properly. Then the manager of Marks and Spencer offered me a job, but the pay isn't very good. I'll have to think of something soon."

"Why don't you work where I work," suggested Pat, "its good money and there's plenty of overtime. I'll give you the address before Malcolm and I go home. We're renting a back-to-back house in Holbeck. I'll give you that address as well and you can come and see us whenever you want."

Shelagh was thrilled as she thought the world of Pat. She couldn't think of anything better than working at the same place as her cousin.

Shelagh arrived back at the Home early the following day and reported to Mrs Jones. After doing so, she ran to the dining room and wrote a letter to Alf Cooke, a large printing firm in Hunslet, asking if there were any job vacancies.

Several weeks later, Miss Porter made her usual monthly visit, firstly to the little house to see that Pat and Joyce were satisfactory. She voiced her concerns to Miss Ratcliffe about the Home closing down. She did not really want the girls to be relocated into another Children's Home, but good foster homes were hard to find.

"Why don't you try Mr and Mrs Wood," suggested Miss Ratcliffe, "they've been acting as foster Aunt and Uncle to Pat for a number of years. I do know they have three children and live on a tight budget as most families do. It's worth a try."

"That's a very good idea," replied Miss Porter, "I'll ask Mr Parnell first and see what he thinks. I'll let you know what the outcome is." With that, she headed towards the big house to see Shelagh; eager to see how the wedding went. She found Shelagh in the hall with her arms folded behind her back.

"What ever are you doing?" she asked.

"I've been told, I'm round shouldered," said Shelagh sharply, "so every now and again I've to fold my arms behind my back for a few hours to pull my shoulders back."

"Well now you can unfold them," laughed Miss Porter, "come and talk to me, and tell me about the wedding."

Shelagh talked non-stop for the next half an hour, telling Miss Porter how beautiful her cousin Pat had looked, seeing her family and admiring the presents they'd received.

"The best is yet to come," Shelagh announced, suddenly running upstairs to her drawer in the dormitory, from where she took out an official envelope and ran quickly downstairs, almost falling as she ran. She handed the envelope to Miss Porter in the sitting room, and burst out,

"I've got an interview for a job next week," Shelagh could not contain her excitement. Miss Porter was delighted. She thought that Shelagh had changed dramatically since that horrible day a few months ago. Although she was not her Care Officer at that time, it was her business to know everything about the children in her care. In her opinion, Shelagh had more than made up for her bad conduct on that awful morning. She had stopped answering back, never questioned anything anymore and never grumbled. Shelagh was indeed growing up into a nice young woman.

To Shelagh's delight, Miss Porter promised to collect her the following week and personally take her to the interview.

"You will need your birth certificate;" she instructed, "I have it in your file in my office, so I will bring it with me."

The following week, as promised, Miss Porter collected Shelagh and remarked how smart she looked. Shelagh was wearing the same clothes for the interview that she had worn for her cousin's wedding.

She accompanied Shelagh to the place where she was to be interviewed by the Welfare Officer.

At the end of a formal discussion, Shelagh was told she would start on the eighteenth of August, which would be her fifteenth birthday, and that she would earn about two pounds, fifteen shillings, per week with stoppages off.

She would start at seven-thirty a.m., and finish at five-fifteen p.m., and be expected to do overtime after her initial training.

After the interview, Miss Porter dropped her off at the Home. Shelagh could not wait to tell Mrs Jones, Mrs Phillips and the rest of the children, especially her sisters. All she needed now was to find somewhere to live.

"At last," she thought, "I'll be leaving the dreaded Orphanage I hate so much." She took a piece of paper from her locker and began to calculate how much longer it would be:

Two months and two days;

= 8 wks and 2 days;

= 58 days;

= 1, 392 hours;

= 5,011,200 seconds to go.

Now the end was in sight!

Chapter 47

During the next few days, Miss Porter made an appointment to see Mr and Mrs Wood.

She arrived at their terraced house in a pleasant part of Woodhouse in Leeds. The rain was pouring down as she knocked at the kitchen door. Mr Wood invited her in and offered to take her wet coat, which he wrapped around the back of a kitchen chair and positioned it near the guarded fire to dry. The flames from the blazing fire were crackling up the chimney.

As soon as she walked into the house, Miss Porter felt warmth, happiness and a sense of security.

Mrs Wood had already put the kettle on one of the four gas rings on top of the cooker, and taking three of her best china cups and saucers, from a fitted cupboard at the side of the fire, she made a large teapot full of tea. They sat together at the square wooden table in the middle of the room. Mr Wood looked a little concerned as to why she felt the need to visit.

"Is there anything wrong?" he asked, a little puzzled.

"Exactly the opposite," Miss Porter replied, her cold red hands were firmly wrapped around the hot cup of tea.

"Were you aware that Headingley Orphanage is to close down in a few months time," she remarked.

Surprised at this news, Mr and Mrs Wood looked at each other and shook their heads.

"Pat's never mentioned it to us," frowned Mrs Wood.

"Well," Miss Porter began to explain. "For a long time now the Home has been having financial difficulties, so the Committee have decided to close it down, and unfortunately it will be in the next few months. That leaves me to find Homes for the children in my care. That's the reason why I am here. Would it be possible for you to take Pat, or if not, do you know anyone who would?" she asked.

They both looked at each other in shock and for a moment, neither knew what to say.

"Well you've really knocked us for six," said Mr Wood. "We do have three children of our own, you know. The two oldest we're very proud of," he continued, "Leslie, our fourteen year old, attends Leeds Central High School, and Trisha, our daughter, is twelve years old, exactly the same age as Pat. Then there's little baby Peter, who's asleep, in his cot for the night, in our bedroom."

"I'm sorry I've sprung this on you," said Miss Porter. "Shall I give you a few days to think about it, and call back in a few days time? What do you think?"

"I don't think there is much to think about," remarked Mrs Wood. "But you're right. We do need to discuss the matter with the children. That's only fair. After all, it's their decision too."

Loud, raucous laughter could be heard from the front room, where Leslie and Trisha were playing. Mr Wood tilted his head towards the inside door that led through to the front room and grinned. After their lengthy conversation, Miss Porter headed towards her car for the long drive home. It had now stopped raining. "What a pleasure to have met such a charming couple," she thought. As soon as she arrived home, she decided to make herself a hot cup of cocoa and write her findings there and then, while they were fresh in her mind from the evening's events. Usually she wrote all her reports in her office but this was one that she felt quite excited about.

Miss Porter began by stating that the home atmosphere was warm and friendly. She wrote that, in her opinion, they showed a genuine fondness for Pat and had acted as foster Aunt and Uncle over the previous eight years. She could not think of a better place for her to live.

She now felt certain that both were very understanding of the needs of children, particularly Mr Wood, who within his capacity as a Housemaster at East Moor Approved School, came in regular contact with young adolescents.

He also earned a good wage of six hundred and ten pounds per annum.

Both were enthusiastic members of a local Methodist Church, where Mr Wood ran a youth club, of which Pat was a member. Miss Porter could not believe that she had met a couple that were so perfect for Pat, and concluded her report by reiterating that in her view, this would be an excellent place for Pat to live. She would not know the couple's decision however, until a few days later.

When a few days had elapsed, an eager Miss Porter returned to see Mr and Mrs Wood.

"Have you made a decision?" she asked, crossing the fingers of one of her hands down by her side. They looked at each other, grinned and then smiled.

"There's nothing to think about is there?" replied Mrs Wood, looking at her husband tenderly, "we knew all along that we would like Pat to be part of our family, didn't we? We just needed to talk to the children."

"If references are needed," butted in Mr Wood, "the Minister at my church will gladly give one, and Miss Ratcliffe has given our application her full backing."

"There is one thing we ask," Mrs Wood asked, "can we tell Pat ourselves."

Miss Porter gave a broad smile and nodded her agreement.

"I don't know whether you realise," she told them, "we will be paying you a boarding out allowance to keep Pat, around thirty shillings per week, plus some pocket money, and every few months, we will send you her clothing allowance."

"Well that's a lovely surprise," remarked Mrs Wood, "that's an added luxury. The money will come in very handy for her, although we would have taken her to live with us anyway, wouldn't we?" she said, looking at Mr Wood. He nodded repeatedly with approval.

"Pat is due her yearly medical at the Education Department in Great George Street, and I will arrange for her to have that before she leaves the Home," continued Miss Porter. "There is one thing I neglected to inform you. Pat's mother could, at any one time, apply for her to be taken back into her care. However, that is highly unlikely, as she has not seen any of her children since she placed them in care, and that is over ten years ago.

On Pat's next visit to the Woods, they asked her if she would like to live with them.

Pat froze for a moment thinking that she was hearing things. They asked her again.

"Can I?" she yelled. "Oh yes please." She began to jump up and down, her eyes sparkling and dancing around. She was so excited that she decided to return to the Home early that evening in order to tell Miss Ratcliffe the news.

"When can I go?" she asked Miss Ratcliffe impatiently.

"Well," answered Miss Ratcliffe, "school will be closing for the summer holidays and we will be going on our usual camping holiday at Scarborough. This time there won't be as many children with us, due to the Home closing. Some have left already, to live with parents or families, so I would really like you to have a holiday with us at the seaside first. Who knows, you might not see the sea again."

"Oh I will," Pat replied, holding her shoulders back confidently.

"Mr and Mrs Wood, Leslie, Trisha and Peter are always going on trips away in their van," she laughed, "and Mr Wood said I can go with them if I want. So can I go with them please and not to Scarborough?"

"If that's what you really want," Miss Ratcliffe sighed. She could see Pat's eyes dancing around and her body shaking with excitement.

Miss Ratcliffe was delighted. She had known the family for a long time and knew that Pat would settle admirably and that it would be an excellent home for her.

She also knew that deep down in her heart Pat, like her older sister, had an intense grudge against the people who had abandoned her and left her in care so many years ago.

A happy, normal life would compensate for this unforgivable act of desertion.

"Miss Porter has been looking at your clothes and thinks you could do with a few more," Miss Ratcliffe informed her, "so she's arranged, through me, to collect you next week and take you to the Supply Department in Easterly Road.

Pat stood, looking and listening to Miss Ratcliffe, with her mouth wide open. She could not believe that in a few weeks time she would no longer be a 'home kid'. She couldn't wait.

The following Friday, the last day of the summer term, Pat arrived home from school to find Miss Porter waiting for her in Miss Ratcliffe's sitting room. Beside her on the floor a small, brown suitcase.

"You've had your hair cut short," she remarked to Pat, "it suits you and makes you look very attractive. The resemblance between you and your sister Shelagh is now remarkable. Are you ready?" she added grinning.

"Are we going to get me some new clothes?" Pat asked hopefully.

Miss Ratcliffe was standing with her back against the fire, laughing.

"Yes I am," Miss Porter replied, "and then I'm going to take you straight to Mr and Mrs Woods to live. I have all your clothes packed into this suitcase," she said, patting the suitcase on the floor beside her.

"Now?" Pat shouted, with a surprised look on her face. "Now?" she repeated her eyes wide open.

"Yes," said Miss Ratcliffe, "I'll miss you dreadfully, but I know you'll be very happy where you're going. You're a very lucky girl. Now you'd better find your sisters and say goodbye to them while I have chat to Miss Porter," suggested Miss Ratcliffe. Pat looked backwards and forwards, not moving her head, hoping Miss Porter would not leave without her.

Pat ran from the sitting room into the kitchen where she knew Joyce was. She was sitting on a high stool holding her face in her hands, her elbows on the table and swinging her legs backwards and forwards underneath. She was eyeing a tray of jam tarts in the middle of the table on a cooling tray and Auntie Ada was watching her from the scullery. Pat quickly told her that she was leaving for good and that she would see her soon. Joyce not really understanding was more interested in waiting for a jam tart.

Pat then ran outside into the yard to look for Shelagh and her friend Valerie.

Miss Ratcliffe began to relay her concerns to Miss Porter regarding Pat.

"I know Pat is going to a very good home," she began. "I worry that she will find it hard fitting into normal family life. She's a very sensible girl for a twelve year old. However, she has been institutionalised in a Children's Home for a long time. Would you please keep me in touch, and let me know how she is?" she asked.

"Well, from what I have seen at the Wood's home, she will be in good hands," replied Miss Porter, "and I am sure she will, in time, adapt to normal family life."

"Yes I know," said Miss Ratcliffe, the worried look still etched on her face. "Pat is a very quiet girl, and easily gets picked on due to her small frame and her placid nature. She tends to bottle things up inside her, and never talks about her feelings to anyone. I just hope that by living in a normal house with normal children, she will eventually overcome whatever troubles she holds inside her."

"Don't worry," assured Miss Porter, "I will keep a very close eye on her, and keep you informed of her progress."

Pat ran outside to the far side of the yard to where Shelagh was playing hopscotch with Yvonne Clarke, a young girl of around thirteen years of age, who was staying at the big house for a few weeks until her mother, who had had major surgery at St James's Hospital, was well enough to take care of her again. Yvonne's mother had brought her up single handedly. She had never known her real father, a GI, who had returned to America before she was born. Yvonne was always saying that one day she would find her father and tell him that she was his daughter.

"I'll come and see you in a few weeks time when you've settled in," said Shelagh, giving Pat a reassuring bear hug. Shelagh also felt sure that she would also be leaving soon, though she did not know where she was going to live.

"If you're looking for Valerie," said Shelagh to Pat, as she looked around the yard, "she's in the shed with some of the other girls."

Pat ran across the yard to the open fronted, corrugated roofed shed, where a group of girls had made a circle around Kim, a sandy coloured, shaggy mongrel, the pet dog of the big girls' house.

The girls had dressed the dog in a dress, cardigan and socks, and wrapped a scarf around his neck, tying it in a knot under his chin. Valerie was arranging a pair of sunglasses over his eyes. They were howling with laughter at the appearance and expressions on the dog's face. Kim jumped into an old dolls pram as though he had done it a thousand times. Holding his head high and wagging his tail, Kim looked at the girls, waiting for one of them to push him around the yard. He loved the children playing with him.

"I've got something to tell you," said Pat, pulling Valerie to one side. "I'm leaving the Home *today*." "I'm going to live with Mr and Mrs Wood."

"Lucky you," Valerie replied, shrugging her shoulders. "When the Home closes next month, I'll be going back to live with my parents. All these years they've never wanted me. Now in a few years time I'll be leaving school, getting a job, and be bringing in some money. They must think I'm daft. Its money they want, not me," she said sadly.

"Well at least they want you back," said Pat. Our parents, wherever they are, don't want to know us. Sometimes I wish I'd never been born."

Both girls were sitting side by side on top of the old table tennis table, holding onto the side and swinging their legs.

"Never mind," carried on Valerie, "living anywhere else has got to be better than living here."

"Yes it has," replied Pat. "I hate it here. I know our Shelagh does as well. She makes it quite clear to everyone. I can't. I just keep it to myself. What's the point of saying anything? Nobody listens or cares about what we think."

"When me and Maureen Flanagan were sent to the big girls' house a few years ago, why didn't you come with us?" asked Valerie curiously.

"I don't know," answered Pat with an angry tone in her voice. "It wasn't fair that all my friends were moved and I wasn't."

"Maybe whoever decides, decided not to separate you and Joyce," suggested Valerie.

"Well it still wasn't fair," grumbled Pat. "At least when I leave, I won't have to get up at the crack of dawn, light fires, set the tables for breakfast, and then get the younger children up and help them to wash, dress and plait the girls hair. I'm sick of it," Pat complained, rolling her head from side to side.

"Well at least you won't get pushed and bossed around anymore by 'you know who'," said Valerie, shoving her shoulder into Pats and looking in the direction of one of the boys, who was well known for being a bully.

"No I won't," continued Pat, "I'll be free. Free, for the first time in my life. I wonder what it's like to live in a real, normal home with normal people." Pat frowned, unsure of how normal people lived.

"I don't know," said Valerie. "We'll soon find out, won't we? Anyway," she continued, "once the school holidays are over, we'll be back at the same school and in the same class. So we'll be able to tell each other what it's like, won't we?"

221

Pat looked into Valerie's face and nodded.

"Yes, you're right, we will," she affirmed. "I'll have to go now; Miss Porter will be waiting for me. I'll see you at school in September," she quipped, as she jumped down from the table tennis table.

"Good luck," Valerie hollered, as she ran across the yard towards the little house.

"My turn now to push Kim around the yard," Pat heard Valerie shouting as Maureen Flanagan came running towards her with Kim still sitting comfortably and fully dressed inside the old dolls pram.

Meanwhile Joyce had eaten a jam tart that Auntie Ada had given to her, and, knowing she would not be getting another, climbed down from the stool and went to say hello to Miss Porter.

"Where's Tony?" Joyce asked, suddenly taking Miss Ratcliffe and Miss Porter by surprise. "We haven't seen him for ages. Doesn't he want to come and see us anymore," she asked inquisitively.

Miss Porter looked at Miss Ratcliffe and then back at Joyce, sighing deeply.

"Well," Miss Porter answered, taking a deep breath, "Tony has a very busy life. He has a paper round every day and he belongs to the Boys Brigade at a church near where he lives. I've asked him time and time again why he doesn't want to visit, and he says he's frightened of orphanages, saying that every time he's naughty, he's threatened that the next time he visits he will be left here. We know that's not true, but he doesn't believe us," she concluded.

Joyce hung her head, pouted her lips, shrugged her shoulders and left the room to find her friend Maureen.

"I think she will miss Pat more than she realises," said Miss Ratcliffe sadly, "and now she thinks she is losing both her sisters, she might subconsciously be trying to cling on to her brother. She's probably thinking she won't see her sisters anymore, but we know that's not going to happen don't we?" remarked Miss Ratcliffe.

Later that evening, after they had been to the Clothes Supply Department, where Pat had been fitted out with a few more clothes, Miss Porter delivered her to her new home. As she entered the kitchen, all the family gave Pat a warm welcome. Pat dragged Miss Porter upstairs to show her that she had a bed of her own in the same room that she would share with Trisha.

After a lengthy chat to Mr and Mrs Wood, Miss Porter left them with an application form for them to read and sign, stating the rules and regulations for a child who was now in their care. She also left some pocket money for Pat, some saving stamps and ten shillings in a Yorkshire Penny Bank book.

As she left, Miss Porter could hear Pat and Trisha talking, and the noise of drawers and wardrobe doors, opening and closing in a bedroom that they would share for many years.

do hereby agree with the Council of the County Borough of Leeds that

(a) I will receive _Patricia Gregson_ into my home, feed, clothe and look after her and bring her up as carefully and kindly as I would a child of my own.

(b) I will help her to become a good citizen, send her to school - work - and to Church - Chapel, and arrange for recreation suited to her age.

(c) I will look after her health and consult the doctor whenever the child is ill, and in the event of her serious illness or accident, I will also notify the Council immediately

(d) I will provide for the cleaning, mending and renewal of her clothing and its proper care.

(e) I will at all times permit any person authorised by the Home Office or by the Council to see the child and her home and clothing, and I will attend to the advice of any such person.

(f) I will allow her to be removed from my home when required by any person so authorised.

(g) I will notify the Council within two weeks if I change my address.

I make this agreement with the Council in consideration of my receiving the sum of _1-10-0_ per week for maintenance, plus _2-6_ per week for pocket money, and clothing allowance at the rate of _10/-_ per week paid quarterly.

3. I acknowledge having received _Patricia Gregson_ into my home on the _28th July 1958_ and agree that she brought with her the following articles of clothing and personal possessions:-

Clothing	Number Bought	Brought	Clothing	Number Bought	Brought
Coat	1	1	Suspender Belt		
Hat			Brassiere		2
Raincoat			Stockings/Socks		
Blazer		1(green)	Handkerchiefs		
Shoes	1	3	Overall/Pinafore		
Slippers		1	Gloves		
Wellington Boots	2		Scarf		
Dress	2	4	Brush and comb		1
Skirt		3	Toothbrush		
Gym Slip			Suitcase		
Blouse		4			1
Jersey		1			
Cardigan		3			
Pyjamas/Nightdress		2			
Vest	2	4			
Underskirt or Set					
Knickers	2	2			

Doctor's Card _____   Personal Savings _____

Signature of foster parent _EWood_
Address _43 Glasgow View Leeds 6._
Witness _Mary Pearson_
Address _229, Woodhouse Lane 2._
Date _28/7/58_   _3._

Chapter 48

Mr and Mrs Morton had recently applied for, and been accepted to act as foster parents for a working girl.

"Perfect timing," thought Miss Porter, as she read their application. In a few weeks time Shelagh would be just that, a working girl.

One warm summer's evening in July; Miss Porter collected Shelagh and took her to meet them.

They lived in the Harehills area of Leeds in a back-to-back house.

Miss Porter knocked on the door, which was partially open. Mrs Morton appeared and invited them in, giving them a warm welcome. After a short time, Miss Porter said that she had another call to make, so she would leave them to get acquainted. She promised that she would call back in a few hours time to take Shelagh back to the Home.

Mrs Morton looked to be in her late sixties. She was very small, very round, and her head seemed to be lost in the middle of her shoulders. Her short, grey, permed hair was a mass of close-knit curls. Her eyes were small and narrow and her voice was squeaky and high-pitched. She was wearing a long sleeved, beige jumper, under a dark grey pinafore dress, and short, black, zip up, suede ankle boots. Mr Morton was standing in the scullery at the side of a Formica table, making them all a cup of tea. He looked to be in his early seventies and was of medium height, with grey hair that was short, thin and sparse. His tortoiseshell glasses were perched on the end of his nose. He was wearing a beige v necked cardigan over a blue open necked shirt, and his trousers looked far too long as they trailed over his slippers onto the floor.

"Milk and sugar?" he asked Shelagh in a soft, gentle voice.

"Yes please," Shelagh answered.

As he shuffled his feet across the floor, carrying a cup and saucer in each hand, Shelagh noticed that his walk was unsteady. His hands were shaking so much that the tea in the cups was spilling over into the saucers. In the absence of Miss Porter, Mrs Morton began to fire questions at Shelagh.

"Where are your mother and father? are they dead?" she began. When did you last see them? Have you got any brothers and sisters? How old are they? Why haven't you been adopted?"

The questions went on and on. Shelagh answered them truthfully. "Nothing to hide now," she thought. After a long inquisition, Mrs Morton, with great difficulty due to her size, escorted Shelagh up the narrow, winding staircase to a small, newly decorated bedroom. The smell of fresh paint still lingered in the air and the large, soft, pink roses stood out on the recently decorated wallpaper.

"This will be your bedroom if you choose to come and live with us," she said kindly, "would you like that?"

"Oh yes please," replied Shelagh, suddenly feeling very humble and grateful.

White sheets could be seen under a pink eiderdown on the small bed behind the door and a small chest of drawers stood beneath the window. Inside the combination wardrobe, which was leaning against the wall, there were shelves and hanging space for coats and dresses. Shelagh could not believe her luck. A bedroom all of her own, even somewhere to hang her clothes.

"There is a little matter of how much board money you will have to pay me out of your wage," said Mrs Morton awkwardly, "but I'm sure Miss Porter will put you right on the matter. Can't keep you on fresh air can I?" she said, giving her a wink.

When Miss Porter returned, she was pleased to see Shelagh's face beaming. She had not seen her smile in a long time.

"I've been having a long talk to Shelagh while you've been gone," Mrs Morton began to say. Shelagh tells me her youngest sister Joyce, who is nearly eleven years old, has nowhere to live. Is that true?"

Miss Porter looked at Shelagh and then back at Mrs Morton.

"Yes that is true," she answered. "She has had a very good foster Aunt for the last eight years but she is a divorced woman and holds down a full time job, so unfortunately can't take her. But yes you're right," she added, "and I'm still looking."

"Well look no longer," exclaimed Mrs Morton." "I've been having a long talk to Shelagh and she would like her to come and live here with us. I have a decent sized attic. It's cold and damp as it hasn't been used in years, but I'm willing if you are. I'm not sure how to take care of a young girl, but Shelagh said she would help. What do you think?"

Miss Porter was stunned. This she had not expected.

"This is wonderful news" she said eventually, "I'm overjoyed. It'll have to be agreed by the Committee, but that's not going to be a problem because you've already been accepted. Joyce is due to go on holiday to Scarborough at the weekend," she said. Then, turning to Shelagh, she added. "So why don't you bring her to meet Mr and Mrs Morton in the next few days?"

Mrs Morton nodded with approval.

"Aren't you going to Scarborough?" Mrs Morton asked Shelagh.

"No," she replied, "I'll be starting work while they are away, so Mr and Mrs Hughes, who are in charge of the big boys' house, said I can stay with them until I leave the home."

Shelagh explained how the little house and the big girls' house always went camping during the first few weeks in August, using the halls of a church in Scarborough. The older boys would spend the last few weeks there.

"In that case," said Miss Porter, "I'll start to arrange for you to be discharged from the Home to here, a few days before you begin work. Is that all right by you?" she asked Mrs Morton.

"That's fine by me," Mrs Morton answered. "As a matter of interest, will you be paying the same boarding out money for Joyce, as Shelagh will be paying me out of her wages?" she added.

"No," Miss Porter replied, "boarding out money is paid on pro rata basis. That means according to age. So it will be around thirty shillings per week, plus pocket money and a clothing allowance."

"Well I don't much agree with that," remarked Mrs Morton, pulling a face and not looking too pleased. "I think it should be the same. After all, it takes more time and energy to take care of a schoolgirl than it does to look after a working girl. Not to worry, I'm sure we shall manage won't we?" she said, looking over at Mr Morton who had been sitting quietly on a chair at the back of the room, not saying a word, but nodding when needed.

A few days later, Shelagh took Joyce to meet Mr and Mrs Morton. They did not stay too long as Joyce, for once, was very quiet and nervous knowing that in the next few weeks she would be leaving the Orphanage. Joyce had spent most of her childhood living with Miss Ratcliffe, who she loved dearly, and had never known any other kind of life. She fidgeted, not once making eye contact with Mr and Mrs Morton all the time that she was there. All she wanted to do was return to the Home as soon as possible to play with Maureen, although her friend was returning home with her brother to their parents in the next few days. Mr and Mrs Morton were not unduly concerned, as they knew that given time, Joyce would soon settle down in her new home.

Mr and Mrs Hughes were a middle-aged couple and had been in charge of the boys' home for a number of years, with two teenage boys of their own. They had taken over from Mr and Mrs Kelly a few years earlier.

During the next few weeks, Shelagh played cricket, kick out ball, hot rice and table tennis in the yard with boys of her own age and loved it.

The boys' house was not as spick and span as the girls' house. In fact, there seemed to be clutter everywhere. There were no strict rules or job rotas to adhere to and everyone helped each other willingly. The house was warm, friendly and always full of laughter. It was indeed a happy home.

The night before Shelagh was to leave; she began to pack all her worldly possessions into a new large, grey suitcase that had been bought for her out of her clothing allowance. She did not sleep much thinking of the new life that lay ahead of her. Eventually, she fell asleep in the early hours of the morning.

After breakfast, Shelagh took a leisurely bath, knowing that it would be the last bath she would have for a long time. There was no bath or even hot water at Mr and Mrs Mortons. Even the toilet, halfway up the street, was shared but that did not bother her at all. The main thing was she would be normal and live with normal people. A few hours before Miss Porter came to collect her, Shelagh asked Mrs Hughes if she could take one last look around the big girls' house. She handed her the key and asked her to collect any post that there might be and put it on the table in Mrs Jones' sitting room. Stepping out of the side door, she walked across to the big girls' house opposite. She unlocked the door and stood motionless for a moment just inside. The house was dark, empty and eerie. Shelagh felt a cold shiver down her spine and her skin was covered in goose lumps. As she began to amble around the empty house, every room seemed to have its own memories. Firstly, the dining room, where she remembered all the strict rules and table manners the children had to adhere to. Then behind the door where the small, metal, handbag lockers stood, where she had kept her writing pad and envelopes, always on the ready to write all those letters to her family over the years, asking them to take them out of the Home, all to no avail. Next, the kitchen with its bare fire grate, that on so many occasions she had failed to light. Then the scullery, where once she was pinned against the wall and a piece of grizzle was rammed down her throat. The cellars underneath the kitchen were next, the dark, cold, damp place where she had spent many an hour chopping wood for all the fires. Shelagh then made her way to the front door, picked up the post and put it on the table in the sitting room. This was where, every Sunday afternoon, they had all queued, around the room and out into the hall, waiting for a handful of sweets from the bureau in the corner beside the fireplace.

Then she began to climb up the sweeping staircase that she had polished so often. Firstly, she walked down the middle of the long dormitory where the younger children slept. The picture with young children standing around Jesus was still perched on the same chest of drawers at the bottom of the room. Shelagh remembered staring at the picture during her first night, and wondered if he was watching her. She had always thought the young girl that he was carrying in his arms resembled Pat, and the boy, carrying newspapers under his arm and looking directly at Jesus, looked like Tony. She picked up the picture, holding it close to her chest with both hands, and then slid it inside her buttoned cardigan.

"If I take this picture with me," she thought, "I will always have Jesus by my side.

Taking a quick look around the big girls' dormitory for the very last time, she hurriedly left the house. When she had locked the door, she ran quickly back to where her case was standing and put the picture inside. Then, as she was giving the key back to Mrs Hughes, Miss Porter arrived to take her to her new home.

Mr and Mrs Hughes gave her a big hug and wished her well for the future.

Shelagh sat on the seat next to Miss Porter as they began to drive away. Her case was stored safely in the boot, and not once did she give a backward glance to the Orphanage where she had lived for almost eight years. How she had hated her time there.

Mr and Mrs Morton gave her a warm welcome when she arrived some time later.

"Why don't you go and put your clothes away," encouraged Mrs Morton, "while I have a talk to Miss Porter. I know there's a lot of paper work for me to read and sign."

Shelagh lugged the heavy case up the narrow staircase to her room and began to unpack all her belongings. The picture took pride of place on the small chest of drawers under the window. After neatly arranging the rest of her clothes on the shelves and hanging her coat and blouses in the combination wardrobe, she joined them downstairs.

Miss Porter was just handing a 'free from infection' certificate to Mrs Morton, requesting that it should be handed to the doctor that Shelagh would be registering with. As she walked towards her car, Miss Porter shouted to Shelagh,

"I'll be back to see you in a months time. If you have any problems, don't hesitate to give me a ring. And good luck in your new job."

Miss Porter gave them a wave as she drove away.

For the first time in her life, Shelagh felt free. She spent the evening in the company of Mr and Mrs Morton, watching television and feeling totally relaxed.

"Before you go to bed," said Mrs Morton "there are one or two rules. Firstly, it goes without saying, it's your responsibility to keep your bedroom clean and tidy.

If you need to use the toilet during the night, there's something for you to use under the bed.

If you have to use it, you must empty and clean it every day, when you come home from work. If you really, really need to go to the toilet during the night, you'll have to use the toilet up the street, no matter what the time is. The key is hung on a hook at the back of the scullery door. We don't have a torch, so it would be better for you if you avoided the need when it's dark. Mr Morton and me are not as young as we used to be," she continued, "so any help around the house will be appreciated. The toilet up the street is shared amongst three houses, so every third week; I would like you to give it a good scrub."

"I'm used to doing jobs," Shelagh remarked, feeling very grateful they had given her a home, "I'll do anything."

"There's no reading in bed," Mrs Morton carried on, "so don't leave the light on. I have a good neighbour opposite, who'll tell me if the light is on too long. Bedrooms are for sleeping in.

If you go out on a night, I want you back in the house by ten o'clock Monday to Thursday, and ten thirty on Friday and Saturday. If I hear you've been in a pub, or you smell of beer on your breath, you will be out on your ear. If you get into any kind of trouble, you'll be out on the street, do you understand?" Her voice sounded serious and meaningful. Shelagh nodded her head.

"There is not much danger of that," she thought. "For one thing, I don't have any friends to go out with, and another thing, I'm too young to go into pubs anyway."

Settling into her new bedroom on that first night, she lay on her back, holding her hands behind her head, and looked at the pretty wallpaper. The Orphanage walls were always painted one colour at the top, usually cream, and another colour at the bottom, either dark green or brown. Before she fell asleep, she looked at the picture on top of the drawers and thanked Jesus.

The following day as Mrs Morton was preparing Sunday dinner, she asked Shelagh if she liked Yorkshire pudding.

"I love Yorkshire pudding," she replied eagerly. "Sometimes Mrs Jones made it for us. Can I help make the dinner?" she asked, trying to be helpful. "I know how to peel potatoes."

"That would be very nice," Mrs Morton replied.

Shelagh took herself into the scullery and began to peel. When the large pan was full of spotlessly clean potatoes, she proudly showed them to Mrs Morton for her approval.

"What have you done?" she screeched loudly, "you've used all the potatoes and there's only three of us," she shouted, screeching even louder.

"Is that why you were in children's home, because you're stupid?" she asked angrily.

Shelagh cowered away, shocked and frightened at her sudden outburst.

"I'm sorry," Shelagh said, "I usually have to peel twice as many as that. I don't know how many to peel for three. I'm really sorry."

"Can't do much about it now," Mrs Morton remarked, after she had calmed down, her voice now being much quieter.

"Potatoes cost a lot of money, so you'll have to pay me out of your pocket money next week for potatoes wasted," she insisted.

Shelagh blamed herself, but agreed to pay whatever she asked.

That night Shelagh went to bed early, knowing she would have to be up at six o'clock for her first days work.

She lay in bed wondering what kind of person Mrs Morton was. One minute she appeared to be kind and caring, and the next flying into a rage at a moments notice, screeching aloud with her high-pitched voice and calling her names.

She was like two different people.

Shelagh's new alarm clock went off at five, forty-five a.m. She dressed quickly, but quietly, made herself a cup of tea, washed her face and cleaned her teeth, then set off in trepidation for her first days work.

She caught a tram to Briggate in the centre of Leeds. Workers had taken all the seats, so she held on tight to a leather strap hanging from a long pole suspended from the roof. Then she took another tram from Briggate to Hunslet in the south of the city. As she was sitting on a seat at the back of the tram, her stomach was churning with nerves and excitement. She had almost forgotten it was her fifteenth birthday.

Arriving at the factory at quarter past seven, fifteen minutes early. Shelagh reported to the Welfare Officer's office, on the first floor of the huge factory, where five other girls, around her age, were standing outside the office.

At seven thirty precisely, Miss Henderson, the Welfare Officer, appeared from inside her office. Firstly, she checked their names and instructed them to follow her to the linen room, where she gave each of them a number and a green overall according to size. Then the girls followed her through part of the factory floor, where the noise from the huge printing machines was deafening. Some of the young lads stopped and stared at the new girls as they passed by. Then they entered another room, called the Box Room, which was twice as big as the one that they had just walked through. Miss Henderson took them to a row of full-length lockers that were leaning against the side of a long wall. After they had each been given a locker, the girls put on their green overalls, locked their belongings inside and followed Miss Henderson towards some tables in the middle of the room. They were then instructed to stand around the tables until she found a supervisor.

As they waited, Shelagh and her companions glanced around the huge room. Men and women were working busily on different sized machines, and there were tables dotted around. Noise and laughter filled the air and some people were actually singing along to loud music that was playing from the wireless, which was being amplified through a tannoy system so that it could be heard across the whole factory floor. A supervisor, who was wearing a beige overall, introduced herself as Mrs Clayton and asked the girls their names. Then grabbing a handful of paper from the middle of the table she began to teach them the art of 'fanning-out' and 'knocking-up' paper and cardboard, procedures that were required, and would be used on a daily basis in the printing industry.

Over the next three days, all six girls got to know each other and chatted about where they lived, their home life, friends and family. Some of the girls had sisters who already worked at the factory. Shelagh did not say too much, as she was not ready to tell them of her background just yet. She wanted to make friends first, and then, maybe.

At the end of the week, Shelagh was given a small sealed brown envelope, which contained her first wage of two pounds, fifteen shillings. She was thrilled. She had enjoyed working in the large factory so much, particularly the sound of men and women laughing and singing as they busily worked. To her it was like being in another world and she loved it.

Shelagh did not see much of her new foster parents, due to the fact that she set off for work in the early hours of the morning and not returning home until around six thirty in the evening.

When she returned home with her first wage packet, she sat down at the small table near the back wall and emptied the contents on to the table. She gave two pounds, five shillings to Mrs Morton, who was sitting opposite her, keeping seven shilling and sixpence for her pocket money, and allocated the remaining half a crown for her tram fare. She wrote everything carefully on the back of the wage packet and left the wage slip inside the envelope. Miss Porter had asked her to do this, stating that she would require all her wage packets and slips to take back to head office.

On her next visit, it had been arranged that Miss Porter would collect Joyce from the Orphanage and deliver her to her new home, a few days before her new school term began. Joyce had been enrolled her at Harehills School, not too far away.

Miss Porter duly arrived with Joyce early one Saturday afternoon. Mr and Mrs Morton and Shelagh were waiting eagerly for her. Shelagh took Joyce's case out of Miss Porter's hand and beckoned Joyce to follow her up the narrow, twisting stairs. Joyce helped push the case from behind, then up some more wooden steps to the attic. The sun was shining through the small, skylight window, giving the dark attic some light. The loft was adequately furnished, with a single bed in the middle of the room, a small wardrobe at the far end and a chest of drawers beside the bed.

"It smells in here," said Joyce, twitching her nose and screwing up a face.

"It's the wooden staircase and floorboards," explained Shelagh, "that's why I've opened the small window in the roof to get some fresh air. Why don't you sit on the bed and tell me about your holiday at Scarborough while I put your clothes away."

Joyce began to chatter non-stop about her holiday at the seaside with Miss Ratcliffe and the rest of the children. Shelagh occasionally detected an air of sadness in her voice, knowing that she would not be going again.

"Miss Ratcliffe sez I can go and see her anytime and I can get a bus at the bottom of the street straight to her house," Joyce said confidently, as she sat on her hands, swinging her legs backwards and forwards.

"What's that?" she asked suddenly, the back of her heels hitting something under the bed. She jumped of the bed and dragged out a white handled pot object.

"What's that?" she asked again, looking even more puzzled.

"Oh that's called a chamber pot," laughed Shelagh.

"A chamber pot, what's one of them?" Joyce asked inquisitively.

"If you need the toilet through the night," Shelagh explained, "that's what you have to use. And if you really, really need to go, then you'll have to come down to my room and I will take you up the street to the main toilet.

"I'm not using that!" Joyce snapped indignantly, sticking her head in the air, pulling her shoulders back and shaking her head vigorously, "and I'm not going up the street through the night."

Shelagh's face was beaming from ear to ear looking at Joyce's reaction and the look of disgust on her face. Then she began to laugh, laughing so much that her sides began to ache. After a while, Joyce saw the funny side too, and began to laugh with her.

"The worst is yet to come," said Shelagh, still laughing.

"The first thing you have to do when you get home from school is to empty it into a bucket and take it up the street and throw it down the toilet," Shelagh tried to explain.

"Oh no, I'm not," replied Joyce indignantly, "if you think I'm walking up that street with a bucket in my hand you can think again, cos I'm not! Everybody will know what's in the bucket, so no, I won't," she reiterated.

"You'll have to," said Shelagh, still laughing at Joyce's face and attitude.

"You'll have to and you'll have to get used to it. I'll do it for you at the weekends," she added trying to help. Joyce however, was like a dog with a bone.

"And another thing," she blurted, "I'm not going to that toilet up the street during the night either."

As far back as Joyce could remember she had always had the use of an indoor bathroom.

"We've been up here a long time," said Shelagh, changing the subject, "we'll have to see Miss Porter before she leaves. When she's gone," said Shelagh, after Joyce had calmed down, "I'll show you where the toilet is. It's in a yard up the street and it's shared amongst three houses, and then we'll have a walk to your new school."

Miss Porter seemed delighted that Joyce had settled in. They had heard them screeching with laughter from upstairs, but had no idea what they had been laughing at.

Sometime later, after Miss Porter had left, Shelagh took the key that was hanging at the back of the scullery door and showed Joyce the shared toilet up the street. Joyce was now sulking, knowing that she would have to do certain things that disgusted her.

As they walked down towards the bottom of the street, the smell of fish and chips came wafting round the corner.

"Fancy a bag of chips?" remarked Shelagh, trying to cheer Joyce up. Joyce nodded, still sulking.

They sat together on a bench just outside what was to be Joyce's new school, eating their chips and scraps and reminiscing about the good and bad times that had happened during the years they had lived in the Orphanage.

During the next few weeks, Shelagh settled extremely well at the factory. She was slowly beginning to make new friends and as yet had not told anyone of the background that she was ashamed of so much. Joyce tried to fit in as best she could at the Morton's, but found adapting to normal life very difficult.

One Saturday, Pat arranged to visit both her sisters, walking the long distance from her home, through Woodhouse into Meanwood, and across Roundhay Road into Harehills.

When she arrived, they decided to walk to Roundhay Park, which they had visited several times over the past years. Every year, Children's Day was held at Roundhay Park, usually on the first Saturday in July.

Each school in Leeds would compete against each other, entering their best athletes, and every year children from the Orphanage would take a packed lunch and spend the day there.

After a long walk, the sisters arrived at the top of the 'Hill Sixty' and stood for a few minutes drinking in the views of lush green hills in the distance, and the flat land surrounding them.

"Can we have a rest?" Joyce asked, promptly sprawling out on the grass.

Shelagh and Pat found a comfortable area on the hill and sat looking down at the arena at the bottom. Joyce, not wanting to be left out, sat in between them.

"There used to be thousands of people here on Children's Day." Pat said reminiscing. "Do you remember?"

"Yes I do," replied Shelagh, "it only seems a few weeks ago that you ran in the relay race for school."

"Shall we have a race now," Pat suggested, jumping up eagerly and running down the hill towards the arena. Shelagh and Joyce followed her down the steep slope.

They began to race each other around the oval stadium. Halfway round Joyce had had enough and was lying on her back with her arms and legs spread-eagled on the grass in the centre of the stadium, acting the fool and pretending to be out of breath. Pat completed the circuit comfortably without any effort with Shelagh not too far behind. Of the three sisters, Pat was the athlete. She had represented her school in the skipping and relay races. Shelagh preferred swimming, but Joyce was not a bit interested in any kind of physical exercise. She just loved life and playing.

"Can we go and play in the maze?" Joyce asked, rolling over onto her stomach with her elbows on the grass and her face held in her hands.

Pat pulled a face, gave a deep sigh and ran towards the maze that was situated at the side of the arena. Shelagh and Joyce took their time and followed her. Soon their loud, raucous laughter could be heard as they played inside the high, green hedges that formed the maze.

"I'm lost," Joyce bellowed at the top of her voice, as she threaded her way through a network of paths inside the maze, "help, come and find me!"

"So am I," yelled Pat. They screeched with laughter as they tried to find each other.

Over the years, the popular maze had been a popular source of entertainment for thousands of children.

After they had exhausted themselves, they found their way back to the entrance.

Parked outside the maze was an ice cream van.

"Want an ice cream?" said Shelagh, "cos I'm buying."

"Two ice cream sandwiches and one ice cream lolly please," she asked the woman who was serving.

"Everybody can hear you three," the woman smiled, as she handed the ice creams over the top of the counter, "all my customers have been laughing at you.

"Can you tell us the time please?" Pat asked, taking a big lick from her lolly, "cos I've got to be home by half past five, in time for tea."

"It's only four o'clock," the woman answered. "So you've got plenty of time," assuming that Pat did not live too far away. As they walked slowly home, the three sisters talked of the past and wondered what the future held for them.

"We'll visit you next time, won't we Joyce?" Shelagh said to Pat as they parted company.

Joyce, whose face was covered in ice cream, just nodded.

"I've got some good news," said Shelagh to Miss Porter on her next visit. "I can start to work over as from next week. I will be working over three nights a week and hopefully every Saturday morning."

"Well that is good news," said Miss Porter, looking pleased, "because I've been looking at the wage slips that you've given me and there's no surplus money left inside your wage packets to help towards your clothing allowance. The Corporation has kept you, your brother and sisters since you were put into care many years ago, and now it's time you were self-sufficient. That means you should be earning enough money to cover all your expenses, as cruel as it sounds, you need to earn as much as you can and stand on your own two feet."

Shelagh just nodded.

"Now then Joyce," said Miss Porter, looking into Joyce's sad eyes and unhappy face, "you don't look too happy. What's the matter with you?"

"I miss Miss Ratcliffe," Joyce whispered softly.

"I've told her," remarked Mrs Morton, "that if it's alright with you, she can visit Miss Ratcliffe every two weeks on a Saturday. She's old enough, at eleven, to travel on a bus on her own."

Miss Porter leaned forward and grabbed Joyce's chubby little hands.

"I'll tell you what I will do," she said, looking at her sad, sorry looking face, "I'll call and see Miss Ratcliffe and if she says you can visit, then that's fine by me. Will that put a smile on your face and make you happy? But you must remember that Miss Ratcliffe is not as young as she used to be and now that she has taken four of the orphan boys to live with her I don't want you making a nuisance of yourself, is that clear?"

"Oh I won't," replied Joyce, shaking her head, "I promise I won't."

"And if you visit I want you to be back in this house by seven o'clock. Is that clear?" she said again. Joyce nodded in agreement

During the first few weeks at the Woods, Pat seemed to settle slowly into normal family life. She was still very quiet, and still very much on her guard, frightened that Leslie and Patricia would not like her. She was very grateful that Mr and Mrs Wood had taken her out of the Orphanage, and that they had given her a home, she had offered without being asked, to assist with the cleaning around the house and take baby Peter for a walk. She would always be the first to offer to go to the local shops if anything was needed. Pat made a point of trying very hard to please everyone.

The weeks passed and soon it was the first day of the new school term. Pat had secretly waited for this day for a long time. It would be the first time she would meet her friend Valerie, since they had both left the Orphanage.

Pat decided that she would set off for school a lot earlier than usual, hoping that Valerie would be there waiting for her. She was. Valerie was sitting on the school wall looking into the direction that she thought Pat would be coming.

"I'm so glad to see you," greeted Pat.

"And I've missed you too," said a pleased Valerie.

"How have you gone on in your new home?" asked Valerie.

"Oh it's lovely," smiled Pat, "I don't miss being in that awful Orphanage a bit. How have you gone on?" Pat returned the question.

"Alright," answered Valerie nonchalantly. "My mother says I've got to get a Saturday job, to help pay the bills."

"What's a bill?" enquired Pat, looking puzzled.

"Everybody gets bills. Don't you know what a bill is?" Valerie continued.

"No," replied Pat, shaking her head.

"Well, everybody gets them," sighed Valerie. "A bill is a piece of paper that tells you how much you owe people."

"What do you mean owe?" Pat asked, frowning and looking even more puzzled.

"Every few months, you have to pay the gas and electric board for the amount of gas and electricity you use. I know my mothers always on about how much she has to pay out," explained Valerie, giving a big sigh and dropping her shoulders.

Pat pulled a face and shrugged her shoulders, not realising that gas and electricity had to be paid for.

"I've decided," said Valerie with determination in her voice, "that when I'm old enough, I'm going to leave home and train to be a nurse. I can live in what's called the Nurses Home. I'll be sixteen in a few years time, and I think that's the age when nurses training begins, so yes, that's what I'm going to do," said Valerie, sounding very positive.

"What are you going to do when you leave school?" she asked Pat.

"I think I'd like to be a vet," Pat replied, "but I don't know if I'm clever enough."

"Why don't you be a nurse like me, and we'll be friends for ever and ever and ever," suggested Valerie.

"Ugh no, I couldn't do that job," responded Pat indignantly, "I could look after poorly dogs, but not poorly people. Besides, I like it where I am. Since I've gone to live with Mr and Mrs Wood, I feel different. They treat me like one of the family and I feel normal. I don't feel like a 'home kid' anymore. It's a nice feeling, and I like it. I like being normal."

The sound of the school bell broke their conversation. After reporting to the teacher in the yard, they headed off together to the class that they would share for the next term, their arms placed around the others shoulder.

Every other week during the next few months, Joyce visited Miss Ratcliffe.

On the days that Joyce visited Miss Ratcliffe, Shelagh began to visit her aunt and uncle in Beeston, again always making sure that she was also back home by seven o'clock, the same as her young sister.

On the days following her visits to Miss Ratcliffe, Joyce was always moody and did not speak to anyone.

Mrs Morton found Joyce extremely difficult to handle, so much so, she would shout and scream in her high-pitched voice and lash out at her. Then she would lash out at Shelagh, blaming her for her sister's moods and tantrums.

"No wonder your mother and father didn't want you, or your family, or anyone else," Mrs Morton would yell, "and now I've changed my mind. I don't want you either. You'll have to find somewhere else to live," she barked, "I've had enough of both of you."

Mrs Morton had developed a habit, that every time she became angry, which was frequently, she would always shout those cruel words to them.

Shelagh, always frightened of her, would apologise, sometimes not knowing why she had to do so. She did not want to leave, because there was nowhere else for them to go.

Joyce never apologised, as she was too stubborn. Consequently, she and Mrs Morton were always at loggerheads. Shelagh asked Joyce repeatedly to try and not to be so cheeky or moody, and to be grateful that Mr and Mrs Morton had given them a home.

Christmas came and Joyce was invited to spend a few days with Miss Ratcliffe and the boys.

Shelagh visited her aunt and uncle in Beeston, who had written to the Children's Care Office, asking permission for her to stay a few days with them over Christmas. Shelagh thought that Mr and Mrs Morton would be pleased, as it would give them a chance to be on their own. She thought wrong. When she and Joyce returned home that day, Mrs Morton began to shout at them again, saying that if they wanted to spend Christmas with their aunt and uncle, then they must think more of them than her. Shelagh just rolled her eyes around, thinking that whatever they did, they just could not win. Joyce gave a sly, smug grin and said nothing, much to Shelagh's relief.

Every Sunday morning Shelagh spring cleaned her bedroom and then helped Joyce to clean the attic. Every Sunday Joyce would say.

"I don't like it here."

"And it shows," Shelagh would reply.

"She hates me and I hate her," Joyce would say. "One day I'm going to live with Miss Ratcliffe."

"You can't," Shelagh would explain, time and time again, "Miss Ratcliffe has no room for you and she has plenty on, looking after four young boys. You'll have to stick it out here until we get older."

One night Joyce had gone to bed early to get out of the way. Shelagh, as usual, was working late and would not be home until around eight fifteen. Joyce wrapped and tied the sleeves of a woolly cardigan around the attic light bulb and began to read a book that Miss Ratcliffe had given to her. A neighbour opposite made her way over to Mrs Mortons to tell her she had noticed the attic light had been on longer than was allowed. Mrs Morton began to climb the stairs slowly due to her large frame. She could smell smoke as she climbed the stairs. Joyce, hearing footsteps coming towards her, realised that the cardigan was on fire. Quickly she grabbed the blazing cardigan, burning her hands, dropped it on the wooden floor, and began to smother the flames with her slippers. She was frightened and shaking. When Mrs Morton finally reached the top of the attic stairs, she was furious, and began to hit Joyce around the head again and again. Joyce was terrified.

"That's it," Mrs Morton shouted, "can't take much more. You'll both have to go," she screeched, "tomorrow is not soon enough."

Sometime later, Shelagh arrived home from work, Mrs Morton, who was now hysterical, told her what had happened, and told her to pack their clothes, as they would be leaving the following day. Shelagh went straight upstairs to the attic and found Joyce was sitting bolt upright in bed in the dark, her body shaking and a look of fear on her face. Shelagh wrapped her arms around her and explained that if she did not apologise, they would both have to leave the next day.

Joyce, knowing what she had done was wrong, went downstairs with Shelagh and apologised, much to Mrs Morton's surprise. She could see by the look on Joyce's face that what had happened had genuinely scared the living daylights out of her. Shelagh took Joyce into the scullery and held her hands under the running cold tap. For a moment, Mrs Morton took pity on the young girl as she winced with pain. She made them a cup of tea and said she would put the matter behind her.

"Although," she added, "I'll have to report it to Miss Porter."

During the next few days, Joyce made it quite clear that she did not like Mrs Morton. Mrs Morton, for her part, found her increasingly difficult to handle.

On her next visit, Miss Porter met Mrs Morton at the bottom of the street. She complained that the girls were very difficult to look after.

"Sometimes, I don't know what to do," complained Mrs Morton. "I find Joyce the most troublesome. In fact, only last week she almost set the house on fire. I'm at the end of my tether."

She recounted the whole incident to Miss Porter, and then said,

"In fact I've saved the cardigan in question to show you."

Miss Porter followed her into the house, where she promptly spread the badly burnt cardigan across the floor. "There," she said, "I've saved the proof. I told her I'd tell you."

When Shelagh arrived home from work around eight fifteen, they were discussing what punishment to give Joyce.

Mrs Morton asked Shelagh to bring Joyce down from the attic.

Joyce stood behind Shelagh at the bottom of the stairs, wiping her sleepy eyes, wondering why she had been woken up. Her face dropped when she saw Miss Porter holding the cardigan.

"What you did was inexcusable," Miss Porter said angrily, with a stern expression on her face, "and it can't go unpunished, can it Joyce?"

"I did say I was sorry," answered Joyce, promptly hiding again behind Shelagh's back.

"Mrs Morton and I have been talking," continued Miss Porter, "and we both agree the best punishment is to stop you from visiting Miss Ratcliffe."

"Please don't," Joyce whimpered, moving her head from behind Shelagh, her face overcome with horror.

"I won't do it again," she pleaded. "Please don't stop me from going to see Miss Ratcliffe."

"If your behaviour improves in the next few weeks," said Miss Porter, "then I will think about it."

Joyce looked sideways at Mrs Morton who had a smug grin across her face. She never hated anybody as much as she hated Mrs Morton now. With tears welling in her eyes, Joyce was determined not to cry in front of them. She took hold of Shelagh's hand as they climbed the two flights of stairs to the cold dark attic.

Mrs Morton had removed the light bulb days earlier.

Now out of sight of Mrs Morton and Miss Porter, Joyce began to cry. The worst punishment that could be given to her was to stop her from visiting Miss Ratcliffe. Shelagh tucked her back into bed. Joyce began to cry angry tears.

"What have we done to deserve this?" she asked Shelagh.

"No point in arguing," said Shelagh, wrapping her arms around her, "it only gets you into more trouble and we'll never win." Joyce's eyes were now swollen with crying and her body was trembling. It broke Shelagh's heart to see Joyce in so much pain. She had never seen her cry so much. Joyce had always been such a happy, bubbly child who loved life.

"It's up to you now," consoled Shelagh, gently stroking Joyce's hair, "just try and prove to Miss Porter that you can behave, and don't answer Mrs Morton back, and then I'm sure you'll be able to visit Miss Ratcliffe in a few weeks time. It's up to you."

"I can't live here any longer," cried Joyce, through her tears, "it's all right for you. In a few years time you'll be eighteen and no longer in care, and then you can leave and do what you want, and go where you want. I've got seven years to go. I can't stay here that long."

She wrapped her arms around Shelagh and rested her head on her shoulder, her body trembling as she sobbed.

"You'll have to," said Shelagh, holding her tightly, "there's nowhere else for us to go. I keep telling you that. So try and behave for both our sakes, and don't be so cheeky for the next few weeks."

One day, during the following week, when Joyce had finished school, she made her way to a bench directly outside the schoolyard. She did not want to go home, but then, she never did. Her mind was wondering what to do next.

Just then, a police patrol car pulled up beside her. The policeman, sitting on the front passenger seat, was resting his elbow on the open window.

"You were sitting there when we passed nearly two hours ago," he asked jokingly, " haven't you got a home to go to?"

"No I haven't," Joyce replied, with a total lack of expression on her face.

"If you don't go home soon, your Mother and Father will begin to worry about you," the policeman continued.

"No they won't," answered Joyce sarcastically, "cos I haven't got a mother or a father. I'm an orphan."

The policeman laughed at her deadpan attitude. He stepped out of the car and sat down beside her, leaving his partner rapping his fingers on the steering wheel, watching and listening to them.

"Now, what's all this about?" he asked, in a soft gentle voice, his elbows resting on his open knees, his chin held in his hand and looking at her with a serious expression on his face. For a few moments, Joyce stared into space, not looking at him.

"Come on, you can tell me I'm a policeman," he encouraged her.

Feeling that she could trust him, she began to tell him her story. When she had finished, she looked into his eyes and insisted that she could not, and would not, go back to her foster home.

"Why don't you let us drive you home," he suggested, "and I'll ring the Emergency Social Services and ask your Care Officer to call and see you tonight."

"No, I'm not going back there," Joyce insisted, shaking her head. She was adamant.

"Can't you take me with you to the police station and lock me in a cell until they find a place for me in a children's home?" she pleaded.

The policeman looked at his partner, who was shaking his head with a look of despair on his face, not quite sure what to say.

"Look we can't leave you here," he said, feeling sorry for the girl. "We'll have to take you back. But I promise, cross my heart," he whispered, crossing his chest with a finger, "I'll get someone to come and see you tonight." He stood up, took her hand and helped her climb into the back seat of the car.

Mrs Morton was surprised when she saw the tall, well-built policeman escort Joyce into the house and silently livid when he informed her that she had not wanted to go home and the reasons why.

When Miss Porter arrived about an hour later, she could see Mrs Morton was furious.

"I've never been so embarrassed in all my life," said Mrs Morton, pointing towards Joyce, who was sitting on a chair at the back of the room. "Out of my house as soon as possible!" she barked. "She's not worth the money you pay. She's been nothing but trouble from the first day she arrived."

As it was now turned eight o'clock, Miss Porter instructed Joyce to go to bed and stay there, promising that she would be back the following evening to see her.

After a lengthy conversation, Mrs Morton and Miss Porter decided between them that it probably would be better to remove Joyce as soon as possible.

"I can't see there being a problem," assured Miss Porter, "but I'll have to speak to Mr Parnell, Head of Children's Department, and I'm sure he will agree with us. I will be back tomorrow evening."

As she was just about to drive away, she caught sight of Shelagh at the bottom of the street, on her way home from work. She had a brief conversation with her and told her of the evening's events. She said that she would be back the following evening, knowing Shelagh would be home, as she never worked over on a Friday. "You mustn't worry about Joyce," she assured her, "things always happen for a reason."

"If that was so," Shelagh wondered silently, "would someone explain to her the reasons why we were abandoned and put into care at a very young age, and why neither of our parents or any of our family members has ever been to see us in the many years that we had lived in the Orphanage?"

She had longed and prayed to be loved and accepted, simply to live a normal happy life with her brother and sisters. Now that was never going to happen. Joyce was right. They didn't deserve the life that they were living.

As soon as Shelagh stepped inside the house, she sensed a dreadful atmosphere.

She could hear Mr Morton shuffling his feet around in the scullery. Mrs Morton was sitting in an armchair by the fire with her back arched and her arms folded stiffly across her chest, staring into the blazing fire. Shelagh crossed the room towards the stairs in the far corner and made her way up the two flights of stairs. When she reached the attic, she could see that Joyce was fast asleep, so she decided that it was best to leave her. Making her way back downstairs, she could hear Mr and Mrs Morton whispering to each other. The room fell silent, as she made her way across the room and into the scullery. Locking the door from the inside with a small bolt, Shelagh put a pan of cold water on the gas ring to boil for a wash and then to make herself a cup of tea.

After she had washed and cleaned her teeth, she passed again through the silent room and made her way to bed. For once, what had happened that night had reduced Mrs Morton to silence, for which Shelagh was extremely grateful.

The following morning, Miss Porter arrived at the Head Office in Woodhouse Lane.

She found Mr Parnell sitting at his desk as usual surrounded by paper work. Pushing the paperwork to one side, he propped an elbow on the desk and held his chin in his hand, rapping a pencil, which he was holding in the other hand, on the desk.

"I'm listening," he said, scowling as he looked into her troubled face. Miss Porter was now facing him in a chair on the other side of the desk.

"It's about young Joyce Gregson," she began, explaining the problems that occurred over the last few months between Mrs Morton and the younger sister.

Mr Parnell threw the pencil to the far side of his desk and folded his arms tightly across his chest.

"To me," Miss Porter carried on, with a look of concern on her face. "I feel that a breakdown has been caused by incompatibility and intolerance on both sides." As she spoke, she kept shaking her head. "All Joyce has ever known has been an institutionalised life and because of that, she has been unable to adjust to a different way of living. To me, Mrs Morton has been unable to appreciate Joyce's difficulties and has expected far too much of her, as I have too. I think that I am also partly to blame. I should have been more understanding."

Pausing for a moment, she looked hopefully at her superior, before continuing.

"In anticipation, I have been in touch with Street Lane Home, and they have been very considerate and are willing to take her back into care today. But before I jump the gun, I would value your opinion."

Street Lane Home was a reception centre for abandoned, orphaned and unwanted children, who would stay there on a temporary basis until a more permanent place could be found in one of the Children's Homes in Leeds. The centre would also take care of children whose parents were going through difficult times. Eventually those children would return home to their parents.

"In that case," remarked Mr Parnell thoughtfully, "I must take some responsibility too."

"Many years ago," he continued, "I took the two youngest sisters off the foster register purely because they had been pushed from pillar to post with different foster parents and I didn't want that to happen again. I think you're right. Joyce is only eleven years old and maybe not quite ready to adjust to a normal home life just yet. Hopefully by the time she is fifteen she may be."

"I spent most of last night worrying and wondering why Joyce hates Mrs Morton so much," said an anxious Miss Porter, "then I realised why."

She began to explain the reasons why she felt some responsibility for the situation.

"We took her from a large house, filled with children and laughter and placed her into a small back-to-back house where she spends every night on her own in a small dark attic. She doesn't see her older sister as much as she would like to, because we expect Shelagh to work all hours that God sends to cover her expenses. No wonder Joyce has behavioural problems."

By now, Mr Parnell had moved his chair away from his desk, stretched out his crossed legs, unfolded his arms and was chewing the end of the pencil that he had picked up from the far side of his desk. Looking over the top of his glasses, he listened intently to what she had to say.

"I agree," he at last managed to chip in.

"On top of that," Miss Porter carried on, "our worst mistake was to take her away from Miss Ratcliffe, the only person who has ever loved Joyce as a mother, from as far back as she can remember."

Miss Porter held her face in her hands. "What have we done?" she asked shaking her head.

"Yes, you're right again," acknowledged Mr Parnell. "We must take most of the blame. The Committee, strangely enough, only approved for Mr and Mrs Morton to take a working girl. We all took a gamble on placing a young girl there, but it didn't work out. You're right," he agreed, "remove Joyce as soon as possible, and I will make sure for future references that's what they will get, a working girl."

That evening, when Shelagh arrived home from work, Mrs Morton was sitting stiffly on a chair at the back of the room with her arms folded tightly across her chest and a look of relief on her face.

"Miss Porter will be here soon," she said coldly. "Your sister is in the attic packing her belongings."

"Your mother and father and none of your family ever wanted you," she remarked heartlessly, "and now I can see the reason why. Well, let me tell you, I don't want you either."

"I'm sick of hearing that," thought Shelagh, as she walked across the room and headed towards the stairs in the corner, trying to shrug off the hurt and swallowing the lump in her throat. Shelagh had learnt never to answer back. What was the point? She made her way up the stairs to help Joyce with her packing.

"Don't try to talk me out of it," Joyce said firmly, holding her hands in the air as Shelagh's head appeared at the top of the attic steps.

"You've got to let me go," she said sternly. "It's better all round if I go back into a children's home and you won't be in the middle all the time. In a few years time you'll be eighteen and out of care, and be able to go where you want, and if I'm not here, it will be a lot easier for you to leave. I hate it here," she said defiantly, "you've got to let me go. You know it's the right thing to do, and it's what I really want. So please don't stop me."

"She was right," thought Shelagh, with a heavy heart. Without Joyce, she would perhaps get on better with Mrs Morton.

"O.K. if that's what you want," Shelagh said eventually, slightly relieved, "I won't stand in your way."

Between them, the girls packed all her clothes and belongings into the same suitcase that Joyce had unpacked only a few months earlier

Shelagh looked around the dingy attic to make sure that Joyce had not forgotten anything and that it was left clean and tidy.

"What are you doing with newspapers up here?" she asked, holding her head back and looking puzzled. Picking them up from the floor in the far corner of the attic, she added, "I've never known you to read newspapers."

"Well that's another story," answered Joyce, hanging her head in shame.

"You know when you said that if I really needed to go to the toilet through the night I was to wake you up and you would take me." Shelagh nodded.

"Well I didn't dare wake you up. Mrs Morton said under no circumstances was I to wake you up during the night, because you get up early in the morning for work. She said I had to stand on my own two feet." With her eyes rolling around her head and giving a deep sigh, Joyce sat on the bed beside Shelagh before continuing.

"So one night I couldn't wait," she explained, "I crept downstairs, took the key from the back of the scullery door, unlocked the outside door and walked up the street. It was pitch black and I could hardly see. Anyway, when I finally opened the toilet door inside the yard, I could feel someone was standing nearby in the yard. I was scared to death and then I saw the red end of a cigarette and a man stood in the corner. He began to cough and he smelt awful. I've never been so frightened in all my life. I did go to the toilet because I had to and I know he was listening to me. I was petrified. So I vowed never to go again through the night."

"So what's the newspapers got to do with that?" asked Shelagh, frowning and looking puzzled.

Joyce blushed and hung her head again with embarrassment.

"After that," she explained, her face now crimson, "if I needed to go during the night, I used to go on top of a piece of newspaper, then wrap it up put it in my satchel, take it to school and put it in the dustbin."

Joyce covered her face with both hands.

"It's best I leave now," she suddenly said, changing the subject, "while I've got the chance. Mrs Morton doesn't like me and never will. And another thing, she hits me everyday for no reason at all. She hides behind the front door waiting for me to come home from school and hits me on me head with a long ruler and it dun't half hurt. In fact I put me hands on top of me head now before I step inside the door and race across the room to the stairs and run up to the attic and stay there. Sometimes if I run fast enough she misses me and that makes her even madder."

"Are you ready Joyce?" A voice echoed up the stairs, breaking their conversation.

"It's time we were going," Miss Porter shouted.

Shelagh and Joyce gave each other a big hug and held on to each other for a few minutes.

"Time to leave," said Shelagh, with a lump in her throat, letting go and picking up Joyce's case.

Miss Porter explained to Joyce that she was taking her to Street Lane Children's Home for a few days until a permanent place could be found for her in another children's home.

A look of sheer delight appeared on Joyce's face. She stood proud and erect as she stepped out of the house, her face now beaming.

"Don't forget to come and see me will ya," she shouted to Shelagh, who was standing on her own in the doorway.

"Course I won't," assured Shelagh, "me and Pat will come and see you wherever you are on your next visiting day."

With a heavy heart, Shelagh waved to Joyce as Miss Porter drove away. Joyce waved back, her face still beaming with happiness.

In the days after Joyce had been taken back into care, Shelagh felt sad, withdrawn and a little guilty. She had made new friends at the factory, one in particular whose name was Mary Smith, a young seventeen year old, a few years older and taller than herself. Mary had a trim figure and her face was covered in freckles. Her short dark hair was a mass of curls and she had a gap in the middle of her top teeth.

"What's wrong?" Mary asked Shelagh one dinnertime, as they were sitting having dinner in the canteen.

"Nothing," Shelagh answered quietly.

"Yes there is," Mary replied, I know something's worrying you, I can tell. We're friends aren't we? You're supposed to be able to tell friends. So come on, tell me what's troubling you," Mary asked again.

They were now alone, sitting facing each other, as the other girls had left the table.

"Come on," encouraged Mary, folding her arms on top of the table and leaning over.

Shelagh remembered that Brenda, her school friend, had always said that that is what friends are for, to listen and help each other. She looked around to make sure that no one was listening to their conversation and then slowly began to tell Mary her story, not leaving anything out. She explained that the reason why she had been quiet over the last few days was that she missed Joyce so much, and felt guilty that things had not worked out for her as she had hoped.

"Now I understand," Mary said comfortingly, "now it all fits into place. On a Monday morning, when everyone talks of where they have been and who they have been with over the weekend, you never say anything you just frown and listen. Is that because you don't have any friends where you live?" she added.

Shelagh nodded slowly.

"In that case," Mary carried on, "I want you call at my house on Friday night. You know where I live. You've been there many a time on our dinner break, and I'm going to take you to meet all my old school friends. Jack is working away, so I won't be seeing him until next week." Jack was Mary's fiancé, who worked in the building trade and often worked away from home. They had become engaged some months earlier, on Mary's seventeenth birthday.

(GIRL)

Agreement of Foster Parent

1. I *Mr & Mrs*   of   *leeds 8*

do hereby agree with the Council of the County Borough of Leeds that

(a) I will receive **Sheila Gregson** into my home, feed, clothe and look after her and bring her up as carefully and kindly as I would a child of my own.

(b) I will help her to become a good citizen, send her to school – work – and to Church – Chapel, and arrange for recreation suited to her age.

(c) I will look after her health and consult the doctor whenever the child is ill, and in the event of her serious illness or accident, I will also notify the Council immediately

(d) I will provide for the cleaning, mending and renewal of her clothing and its proper care.

(e) I will at all times permit any person authorised by the Home Office or by the Council to see the child and her home and clothing, and I will attend to the advice of any such person.

(f) I will allow her to be removed from my home when required by any person so authorised.

(g) I will notify the Council within two weeks if I change my address.

2. I make this agreement with the Council in consideration of my receiving the sum of **2-5-0** per week for maintenance, plus **7-6** per week for pocket money, and clothing allowance at the rate of **12-6** per week paid quarterly.

3. I acknowledge having received **Sheila Gregson** into my home on the **16th Aug, 1968** and agree that she brought with her the following articles of clothing and personal possessions:-

Clothing	Number Bought	Number Brought	Clothing	Number Bought	Number Brought
Coat *Duffle Coat*		1 & 1	Suspender Belt		1
Hat			Brassiere		2
Raincoat		1	Stockings/Socks		3
Blazer			Handkerchiefs		
Shoes		3	Overall/Pinafore		2
Slippers *Sandels*		1	Gloves		2
Wellington Boots			Scarf		5
Dress		3	Brush and comb		1 & 1
Skirts *cloth & cotton*		3-4	Toothbrush *provided*		1
Gym Slip			Suitcase		1
Blouse		5	*Dressing Gown*		
Jersey		2	*Bathing costume*		1
Cardigan		4	*Umbrella*		1
Pyjamas/nightdress		4			
Vest		4			
Underskirt or Set		2			
Knickers		4			

Doctor's Card   Personal Savings

Signature of foster parent   *63*

Address   *Leeds 8*

Chapter 49

When Shelagh arrived home, she asked Mrs Morton if she could go out with her new friend Mary on Friday night. Mrs Morton agreed and said she was pleased that at last she was going out and making new friends of her own age, and getting out from under her feet.

After work, on Friday, Shelagh dashed home as fast as she could, grabbed a sandwich and a drink, quickly washed and dressed herself in her best clothes. Looking in the mirror on the wardrobe door, she put on some lipstick and then stepped back to admire herself. Quite pleased with what she saw, Shelagh wrapped a silk scarf around her head, put on a warm winter coat, and set off to Mary's house. It was a cold February night.

"Don't forget I want you back in here by ten thirty," shouted Mrs Morton, "no later, or you'll know why. I'll lock you out and then where will you go?"

Shelagh felt both excited and a little nervous at the thought of meeting new friends. She took a tram to Briggate and then another to Dewsbury Road. When she arrived, Mary was waiting for her. They linked arms as they chatted and walked the short distance to the La Strega Coffee Bar in the middle of a parade of shops on Dewsbury Road. As they got nearer, the sound of rock and roll records could be heard from the jukebox and the smell of fresh coffee was wafting through the open door.

Mary introduced Shelagh to lots of her ex-school friends, both boys and girls, who congregated in the coffee bar every Friday evening, where they would play the jukebox in turn and drink coffee from heatproof glass cups and saucers. Everyone was friendly and made Shelagh feel welcome and comfortable.

One ginger haired, freckled face young man wearing a Teddy Boy suit and thick crepe sole shoes slotted his money into the jukebox and pressed a button for his choice of record. Within seconds, Buddy Holly began to sing 'Rave On', a record that had been in the charts for some time. A few young couples began to jive in the small area in front of the jukebox.

"Fancy a bop?" He asked Shelagh looking directly at her.

Shelagh shook and lowered her head, her face crimson with embarrassment.

"Go on," said Mary encouragingly.

Shelagh took off her coat, wrapped it around the back of the chair and nervously took hold of his outstretched hand.

Time passed quickly, and all too soon, it was time for Shelagh to leave.

"What's the rush?" Mary asked, "It's only nine o'clock."

"I have to be in by half past ten," Shelagh said anxiously, "and I've got two trams to catch. So I'll have to go. I don't want to get locked out."

"Come on Cinderella," shouted Michael, watching her hurriedly putting on her coat.

"I'll walk you to the tram stop," he said, taking her arm.

She did not have long to wait, as one arrived a few moments later.

"I'll see you next Friday," Michael shouted encouragingly, giving her a wave as the tram pulled away.

When Shelagh got home, it was ten twenty five and Mrs Morton was standing in the open doorway waiting and looking for her.

"Let me smell your breath," she said, pushing Shelagh against the wall just inside the door.

Once Mrs Morton was satisfied that Shelagh had not been drinking, she let her into the house.

"I've decided not to go to the coffee bar every Friday," Shelagh told Mary a few weeks later.

"Why not?" Mary asked, "I thought you enjoyed it,"

"I do," Shelagh answered," by the time I get there, I can only stay an hour and then I have to set off back home again. It's not worth it, and besides I can't really afford to go every week, what with tram fares, buying coffee and playing records on the jukebox I hardly have anything left out of my seven and six pocket money," she explained.

"I understand," said Mary. "Next time me and Jack go to the pictures, why don't you come with us. We usually go to the Rex Cinema at the top of Dewsbury Road and we always go to the first half on a Saturday night. So you'll have plenty of time to get home."

"I will," Shelagh replied, with a smile on her face.

"That would be something to look forward to," she thought.

The last time Shelagh had been to the cinema was to see 'Rock Around the Clock', starring Bill Haley and the Comets at the Hyde Park Cinema, and that was over a year ago.

One day, while Shelagh and a few other girls were busy working on the same machine and singing loudly to the wireless, a message came over the tannoy.

"Will Shelagh Gregson report to the Time Office door, where someone is waiting to see her?" it announced.

Shelagh froze for a moment. She felt a cold shiver run down her spine and her skin was covered in goose lumps.

"Who would want to see me?" she asked, looking at Mary.

"You never know it might be your knight in shining armour," laughed Kathleen, one of her other friends.

"I wish," Shelagh answered, and then asked Bill, who was in charge of the machine, if she could be excused.

Walking through the factory with a puzzled look on her face wondering who could possibly want to see her, Shelagh turned a sharp corner and bumped smack into a young apprentice guillotine operator. He instinctively grabbed her by the shoulders. Shelagh's face was crimson with embarrassment.

"Don't look so worried," the young man said, in a happy go lucky voice and a twinkle in his eyes.

His voice was deep and strong and his large brown eyes sparkled as he looked directly into her face. He let go of her shoulders and tousled her hair as he left, carrying on to where he was heading.

The young guillotine operator's name was Peter Flynn, a young twenty year old who was around five feet, eight inches tall. His hair was dark and cut in a crew cut style. He was wearing a red crew neck sweater, the sleeves of which were pushed up to his elbows, grey corduroy trousers, and grey suede, lace up, crepe-soled shoes. Shelagh had watched him many times at the far side of the factory, listening to his non-stop infectious laughter. He always seemed happy and full of life. For him to be as he was, he must have a happy home life, and she envied him. Shelagh passed through several Departments before she reached the Time Office, which was situated on the left, near the side door, which opened into a large concrete yard outside. On either side of a clock, which was situated to the right hand side of a long wall, were numbered clock cards, one to clock in and one to clock out. She remembered the Welfare Officer telling her and the other girls on their first day, that it was an immediate sackable offence to clock anyone else's clock card in or out.

"Hello," greeted a young woman, as Shelagh stepped outside the Time Office door into the outside yard. She was leaning against the factory wall smoking a cigarette.

"Remember me?" she asked smiling. "My name's Iris and I used to live next door to your Grandmother before I got married. Do you remember me?" she asked again.

Shelagh breathed a sigh of relief knowing that nothing had happened to her brother and sisters.

"Yes I do," she answered, "you used to do my grandmothers shopping and once when I visited, you were there. How did you know where I work?" she asked, a little intrigued.

"Well last Sunday, when I visited my mother and father, I bumped into your Cousin Pat and her new baby daughter. I asked how you were and she told me where you were working. I only live two minutes away from here and I thought it would be nice if you came for dinner. We could have fish and chips. I don't work, so I would enjoy your company. I could meet you outside the factory gates at twelve o'clock on Friday. What do you think? Would you like that?"

Shelagh was surprised, for a change; it was nice that someone had actually come to see her. She had always been the one to visit everyone else. "Besides," she thought, "if Iris regularly visits her parents, I will be able to ask her if my own mother ever visits my grandmother.

"Why don't you come out with me and Walter next Saturday night," asked Iris, a few Fridays later. "You can stay the night. You can sleep with me, and Walter can sleep in the armchair. We go to the local pub just around the corner from here and have a sing-a-long. You'd like that."

Shelagh looked at her with a blank face and shook her head.

"It's not that I don't want to," she replied, "I'm not old enough. I'm only fifteen, not old enough to go into pubs and I'm not allowed to stay out overnight anywhere, unless a letter is written to Mrs Morton and Miss Porter, my Children's Care Officer, saying who you are and where I will be staying."

"Oh don't you worry about that," Iris replied, "I'll meet you outside work when you've finished later this afternoon, and I'll go home with you, and we'll pretend that I'm your real auntie, and I'll say I'd like to take you to the pictures."

Later that afternoon, as promised, Iris was waiting for Shelagh outside the main gates.

"You'd better start calling me auntie Iris, seeing as that's what I've said I am in these two letters that I have written," she quipped, waving them in front of Shelagh as they travelled home on the tram. Shelagh was still not sure if she really wanted to go out or even stay the night with Iris and her husband. She was frightened that if Mrs Morton found out that she was lying, she would be in a lot of trouble. Then again, Shelagh was grateful that Iris had taken an interest in her, and she did not want to hurt her feelings.

She hoped that when she arrived home Mrs Morton was in a good mood. She was in luck.

Mrs Morton listened to Iris, not sure at first to believe that she was Shelagh's aunt, but after a lot of persuading from Iris, she agreed, saying the final word would be Miss Porter.

Iris gave her one letter and posted the other to Miss Porter at the Children's Care Department, Head Office, Woodhouse Lane.

Within a few days, Iris received a reply from Miss Porter saying that seeing as she was Shelagh's aunt, she would allow Shelagh to stay overnight the following Saturday.

The following Saturday around seven thirty in the evening, Shelagh arrived at Iris' home.

"Pleased to meet you," Walter, Iris' husband, said, holding out his hand for her to shake,

"I've heard such a lot about you. Tonight's going to be a night for you to remember."

Walter was a tall, well-built, stocky man. He was wearing a dark suit over an open necked white shirt, and his blonde Brylcreemed hair was combed to the back of his head, sporting a quiff at the front.

Shelagh shook his strong hand and looked into his large, blue eyes. Something about him made her feel uncomfortable. As they walked the short distance to their local public house, they all linked arms, with Shelagh in the middle. Once inside, Shelagh sat beside Iris, on a seat attached to the back wall, her back arched and a little nervous.

"There you are," said Walter, placing a glass of beer each in front of her and Iris, "get that down you. It will do you good, and there's plenty more where that came from." He walked away and began to talk to a group of men standing at the bar.

After an hour of looking at the beer, Shelagh took a sip causing her body to shake, and a look of distaste on her face.

"Want another," asked Walter, sitting down beside her. "Come on, drink it up." He leaned forwards and looked into her face.

"I don't like it," replied Shelagh meekly. "I'd rather have a bitter lemon. I shouldn't be drinking beer, I'm only fifteen."

"Sh," Walter whispered, holding a finger to his puckered lips. He brought over a small bottle of bitter lemon and then returned to his friends at the bar.

By now Iris had had quite a lot to drink, and was singing merrily and loudly next to Shelagh. She was thoroughly enjoying herself.

Shelagh looked around the public house. The air was full of smoke and scruffy men, sitting on high stools at the bar, who occasionally turned round to stare at her. She felt extremely uneasy, uncomfortable and out of place. When last orders were shouted at ten thirty, she breathed a sigh of relief.

Eventually Walter, Iris and Shelagh arrived home. The return journey had taken them twice as long as Walter and Iris were both blind drunk and wobbled all the way home.

"Take a seat," Walter said to Shelagh in a slurred voice, as they stepped inside the house. He pointed to an armchair at the far side of the table in the middle of the room. "While Iris makes us a good strong cup of tea," he flopped down on the other armchair at the other side of the table, staring into the fire that had long since died out.

Iris placed a mug of tea each on the table, and totally unexpected and out of the blue announced,

"I've got to go out, I won't be long." She disappeared out of the door into the darkness.

Shelagh was horrified and scared.

"Don't look so frightened, you're as safe as houses with me," said Walter, looking into her terrified face. "She won't be long. Meantime why don't you tell me about yourself? How old did you say you was?"

"I'll be sixteen next month," Shelagh replied, her voice quaking.

"Have you got a boyfriend?" he persisted.

"No," Shelagh answered quietly.

"No" he remarked, "a pretty young thing like you. They don't know what they're missing. Why don't you come and sit on my knee and tell me all about yourself," he suggested, patting his knee with his large hand.

Shelagh shook her head uncomfortably.

"Aw come on, I promise I won't hurt you," he continued. "Iris will be back in a few minutes. So come on, I wouldn't hurt a pretty thing like you. So come on." He beckoned to her patting his knee again.

Shelagh could feel her heart thumping inside her chest. She didn't want to make him angry and she was grateful that Iris and Walter had taken an interest in her, and besides every night away from her foster home was a bonus. If she did not do as he asked, she reasoned, he might tell Mrs Morton that she had not gone to the cinema, and tell her where she really had been. Nothing could be worse than her finding out the truth. Nervously, Shelagh crossed the room and sat on his knee. She had never ever been so frightened. Terror and fear churned inside her stomach. His eyes were hazy and his breath stank of alcohol. Drunkenly, he held her chin in his hand and began to move a finger slowly down her neck, touching the top of her blouse and then slyly and slowly undoing the top button.

Shelagh froze, petrified.

"Please don't," she asked.

"I told you I wouldn't hurt you," Walter murmured in a slurred voice, his fingers slowly creeping towards the second button.

Suddenly finding the strength and the courage, Shelagh jumped off his knee and ran as fast as her legs would carry her up the stairs. She jumped into bed fully clothed, sat upright with her back against the headboard, bent her knees and covered herself with the blankets, not taking her eyes of the bedroom door for a moment. She thought that if he had followed her, she would not stand a chance against such a strong man. Shelagh's head was exploding with thoughts of what could happen next. She hoped that in his drunkenness he would fall asleep in the armchair and prayed to God that he would not follow her to the bedroom.

After what seemed an eternity, Shelagh heard the outside door open and Iris' voice. Breathing a sigh of relief, she undressed quickly and put on her baby doll pyjamas before jumping into bed.

A few moments later, Iris climbed the stairs, undressed and slid in beside her.

Shelagh pretended to be asleep.

The following morning, Shelagh said that she needed to get home early, as she wanted to wash and iron her clothes for work the following day.

On her way home, Shelagh's stomach was churning as her thoughts strayed back to the previous evening.

"How could he do that to me? Maybe he thought he could, because I was brought up in a children's home. He said that he had heard all about me. Iris must have told him all about my background. So he must know that there is no one I can turn to."

Her head was in turmoil.

"Should I tell Mrs Morton the truth? What would she do, if she knew that I had lied? I know what she would say. Serves you right, yes, that's what she would say. That's what you get for not telling the truth. You must have done something to encourage him." Mrs Morton would have no sympathy, and blame everything on me, Shelagh mused. "Then she'd revel in the idea of telling Miss Porter. I not only lied to Mrs Morton, I also lied to Miss Porter. What if Miss Porter took me away, and put me in a remand home until I was eighteen. I could not stand going into another home."

Thoughts were exploding inside Shelagh's head.

She decided that if she kept it a secret, and did not tell anyone, or think about it, then maybe it would go away. That's what she hoped.

Arriving home later that morning, she was greeted by Mrs Morton on top form as usual. Before Shelagh had chance to take her coat off, she began to bombard her with questions.

"Did you go to the pictures?" she asked impetuously. The questions came thick and fast.

"Which picture house?

What did you go see?

What time did it start?

What time did it finish?

I want you to sit down and tell me all about it," she said eventually.

Fortunately, Shelagh had been with Mary and Jack a few weeks earlier to see 'The Fly' at the Rex Cinema at the top of Dewsbury Road and even better, she still had the stub from the cinema ticket in her coat pocket to prove it.

Shelagh never told anyone what had happened that night. After all, who would believe a fifteen year old?

Neither did she see or hear from Iris and Walter again.

Walter, Iris's husband was right, that was indeed a night to remember. A night she would never forget.

Occasionally, that secret Shelagh held inside her, would surface, and fill her with fear of what might have happened that awful night. It would be many years before she was able to talk to anyone about the incident, and realise that she was in no way to blame.

Chapter 50

In the July of 1959, the work forces at Alf Cooke's were instructed by their union representatives to strike. The printing industry, which included the publication of daily newspapers, brought the country to a standstill.

Shelagh, along with everyone else, was told where, when and at what time to collect their strike pay.

"What shall I do?" Shelagh asked Mrs Morton when she arrived home on the Friday that the factory had closed down, "I've been told my strike pay will only be seventeen shillings a week. What do you think I should do?" she asked again.

"Well I don't rightly know," Mrs Morton, replied, a little surprised. "I can't keep you on seventeen shillings, that's for sure. I think you ought to make an appointment to see Miss Porter, and if they can't give you any money, then you'll have to find another job. The sooner the better," she added.

Shelagh took her advice, and walked the short distance to the nearest public telephone.

Holding the 'phone in one hand, she slotted two pennies into the black box attached to the wall inside the 'phone booth, pressed the 'A' button to be accepted and then the 'B' button to be connected. She explained briefly to Miss Porter why she needed to see her, and made an appointment for the following morning at eleven o'clock.

The next morning, Shelagh boarded a bus full of passengers, who were on their way to the city centre to do their Saturday shopping.

When she arrived, Miss Porter was waiting for her. Pointing to a chair, she invited Shelagh to take a seat at the other side of her desk.

"Don't look so worried," she assured Shelagh, "it's not your fault that the factory is on strike. It won't be forever. Mr Parnell and I have been discussing what to do. The strike might be over in a few weeks so there's no point in you looking for another job. We've decided," she paused for a moment, before continuing. "For every week that you are on strike, we'll send Mrs Morton your full boarding out allowance. However," she said folding her arms on top of the desk and leaning over, "as soon as you have collected your strike pay, along with a receipt, I want you to come and see me straight away and I will give you your usual pocket money and fares."

Shelagh breathed a huge sigh of relief. She enjoyed working in the factory, as she had made new friends, and did not really want to work anywhere else.

Expressing her gratitude, she stood up to leave.

"There is one more thing," Shelagh wanted to know, "the trams have been taken off Roundhay Road and have been replaced with buses. I was allowed two shillings and sixpence for tram fare, but buses are a lot more expensive, at three shillings and four pence. So could I be allowed the extra fare please?"

"That's not a problem," Miss Porter answered, "I'll increase your travelling costs accordingly. Now if you go and sit in the waiting room I'll be going myself in about 10 minutes," she said, looking at the dainty wristwatch on her slender wrist, "so I can give you a lift home."

"Thank you kindly," Shelagh remarked, "but I'm not going home. I've made arrangements to have dinner at Pat's house, and then we're going to see Joyce."

"So I'll see you next week, when you bring your strike pay," Miss Porter smiled, as Shelagh left the office.

It did not take Shelagh long to walk to Pat's house in Woodhouse, as it was not too far away from Head Office.

Pat was full of beans and excitement when Shelagh arrived. She talked incessantly about the holiday to Ingleton, Mr and Mrs Wood had planned for her and the rest of the family during the following week. Shelagh was pleased that she had settled in straight away and loved being part of a normal happy family. "In fact," Shelagh thought, "Pat had been the luckiest of us all."

After dinner, Shelagh and Pat set off to see Joyce, who, some months earlier, had been transferred from Street Lane Home to the Keldholme Children's Home in Headingley.

It was a beautiful, sunny summer's afternoon, as they meandered through the many narrow cobbled back streets and ginnels through Headingley that brought them to the top of Woodhouse Ridge, then winding down a long, woody path and over a narrow bridge that crossed a stream towards Keldholme. As they walked, they laughed and reminisced of the times they had spent at the same school and of good and bad times in the Orphanage. Shelagh told Pat that she was on strike and that although she did not know how long it would last, she hoped that it was not for long. Eventually they reached Keldholme, a huge, impressive detached house that was surrounded by well-kept lawns edged with colourful summer flowers.

Joyce had been watching and waiting for them. When she saw them approaching, she ran down the long, winding path, impatiently to meet them and guided them to a wooden bench, eager to see what Shelagh had brought. Every time Shelagh visited her sisters, she would spend her pocket money on comics, sweets and chocolate for Pat and Joyce to share. Shelagh gave Joyce the carrier bag which she promptly emptied and spread the contents onto the grass.

"Don't forget to save some for Sunday," Shelagh reminded them, as she always did when they shared out the sweets.

"We won't," they answered in unison. They both laughed as they looked at her.

After years of queuing round Matron's Office after Sunday dinner to be given a handful of sweets, it had become a habit for Shelagh to eat them only on a Sunday.

Joyce had settled immediately in Keldholme and loved being back in a children's home with boys and girls of her own age, and had returned to being her normal happy bubbly self. She had even passed her scholarship at eleven years of age, applied and been accepted at Allerton Grange High School. Better still, she had begun to visit her beloved Miss Ratcliffe as often as she could.

Eventually visiting time was over, and it was time for Shelagh and Pat to leave.

"Don't forget if there's anything you need just write to me," Shelagh said to Joyce, as they began to walk home to Pat's house, where she had been invited to stay for tea.

When Shelagh arrived home later that evening, Mrs Morton was eagerly waiting to hear what advice Miss Porter had given concerning her job. She breathed a sigh of relief when Shelagh told her that the full boarding allowance would be sent to her by post every week until the printer's strike ended.

During the weeks of the strike, Shelagh occupied her time with different activities. She helped Mrs Morton spring clean the house from top to bottom. She visited her aunt and uncle in Beeston, and spent a day with Tony, who was on holiday from school. Tony told her he had applied, and been accepted as a plumber's apprentice, when he left school at Christmas, which was only a few months away. He always asked her the same questions when they met.

"Have you heard from our mother or father?" he would ask.

The answer was always the same, "No."

Shelagh knew that Tony had secretly hoped to meet his brother Robert, who he had never met, and that one-day he hoped that they would all be back together again as a family. That hope, however had long since gone.

On the last Saturday of every month, Mrs Morton would shop in Wakefield, as she always said that the shops there were better than those in Leeds. Shelagh always thought it very strange that, when she returned home, late in the afternoon, all she ever brought home was herself and her handbag.

One Saturday, when Mrs Morton had gone to Wakefield, Shelagh spent the whole day with Mr Morton. He was a lovely, gentle old man and was different again without the presence of his wife. He told Shelagh many stories about when he was a soldier in the First World War and how he had lost many friends in the trenches. His first wife was killed in the War and he always said that he regretted not having any children of his own. He had met and married Mrs Morton some fifteen years ago. Shelagh had sensed a long time ago that it was an unhappy marriage on his part. Mrs Morton was definitely the more assertive person and it was easier for her husband to do everything she asked of him and agree with everything she said. Some days Mrs Morton would scream at him, yelling verbal abuse in her high-pitched voice, making him cower away. He always did the best he could to please her, and never dared complain or voice an opinion, if it was different to hers.

Mr Morton often bought Shelagh a jam doughnut from the local bakery. He would secretly hide it in the kitchen cabinet behind the scullery door, and push it into her hand at a convenient moment for her to take to work for her morning break. He would always hold a finger to his closed lips, silently asking her never to reveal anything.

Shelagh meanwhile longed for the strike to be over, and eventually, after around six weeks, an agreement was made between the management and the unions, and much to everyone's delight they returned to work.

There was much work to catch up on, and Shelagh looked forward to working overtime as much as she was asked.

One early Saturday evening, Shelagh was sitting in an armchair watching, 'Oh Boy', a rock and roll programme on which celebrity guests would appear, Cliff Richards, Adam Faith, Billy Fury and Marty Wilde, to name but a few.

Mrs Morton bought a large cumbersome tape recorder and after showing Shelagh how to use it, told her to record all the songs from the programme. Shelagh did so every week, and would play back the songs slowly to learn every word off by heart.

One day, however, the tape recorder broke, and Mrs Morton when she had had it repaired, complained to Miss Porter that Shelagh had broken it by using it too much, and that she would like to be compensated. Miss Porter told Shelagh that, because she had used it more than Mrs Morton did, she must have broken it, and so she should be the one to pay for the repair. She instructed Shelagh to pay Mrs Morton two shillings and sixpence every week, out of her pocket money, until the debt had been fully paid.

For the next few months, not having much money left, Shelagh was unable to leave the house, with the exception of visiting Pat and Joyce.

Early one Saturday evening, as Mr Morton was shuffling and pottering around in the scullery, and Shelagh quietly reading a book, Mrs Morton was reading the evening paper.

"There's a job here for you," she said unexpectedly, looking at Shelagh from over the top of the newspaper. Shelagh glanced sideways at her, puzzled.

"I don't mean a day job," she carried on, "I mean an evening job."

Shelagh looked at her even more puzzled.

"Well you never go out," she pointed out, "you're in a rut, you mope around every weekend, never attempting to go anywhere, and it's time you did. A couple are advertising for a young girl to baby-sit their young son every other Saturday. They say they will pay seven shillings and sixpence. Why don't you go and 'phone them?"

Shelagh agreed, and made an appointment to meet the couple the following day.

On a rainy Sunday afternoon, Shelagh arrived at a beautiful, semi-detached house in Cross Gates, and nervously and gently rapped the small, wrought iron knocker.

A very smart man, in his early forties, answered the door.

"Hello," he said in a friendly voice. "Pleased to meet you. My name is Mr Read.

He was of medium height and was wearing a crisp open necked shirt. His beige slacks were held up with black braces, and his black hair was full of waves. Perched on the end of his nose, were dark rimmed, thick glasses.

Mr Read showed Shelagh into the lounge and invited her to sit in a large armchair by the window.

A young boy around seven years old was sitting on the settee, his face hidden behind a 'Beano'.

"Hello," the boy said sheepishly, peeping over the top of the comic.

Shelagh could hear sounds of chinking crockery and a woman singing through an open door.

A few moments later, she appeared in the doorway carrying a tray holding matching china cups and saucers, a milk jug, sugar basin, and a large teapot full of freshly made tea. Half-covered chocolate digestive biscuits were placed on a matching plate.

Mrs Read was a petite, very attractive woman in her late thirties, who was wearing a blue and white cotton polka dot dress. Her short, blonde, bouffant hair was immaculate

As they drank tea, Mr Read began to ask Shelagh the usual questions.

"How old are you?" he began.

"Sixteen," she answered.

"Where do you live?

Tell us about your mother and father?

Have you any brothers and sisters?

Which school did you attend?

Do you have a job?"

As the questions continued, Shelagh answered them truthfully, giving them a brief history of her life.

Mr Read asked to be excused for a moment and disappeared upstairs whilst his wife collected up the cups and saucers, replaced them on the tray, and took them into the kitchen. Shelagh glanced around the lounge. "What a beautiful house," she thought and secretly wondered if they were rich. She walked across the room and sat beside the young boy, much to his surprise. He told Shelagh that his name was David and that he was seven years old.

Within moments, they were stringing along a conversation, and had become firm friends.

Now back in the lounge, Mr and Mrs Read looked at each other and, much to Shelagh's delight nodded their approval and promptly offered her the job.

"You won't be like everyone else and leave will you?" David asked Shelagh.

"Of course I won't," Shelagh answered, looking at Mr Read and then at Mrs Read with a puzzled expression.

"He's right," Mrs Read remarked, shrugging her shoulders. "We've had a number of girls. Some only stay a few weeks, and some a few months, giving the excuse that they would rather be out with their friends on a Saturday night dancing. You won't let us down will you?" she asked.

"No I won't," replied Shelagh, shaking her head.

"Come on, I'll take you home, seeing as it's raining heavily, and I can introduce myself to Mrs Morton," said Mr Read kindly.

He drove a large, two-toned coloured car out of the garage and beckoned Shelagh to sit on the front passenger seat beside him. As he drove through Cross Gates towards Harehills, people stared at the conspicuous car. Shelagh felt like a queen sitting on the plush, comfortable, cream leather seats.

Mrs Morton was immediately impressed with the smart man that had brought Shelagh home.

He told her that he was the managing director of an engineering firm and that every few weeks he liked to take his wife out for a drink and, as she spent all her time taking care of him and their son, round the night off with a meal at a good restaurant.

"If Shelagh could make her own way to our house by seven thirty," he asked Mrs Morton, "then I will make sure she gets home safe and sound no matter what time it is. I will personally drive her home." As he left, Mrs Morton shook his strong hand and smiled at Shelagh approvingly.

Every two weeks, for the next few months, Shelagh baby-sat for young David. They would play games such as Ludo and Snakes and Ladders, and she would read him a story before he went to bed. On each occasion, Mrs Read would leave Shelagh a china cup and saucer, and cheese sandwiches, neatly cut into triangles on a tray, and would tell her to help herself to tea or coffee.

After David had gone to bed, Shelagh would drink tea and eat sandwiches while she watched the big screen television. She loved those peaceful hours on her own.

One late night, when Mr Read dropped Shelagh off, he leaned over from the driver's seat and gave her a quick peck on the cheek. Shelagh did not like it, but decided not to say anything, as she did not want to offend him for fear of losing her job.

Again, a few weeks later, when he took her home, he leaned over and kissed her on the cheek, and once more, she did not say anything.

The next time that Mr Read took her home, he grabbed and held her face between his hands and attempted to kiss her on the lips, his thick glasses pressing into her face. Shelagh winced and pushed him away. His breath stank of whisky. Mr Read always drank whisky, never beer.

"Aw, come on, be nice to me," he said.

Shelagh shoved him away with both hands and jumped out of the car, almost losing her balance. Slamming the car door behind her, she ran home, fumbling for the key in her handbag, quickly opening the door, and falling into the house. Mr Read drove away into the night.

As Shelagh lay in bed on her back, with her hands folded behind her head, she wondered why she attracted the wrong kind of man.

"It could have been a lot worse," she thought. Fear flooded her body as her dark, secret, began to surface, reminding her of that terrifying night, not so long ago.

"This time," she thought, "I'm going to have to tell Mrs Morton about Mr Read. If I don't, she will want to know why I don't baby-sit anymore."

Once again, she decided to bury 'her secret' deep down inside her. Hoping, once again that it would go away.

Then she remembered Mrs Read had said all the baby sitters had left after a short time, now she knew why. Mr Read must have been the reason. With that in mind, she felt a little easier.

Shelagh told Mrs Morton the following morning that she would not be going again and the reasons why. Strangely enough, Mrs Morton believed her, and said that if she ever saw him again, she would give him a piece of her mind.

In the months that followed, Tony left school and began to work as a plumber's assistant, with a view to an apprenticeship when he was sixteen years old. Pat was extremely contented at the Wood's and Joyce, having passed her scholarship, was happily attending Allerton Grange High School. She had immediately settled back into a children's home, where she had become her normal, boisterous, bubbly self.

Each morning, as Shelagh and her colleagues busily worked on their machines, singing and shaking their bodies in unison to Rock and Roll on the tannoy, the music would stop and a loud buzzer sounded a signal to stop what everybody was doing for a fifteen-minute break. Everyone sat at the end of their machines and ate a quick snack, chatted, and drank tea provided by Jesse the tea woman.

One particular day as they were sipping their tea, Mary, Shelagh's friend, said to her.

"Every week I ask you if you would like to go to the Mecca on a Saturday night, and every week you say no." looking directly at her, Mary continued.

"It's obvious you like Rock and Roll as you're the only person who knows and sings every word. You would enjoy it. Everybody dances all night, and if you ask the D.J., Jimmy Saville nicely, he will play a record of your choice."

Shelagh shrugged her shoulders, as she always did.

Sighing, Mary paused for a moment and then said.

"Me and Jack are going this Saturday night, so why don't you meet us outside the Mecca at half past seven? You'll never meet anyone if you never go out," she added, sighing again.

A loud, clear, shrill whistle could be heard across the factory. Shelagh looked over to the far side of the room at Peter Flynn, who was standing on a wooden box, with his hands on his hips, his neck stretched in the air, whistling and trying to get the attention of his friend Tony in one of the offices.

"And it's no good waiting for him to ask you out either," snapped Mary, looking over her shoulder. "He doesn't know you exist, and besides you're far too young for him. If you don't turn up on Saturday night, I'm not going to ask you again. I'm fed up of asking you. This is the last time," said Mary, angrily standing up and walking back towards her machine.

"Alright," Shelagh relented, not looking very enthusiastic as she caught Mary up, "I'll meet you if that's what you want."

Mary and Jack were waiting for Shelagh outside the Mecca Laccarno Ballroom, in the centre of Leeds, on Saturday night at half past seven. As she approached them, Shelagh smiled as they clapped their hands sarcastically in ironic greeting as she approached them.

Shelagh danced all the night away to popular records, thoroughly enjoying herself, even asking Jimmy Saville to play a record for her, 'Let's Jump the Broomstick'.

That was it. Shelagh was hooked on the Mecca, and for months, every Saturday night, she danced the night away. Mrs Morton even allowed her to stay out until eleven o'clock, half an hour later than her previous curfew, but was always waiting for her when she returned home, smelling her breath in the doorway, before she entered the house.

Chapter 51

One day, Shelagh received a letter from her brother Tony, asking her to meet him in front of the Malvern Picture House in Beeston at twelve o'clock. The following day would be her seventeenth birthday.

When Shelagh arrived, Tony was sitting on the flags outside the Picture House.

"Happy birthday," he greeted her, holding out his hand for her to pull him up, while giving her a birthday card with the other hand.

"Let's go for a walk in Cross Flatts Park," he suggested.

Shelagh looked at him a little puzzled, and sensed that he had something important to tell her.

Tony called at a fish and chip shop that they were passing and after a few minutes, he re-appeared carrying two bags of chips smothered with scraps and salt and vinegar.

"Here, that's your birthday present," he grinned, handing her a bag of chips and laughing.

They made their way to Cross Flatts Park and parked themselves side by side on a swing, finishing their chips, as they swung backward and forwards.

"I've got something to tell you," said Tony.

"I knew you had," Shelagh answered, bringing the swing to a sudden halt.

"Go on then tell me," she said, holding onto the side of the swing and glaring at her brother.

"I've joined up," he said, quietly and quickly.

"What do you mean you've joined up?" Shelagh replied unbelievably.

"I've joined the Royal Engineers Regiment; I'll be sixteen years old in a few months. I've already passed a medical and signed all the papers. It's all been approved by the Children's Care Office."

Shelagh was shocked. She had not expected this news.

She began to bombard him with questions.

"Why?

What for?

How long for?

What about your job?

What about Mr and Mrs Hawkins?"

Once she had stopped asking questions, Tony began to answer them.

"I've signed up for twenty two years, with a nine year option," he explained.

"Twenty two years," Shelagh shouted, with a look of horror on her face, "why all them years?"

"Well," Tony answered, taking a deep sigh. "Mr and Mrs Hawkins are getting divorced. In the Army, I'll have roots and security, and they've told me I can do a plumbing, electrical and engineering apprenticeship all at the same time. I'll be able to travel and see the world, and it won't cost me anything. I'd be a fool not to. I'll write to you all the time," he said, trying to reassure her.

Shelagh shook her head.

"I've never thought of joining the Army," Shelagh said, suddenly, with a sparkle in her eye, "maybe *I* will one day."

Tony glared at her with his mouth open. Then they both laughed heartily as they took it in turns to push each other higher and higher on the swings.

When Tony was sixteen years old, he did join the Army as a member of the Royal Engineers Regiment, and he and Shelagh began to write to each other regularly as they had promised.

"I'm writing to a soldier," Shelagh would brag, showing off to her friends at work by waving the blue air mail envelope in the air, then laugh and own up to it being her brother's.

After dinner, one spring day, Shelagh, Kathleen and Mary were on their way back from the canteen when Mary stopped to look at the notice board.

"Here," said Mary, pointing to a newly printed notice, "it's the shop dance in a few weeks. Do you fancy going with Jack and me?" she asked Shelagh.

"You've got to be kidding," Shelagh laughed, "have you seen the time it finishes?

One o'clock in the morning. Mrs Morton will never let me stay out that late, even for a special occasion. So the answers no."

"Yes she will," said Mary, "me and Jack will come and ask for you."

"Will ya?" Shelagh replied, surprised and excited, "she might say yes if someone else asks for me."

Later that day, Mary and Jack appeared on Shelagh's doorstep. Shelagh asked them in and invited them to sit down. Mrs Morton looked at Shelagh and then at Jack and Mary, cautiously

"What's all this about?" she enquired.

"We were wondering if you would let Shelagh go to the shop dance with us in a few weeks?" said Jack. "We'll look after her."

Mrs Morton looked a little puzzled wondering why they felt the need to ask her and not Shelagh.

"It doesn't finish until one in the morning, so it will be late when she gets home," explained Mary. Mrs Morton moved her shoulders back, lifting her head and eyebrows in the air.

Shelagh was standing in the doorway leaning against the wall, not daring to say anything, listening and holding her breath.

"Oh I see," remarked Mrs Morton, looking across at Shelagh.

Shelagh hoped that Mrs Morton would not lose her temper and start screeching at them, she crossed her fingers on both hands and held them behind her back.

"Well I have to say," began Mrs Morton, dropping her shoulders and sounding quite relaxed. "I've been very poorly over the last few weeks with flu and bronchitis and Shelagh has been a God send to us, hasn't she?" She looked across at Mr Morton, who was standing leaning against the scullery doorway, who nodded in agreement. Then looking sideways at Shelagh and smiling, she continued.

"Nothing has been too much trouble for her," she assured, "so I'm going to say," she paused for a moment, as the room went deadly silent, "Yes," she blurted out.

"But there's one condition," she said, holding a finger in the air and looking across at Shelagh's smiling face, "I don't want you to drink any alcohol. At seventeen, you're still not old enough and you're still in my care. Is that a deal?" she asked, leaning her head to one side and raising her eyebrows.

"Yes, I promise," answered Shelagh, now jumping up and down with delight.

During the next few weeks, Mrs Morton and Shelagh went shopping into Leeds. After dining on fish and chips in Youngman's famous fish shop in Briggate, they wove in and out of the many shops, eventually finishing at Etams. Mrs Morton helped Shelagh choose a square- necked, white, silky dress, patterned with large, grey roses, and a three-quarter, white cotton coat. Then they bought a pair of white stiletto shoes from Stylo shoe shop and a matching white handbag for the shop dance, all out of her clothing allowance. Miss Porter had asked Mrs Morton to always accompany and advise Shelagh whenever she bought new clothes, saying on no account must Shelagh shop on her own. In her opinion, she was too young and inexperienced to choose her own clothes, much to Shelagh's disgust.

Chapter 52

Weeks passed, and the night of the shop dance finally arrived. Shelagh raced home from work, grabbed and quickly ate a sandwich, while she washed in the scullery, before racing upstairs to put on her new clothes. As she waited excitedly for Mary and Jack to arrive, Mrs Morton complimented her saying how pretty she looked.

As promised, Mary and Jack arrived promptly at half past seven and together they walked the short distance up Roundhay Road towards the Astoria Ballroom, where the dance was being held.

Around nine o'clock the ballroom was buzzing alive.

The band played all kinds of music, to waltzes, quickstep, cha cha and rock and roll, to name but a few, and very soon, the dance floor was packed with excited dancers. As the dance ended, Mary and Jack left the dance floor and headed back towards Shelagh who was sitting at a table at the far side of the room drinking a bitter lemon and looking around the ballroom.

"Guess what," said Mary, as she approached Shelagh. "You'll never guess who's sitting right down at the bottom of the room with his friends?"

"Don't know," Shelagh replied, shrugging her shoulders, "who?"

"Peter Flynn," Mary said excitedly. "Why don't you go and make a nuisance of yourself, and with a bit of luck he might notice you and ask you for a dance."

"I can't do that." Shelagh replied, shaking her head, a little embarrassed. "That's rude and it's bad manners. No."

"Well you won't get another chance like this," Mary persisted, "this is perfect timing, isn't it Jack?"

Shelagh looked at Jack, who raised his eyebrows and nodded.

"Mary's right," he answered, "what have you got to lose?"

Cautiously and nervously, Shelagh walked slowly down to where Peter and his friends were sitting, talking and drinking.

Directly in front of where they were sitting was a round white, marble column. Shelagh leaned against the front of the column, keeping out of sight and occasionally peering round the side.

After a while, she had had enough, as her feet were killing her in the new stiletto shoes she was wearing.

"Do you know that girl hiding behind that post?" said the girl, sitting beside Peter.

Peter tilted his head to one side, momentarily catching Shelagh taking a sneaky look at him. Shelagh shot back out of sight.

"Yes," he replied, "she's one of the young girls who works in the Box Department."

"Well I think she fancies you," Peter's friend observed. "She keeps looking at you from round that post. I bet she's waiting for you to ask her for a dance. Why don't you go and ask her and put her out of her misery?" she suggested. Just as Shelagh had had enough of waiting and was about to head back to her friends, she felt a tap on her shoulder from behind.

"Can I have the next dance with you please," Peter asked in his deep voice.

"Me?" she replied, holding her hand to her chest and pretending to be surprised.

"Yes you," Peter smiled.

He took Shelagh by the hand and headed towards the dance floor where they danced one dance after another. Every time they passed Shelagh's friends, Jack, gave her an approving wink.

After several dances, Peter took Shelagh over to the table where he had been sitting with his friends and invited her to join them, pointing to the empty space where he had been sitting.

"This is my friend Geoff," Peter said, introducing Shelagh, "and this is my sister Pat and her husband Bob."

Finally, the band announced the last waltz and everyone, including Peter and Shelagh, made their way to the packed dance floor. After it was over, everybody began to form a queue for the cloakroom.

"Where do you live," Peter asked Shelagh.

"Oh not too far away," she answered, "just down the road."

"Can I walk you home and make sure you get there safe and sound?" Peter asked.

"Yes," Shelagh replied, pinching herself.

Shelagh turned around, looking to see if she could see Mary and Jack's heads bobbing up and down in the cloakroom queue. She spotted them in the distance and caught their eye.

"Peter's walking me home," she mouthed to them.

With a pleasing look on his face, Jack stuck his thumb high in the air and nodded.

Peter did walk Shelagh home that night, and arranged to meet her early the following evening outside the Clock Cinema, where they had planned to see the film, 'Saturday Night and Sunday Morning', starring Albert Finney.

Shelagh could not sleep that night. She could not believe that the boy she had had a crush on for years had walked her home, and even better, he had asked her for a date the following day. She pinched herself and hoped that he would turn up. There was no guarantee. She fell asleep with her fingers crossed.

Early the following evening, Shelagh walked the short distance to the Clock Cinema, where she had arranged to meet Peter, all the while wondering if he would turn up. She need not to have worried as she could see him parking his Lambretta scooter against the cinema wall as she crossed the road. He purchased two tickets for the upper circle and even bought her a small tub of ice cream during the interval. After the film was over, there were still a few hours of daylight left, so they made their way out of the cinema and down the crescent of steps outside.

"Come on, I'm taking you home to meet my mother," said Peter, to Shelagh's surprise. He took hold of her hand and headed towards his parked scooter. He patted the back of the seat, beckoning her to climb on behind him.

Shelagh did as he asked, and folded her arms around his waist, holding on tight. The wind was blowing her hair in her face as he drove to his house. When they arrived, he took her through a long, dark passage to the back of the house, walking through the back door that led directly into a square kitchen. The house was in darkness. The only sound that could be heard was from a television in the adjoining room. Peter disappeared from the kitchen into the room for a few minutes, leaving Shelagh in the kitchen leaning against a square wooden table along the back wall. Then a woman's voice whispered.

"Don't you dare put the light on?"

Peter appeared in the kitchen with his sister Pat, who Shelagh had met at the dance.

"Mum's not very well," said Pat, as she hurried across to fill the kettle. "She's asked me to ask you if you would like to come for tea tomorrow." Pat sat the kettle on top of an old gas cooker, lighting the gas ring with a twisted piece of paper from the fire. She came closer to Shelagh and whispered in her ear.

"Mum's not poorly," she explained. "She wasn't expecting company." She looked daggers at Peter.

"She's too embarrassed to meet you," Pat apologised. "She's wearing an old overall, her hair is in pins under a hairnet and more embarrassingly, she hasn't got her teeth in."

Shelagh smiled and secretly wondered if Peter did not have a father, as there seemed to be no man in the house.

"Come on, I'd better take you home," said Peter, some time later. "You said you have to be in by eleven o'clock. I don't want you getting into trouble."

Once again, Shelagh climbed on the back of his scooter, wrapping her arms tightly around his waist, and snuggled into his back as he drove her home in the dark. They stood for a long time talking at the bottom of the street. Peter told her that his father was working a night shift. He worked as a stoker for the Gas Board. Bob his brother-in-law was a bus driver who regularly drove the number fifty-four bus route from Pudsey to Halton Moor. Peter explained how Pat would meet Bob later that night at the bottom of their street on his last run, where she would board his bus so that they could head off home together.

Shelagh talked mainly of work, eventually slipping into the conversation that she lived in a foster home. She was relieved when Peter did not ask why.

Next day, Shelagh went for tea at Peter's house and was introduced to his mother.

"Just call me Hilda," she said, smiling at her. Peter's mother was a lovely woman. She was small and in her late forties, and was dressed in a pale green, cotton dress. Her auburn hair was full of close-knit curls. Peter's father appeared from upstairs.

"And you can call me Charlie," he said, introducing himself to Shelagh. She noticed, as he smiled that he had only two, long, middle teeth at the top. Pat and Bob had also been invited for tea.

Pat caught Shelagh's eye and pointed a finger to her teeth and then to her mother, indicating the older woman had her teeth in. They all made her feel so welcome and she felt comfortable in their presence. She thought what a happy close family they were. How she envied them.

During the next few weeks, Shelagh and Peter saw each other regularly, two or three times a week. They went for walks in Temple Newsam Park, which was not too far away, or to the many picture houses in the area, and when Peter's mother and father went out for the evening, they stayed in and watched television and ate fish and chip suppers. Shelagh was always reluctant to take Peter back home, knowing that if and when she did, Mrs Morton would tell him of her background and bombard him with questions. Shelagh chose to visit Peter rather than he visit her, as she wanted her background to remain a secret.

"I need to meet this young man of yours, that you spend so much time with," said Mrs Morton one day. "While ever you're under my roof, you're still in my care, and you're still my responsibility." Shelagh knew that this day would come, so she asked Peter to call for her early one evening to meet Mr and Mrs Morton. He had only been in the house two minutes before she began to ask him questions.

"How old are you?" she wanted to know.

"Twenty two," he answered politely.

"Where do you live?

Have you a mother and father?

Do they work?

What do they do?

Have you any brothers or sisters?"

Then suddenly, turning her head, looking at Shelagh who was standing beside Peter, and wishing that a hole would open beneath her feet and swallow her up, she asked. "Do you know what you are taking on?" Shelagh, her face now red with embarrassment, looked at the glass-domed clock on top of the tiled fireplace. Eager to get Peter out, she pushed him into the doorway, saying.

"Come on, we'll be late for the pictures."

"Which picture house are you going to," Mrs Morton shouted across at them.

"The Regal in Cross Gates," Peter answered.

By now, Shelagh had opened the outside door and was pushing Peter out from behind.

Once outside on the pavement, she breathed a huge sigh of relief.

Every few weeks, Shelagh continued to visit Pat and Joyce and, on each occasion, she took them sweets, chocolate and comics. She told them all about Peter and his happy family. Pat, by now was fifteen years old, and about to leave school in a few months time and had been offered a job at Reynolds and Branson, a pharmaceutical company, where she would be employed in the storeroom as a packer. Her working hours would be from eight thirty to five thirty and her wage would be three pounds per week.

Joyce, at fourteen years old, was making excellent progress at Allerton Grange High School, and was still very happy and contented living in a children's home.

As Shelagh returned from work one Saturday morning, she shuddered as she neared her foster home. In the distance, she could see Peter's scooter parked outside her home. He wasn't expected, as they had arranged to meet at his house later that evening. She wondered how long he had been there. Fear flooded her body, making her stomach churn, worrying what Mrs Morton might be saying to him. Shelagh's mind was exploding, remembering vividly what Mrs Morton had said to her in the past months.

"Have you told him?" she would ask again and again, referring to Shelagh's background.

"No," Shelagh had always answered.

"Well when you do," she replied heartlessly, "he'll drop you like a ton of bricks and you can't blame him. You've got nothing to offer. Men don't want girls like you with no background."

Shelagh fully expected Peter to walk out of the house before she got there and ride away as fast as he could. Suddenly she found the energy to get into the house as quick as possible, reasoning that the less time Peter spent with Mrs Morton, the less she could tell him.

"What are you doing here?" Shelagh asked Peter, as she stepped inside the door, "I wasn't expecting to see you until tonight."

"Well, I thought seeing as it's such a nice day, we could go for a walk round Temple Newsam Park," he replied cheerfully, "then back to my house for tea."

Shelagh looked at Mrs Morton who was sitting by the fireplace, and then back at Peter who had a serious look on his face. She wished that she knew what Mrs Morton had confided in him.

"I'll be two minutes," Shelagh replied, running upstairs to change quickly into a clean set of clothes.

She did not want to leave Peter with Mrs Morton a moment longer than necessary.

Riding pillion behind Peter on their way to Temple Newsam, Shelagh decided that this was the moment that she would have to tell him of her background. The thought filled her with dread. If Peter dumped her, as Mrs Morton hinted, then there was nothing that Shelagh could do about it.

The park was full of people, mostly elderly couples strolling together and parents who were playing football with their children on the vast, open grassland. A group of youngsters were throwing bread to the ducks near the stream.

As Shelagh and Peter strolled along the winding path, small rhododendron blooms, in their full glory, were blooming on either side. In the rose garden, surrounded by beautiful, different coloured roses, Shelagh stood for a moment, took a deep breath and sighed.

"I have to talk to you," she confessed, "I've got something to tell you before someone else does. I should've told you a long time ago. I've been too scared to tell you." Her face was drip white. She had dreaded this moment. Peter led her to a bench and sat her down. He sat sideways with his knee resting on the bench, and his foot across the other knee, his elbow leaning over the back of the bench, and his head resting on his hand. He stared at her with his big, brown eyes. Shelagh could feel her heart thumping in her chest. Staring at the ground, she began to tell him of her life in care. As she spoke, her fingers were entwined and her thumbs rolled around each other.

"And that's why I live in a foster home," she eventually concluded. For a few moments, there was silence.

"Haven't you got anything to say?" Shelagh asked nervously.

Peter half grinned at her.

"I know," he answered softly.

"You know," Shelagh exclaimed, dumbfounded.

"How do you know?"

Then with a look of confusion on her face, she asked, "Who told you?"

Then, biting her lip, she added, "did Mrs Morton tell you?"

"No she didn't," replied Peter assuringly. "I've known for years. Your cousin Pat told me a long time ago. I used to go out with one of Pat's friends, and when she started going out with Malcolm her husband, we all used to go out regularly as a foursome. I've been to your Cousin's house many a time."

Shelagh felt as if a weight had been lifted from her shoulders.

"Why didn't you tell me you knew? She burst out. "You've no idea how hard that's been for me to tell you. Why didn't you tell me you knew?" she asked again, with a puzzled look on her face.

Peter leaned forward and held both her hands in his.

"I've been waiting for you to tell me yourself," he said kindly. "I wanted you to tell me when you felt it was the right time. You've got nothing to be ashamed of. You've done nothing wrong. It wasn't your fault that you were put into a children's home. Stop being afraid of what other people think. People will like you for who you are."

"Mrs Morton says you will dump me when you find out," Shelagh remarked.

"And what kind of a person would that make me?" Peter replied wearily. Have a little more faith in human nature, I don't care what background you come from. In fact, now you've got that off your chest, there is something I want to ask you."

Shelagh looked at him, with a knot forming in her stomach once again.

"Next month you'll be eighteen," he told her, "so why don't we get engaged on your birthday?"

"Are you serious?" Shelagh gasped, jumping up and down. "Do you really mean it?" She jumped up from the bench, her heart now pounding with excitement.

"Is that a yes or a no?" Peter asked, laughing at the excitement in her eyes and on her face.

He stood up and flung his arms around her waist and began to swing her around and around in the air.

"Well," he asked again, firmly planting her feet back on the ground, "Is that a yes?"

Shelagh began nodding her head vigorously, her face beaming with happiness. As he knelt down on the ground beside a rose bush, Peter broke off the stem of a red rose, pricking his finger at the same time from a sharp thorn, which caused her to laugh.

"Look, I've even drawn blood for you," he declared, showing her his bleeding finger. As he handed her the rose, he stuck his finger in his mouth, which made Shelagh laugh even more.

The following morning with her head still on cloud nine, Shelagh told Mrs Morton that Peter had asked her to get engaged the following month.

"I'm really pleased for you," Mrs Morton replied, a little coldly, "I just hope it comes off." Shelagh looked at her and half shook her head.

"And it's no good shaking your head at me and rolling your eyes around," Mrs Morton continued. "I'm only trying to prepare you in case it doesn't happen."

"Oh I know it will," Shelagh assured her timidly.

"You do know you'll have to let Miss Porter know," Mrs Morton insisted. "I don't know what's she's going to think. To me, you're far too young and very naïve. I hope, for your sake, he's not stringing you along, but only time will tell. I'll believe it when I see it."

Shelagh took herself to her bedroom out of the way. Mrs Morton always looked on the bad side and never on the good side, causing Shelagh to wonder if something had happened in her past life to make her so bitter.

A few days later, as Shelagh was tidying her bedroom, Mrs Morton shouted up the stairs.

"Miss Porter's here to see you."

Dropping everything Shelagh ran down the steps eager to see her. As she reached the bottom, she could hear Mrs Morton was telling her that Shelagh was hoping to get engaged on her eighteenth birthday.

"That's the best news I've heard all day," declared Miss Porter, looking very pleased at Shelagh. "In fact," she carried on, "what a lovely leaving present that would be on the day you will pass out of care."

"I hope he doesn't let her down," remarked Mrs Morton, pretending to sound very sweet and caring.

Mrs Morton was always the perfect woman in the presence of Miss Porter.

"Today will be my last visit to see you," announced Miss Porter, "I've made an appointment for you to have your last yearly medical at the Education Department in Great George Street, in the next few weeks, before you are officially out of care."

"She might be out of your care, but she'll still be in my care while ever she lives here," butted in Mrs Morton in a pleasant voice, "and I'll always be here to steer her in the right direction."

"I've known you for a number of years," remarked Miss Porter, looking at Shelagh, "and I've seen you go through some difficult times, but you've come through, and I'm very proud of you. If at any time you need to talk to me about anything, you know where I am. I sincerely hope you do get engaged. You deserve to and I hope you have a happy life."

Shelagh swallowed the lump in her throat and said that all being well, she would keep in contact.

She followed Miss Porter to her car and watched her climb into the driver's seat.

"I sincerely wish you all the best for the future," Miss Porter said kindly. "The future's in your own hands, and what you do with it is entirely up to you," giving Shelagh a big wave, as she drove away for the very last time.

Shelagh, Peter, Bob and Pat

Chapter 53

On Saturday, 18 August, it was Shelagh's eighteenth birthday. She received a letter in the post from the Children's Department, informing her, that from this date, she was now out of care.

Shelagh kept on looking at the letter, suddenly feeling relieved and very grown up. From today, no one would have to write and ask permission for her to stay out overnight and never again would she be accountable to the authorities. She would even have full control of her own wage packet. Miss Porter had encouraged her months ago to save a small amount of money out of her wage each week and put it into the bank, and now she had twenty six pounds and ten shillings in a Yorkshire Penny Bank account.

Shelagh showed Mrs Morton the letter that she had just received, stating that now she was officially out of care.

"You might be eighteen and out of *their* care," Mrs Morton snapped, "but while ever you're under *my* roof, you're still in *my* care and don't you forget it."

Shelagh ran upstairs with the letter and putting it safely in a drawer, began to get ready to meet Peter in Leeds City Centre.

She had arranged to meet him opposite the main bus station at twelve o'clock and sitting on the bus that was packed with Saturday shoppers, she hoped that Peter would turn up. There was an element of doubt in her , Mrs

Morton had seen to that, always reminding her that one day he would drop her like a ton of bricks.

She arrived at the bus station at five past twelve, five minutes late. There was no sign of Peter. Shelagh stood and waited for a while, then looked across at the clock on the tower of Leeds Parish Church. It was twelve fifteen. Her mind began to play tricks and she became increasingly anxious. By half past twelve, Peter had still had not arrived. Now Shelagh did not know what to think.

"Perhaps the Parish Church clock is half an hour fast," she reasoned, though she knew that she was kidding herself. Shelagh did not want to think the worst, but maybe Peter had changed his mind, as Mrs Morton had said he would.

"No, he wasn't like that," she argued, trying to convince herself. But where was he? The time on the Parish Church clock was now twelve thirty five.

"I'll give him another ten minutes, making him forty five minutes late," she decided, "and then, if he's not here by then, I might as well go home and face the music. Mrs Morton will be in her element."

At that moment, she spied him in the distance riding towards her on his Lambretta.

"I'm really sorry," he spluttered, after he had parked the scooter and joined her. "I really am sorry I'm late. I bet you thought I wasn't coming, didn't you."

Shelagh nodded with a look of relief on her face.

"I couldn't get my bike to start," Peter began to explain, "and it was too late to catch the bus, and when I did find out what was wrong with it, I had to start and mend it," he gasped, not stopping for breath.

"Thankfully you're here now and that's all that matters," Shelagh smiled, now looking very relieved. After strolling around the shops, they finally came across a small jewellers on Boar Lane called Kelvingtons. In the window, they saw an eighteen-carat gold, solitaire, diamond, platinum-setting ring. Once Shelagh had put the ring on her finger, she was reluctant to take it off. The jeweller kindly gave them a box of silver teaspoons as an engagement present.

"It's a lovely day," said Peter impulsively, "why don't we spend the rest of the day at Roundhay Park?"

It was a warm, sunny August afternoon, and the park was full of visitors. As they sauntered around the park towards the lake, Shelagh was in a dream.

She wondered if any of the many visitors could tell how happy she was by the look on her face. Standing in the long queue waiting for a rowing boat, Peter held and kept squeezing, her hand. Eventually they stepped down into a small rowing boat and Peter rowed out onto the lake. The sun was glistening on the water as Shelagh threaded her left hand through the ripples, making her ring shine even more. After the boat ride, they sat on a bench and ate ice cream.

"One day, we'll have a house and a garden of our own and lots of children," said Peter grinning, "maybe a football team!"

Shelagh simply smiled and nodded. She could not allow herself to think that far ahead in case it did not happen. All that mattered at that moment was that she was the happiest girl in the world. Wiping the side of her face to show off her new sparkling engagement ring, she hoped that passers-by would notice that she was engaged to the most handsome boy in the world. She loved Peter so much.

After their idyllic afternoon together, they eventually returned to Peter's home for tea.

All too soon however, the day ended, and later that night, Peter took her home. As they stood at the bottom of the street, leaning against a wall, Peter wrapped her inside his coat and folded his arms around her.

"This has been the best day of my life," Shelagh confided, her head resting sideways against his chest and feeling the warmth from his body. As they embraced, Peter spoke again of a house with a garden and children.

"But," he added. "Before that, I haven't had a holiday for a long time. Once we get a mortgage, we might not be able to afford one for a long time, so I think we should save up and have a good holiday before we settle down. What do you think?" he asked Shelagh.

"Well if I had my way, I'd run away to Gretna Green tomorrow," said Shelagh excitedly, "but I know that's not possible. So alright, that's what we'll do. We'll have a really good holiday first," she agreed.

During the next few months, Peter and Shelagh had saved enough money for a deposit and booked a week's holiday for the following year at Middleton Towers Holiday Camp, just a few miles outside Morecambe. Home life for Shelagh did not change, as Mrs Morton was as unpredictable as ever. Some days she could be pleasant and caring, whilst on other days, if anything upset her, however small the incident, she would screech at the top of her voice yelling abuse and cruel words at Shelagh and Mr Morton. Shelagh tried to spend as little time as possible at home.

The months passed quickly and soon it was time for their holiday. Early one Saturday morning, Peter and Shelagh took a train to Morecambe, where they were met by a number of 'blue coats', the entertainment staff, who directed them to courtesy buses. The Camp was divided into different categories, families, single men and single women; a single chalet consisted of a small room, and contained a metal framed bed that filled one side and a small chest of drawers, a tiny wardrobe and a sink occupied the other wall. The toilet blocks were dotted around the camp. For the rest of the day Peter and Shelagh familiarised themselves by exploring the camp, and later that evening, after a tiring day, they made their way back to their chalets which were at the opposite ends of the camp, apart from each other. Around eight o'clock the following morning, a loud clear voice on the tannoy echoed across the campsite.

"Good morning campers," a woman would broadcast, "we are now serving breakfast in the dining room."

Men, woman, and children of all ages, appeared from everywhere, running to the dining room and almost knocking each other over in their haste to arrive in time.

Later that morning, Peter was playing pool in the games room and Shelagh was sitting beside him reading a magazine.

"Can I join you," a voice asked Peter. Peter looked up and to his surprise identified the speaker as one of the lads that frequented the club that he and his dad were members of back in Leeds. His name was Ralph and he and his wife Shirley were staying at the camp for the week. They all soon became close friends.

One day, they all took a taxi into Morecambe, where they spent a few hours on the many rides in the fairground, before taking a long, brisk walk along the promenade.

"Fancy a ride on one of those?" Ralph asked, seeing a young man on the beach holding the reins of several horses."

"No thank you," said Shirley indignantly.

"Me neither," echoed Shelagh.

"Looks like me and you then Ralph," laughed Peter.

The two men jumped over the railings and ran to the horses. Ralph mounted a black horse called Jet and Peter climbed onto the back of a brown horse called Toffee.

"Don't worry about the route," shouted the owner of the horses, "they know their way back. You'll only be about twenty minutes."

Shirley and Shelagh stood and watched, holding onto the railings at the side of the promenade. For the first few minutes, Peter and Ralph chatted to each other as the horses strolled leisurely on the sand, but then Peter gently tapped his horse's bottom causing it to bolt and gallop towards the sea in the distance.

"Oh no," Shelagh gasped. She had visions of the horse throwing Peter over its head into the sea. She closed her eyes and covered her face with her hands fearing the worst.

"I shouldn't worry if I were you," laughed Shirley. "He's taken to that horse like a duck to water. He's managed to stand up in the stirrups, take hold of the reigns and take control."

Shelagh opened an eye and spread her fingers open to see Peter calmly and in full control, riding the horse back to where Ralph, who had already dismounted his horse, was waiting for him.

"I didn't know you could ride a horse," remarked Ralph, looking very surprised as Peter dismounted Toffee.

"Neither did I," Peter answered. "That's the first time I've ever been on a horse," he grinned, looking very pleased with himself.

"Well you rode that horse like a true jockey," complimented Ralph.

"Well done," said the owner of the horse, tapping Peter on the shoulder.

Shirley and Shelagh began to laugh as Peter walked slowly towards them, moaning, groaning and rubbing the back of his bowed legs with his hands. Eventually he too saw the funny side and joined in the laughter along with Ralph, who was now almost hysterical.

Feeling a little saddle sore, Peter suggested that they should head back to Camp.

Bob, Peter's brother-in-law, and his mother and sister Pat, had arranged to visit them during their week's stay at Middleton Towers. Peter and Shelagh met them in the visitor's car park, where Bob parked his two-tone Ford Zephyr Zodiac. Hilda, Peter's mother, was eager to be shown around the campsite, so Peter showed her his small and dismal chalet in the middle of the men's quarters, then across the camp to inspect Shelagh's accommodation.

"That's made my mother's day," Pat whispered into Shelagh's ear. "She can go home and sleep easy in her bed tonight, happy in the fact you've both got separate chalets."

After their grand tour of the camp, they decided to take the short drive into Morecambe. As they strolled leisurely by the sea, sounds of loud clapping and noisy cheering could be heard from inside the open-air swimming pool where the 'Miss World' contest was being held. Bob spotted the horses for hire on the beach and asked Peter if he fancied a ride.

"No thanks," Peter laughed, rubbing the back of his thighs before relating the story of Toffee the horse.

Later, as Bob drove back to the camp, a voice interrupted the record that was playing on the car radio.

"We have a news flash," it announced.

Norma Jeane Baker, more popularly known as Marilyn Monroe had been found dead in her home in Brentwood, California. She was thirty-six years old.

The date was the fifth of August nineteen sixty two.

Over the next few days, the sudden death of the film star was the talk of the camp.

The week passed all too quickly and soon Peter and Shelagh were making their way back home to Leeds on the train.

"I don't want to go back there," said Shelagh to Peter, meaning to Mr and Mrs Morton's house.

"Well hopefully it won't be for much longer," Peter answered, "we need to start saving every penny we can get hold of to get married and buy a house."

Those words seemed like music to Shelagh's ears. She had lived with Mr and Mrs Morton for four years, so one or two more would soon pass by. With that in mind, Shelagh could now see a light at the end of the tunnel.

Peter and Shelagh

Chapter 54

When Shelagh arrived back home, she dragged her case up the three steps leading to the door and into the room. Mrs Morton was standing in front of the fireplace with her hands folded behind her back and, after asking Shelagh if she had had a nice holiday, she told her to take her case upstairs and then come straight back down as she wanted to speak to her. Mrs Morton, very much out of character, appeared to be in an excellent mood, but puzzled as to why she wanted to speak to her. Shelagh took her case upstairs and returned immediately. Mrs Morton was now sitting on the two-seater settee.

"Come and sit beside me," she patted the empty space beside her. "There's something I want to talk to you about."

Shelagh sat down, suddenly feeling very nervous and uncomfortable.

"You know I have a son called Roger who has been working away from home for some time," she began. "Well," she said, pausing for a moment and breathing deeply, "he's coming back home and he wants his bedroom back. To tell you the truth, he has been kind of working away from home, but not as you think."

Shelagh frowned looking even more puzzled.

"He's been a prisoner in Wakefield Jail," she said quickly, for once looking a little ashamed and embarrassed. "I've never told the authorities because I didn't think it any of their business, and besides, it doesn't matter now you are out of care."

Suddenly it all began to fit into place. That is why Mrs Morton went to Wakefield every month and never came back with any shopping. Shelagh was curious to know what Roger was like and why he was in jail. She had never known anyone who had been in trouble with the police, never mind anyone in jail.

"Roger's coming home in the next few days," Mrs Morton continued, "so I want you to move all your belongings out of your bedroom and into the attic. Is that alright?" she asked Shelagh.

"That's alright by me. I don't mind," Shelagh answered. "In fact," she reasoned, "if someone was living in the same house who had been a prisoner in jail, she would rather be in the attic and out of the way." After she had moved all her clothes and possessions, Shelagh put everything away neatly into drawers and into the small wardrobe, placing the small picture of Jesus, that she had stolen from the orphanage, on top of the chest of drawers. As she sat on top of the bed surveying the room, she thought of Joyce who for five months used this bedroom, hating every minute of living here. She began to wonder what Roger was like, and why he had been in jail for such a long time. She felt very nervous at the thought of meeting him.

Shelagh did not have long to wait to meet Roger. A few days later, when she returned home, Roger was standing in front of the fire with his hands firmly wrapped around a large white mug filled with tea. He stared at her as she hung her coat on a hook at the back of the room door, which led directly out onto the street.

"I'm Roger," he greeted, "I presume you must be Shelagh."

She nodded at him a little nervously.

"Come and sit down and tell me all about yourself," he said, pointing to the two-seater settee.

He sat beside her, placed his mug of tea on top of the tiled fireplace, took a packet of twenty Players extra strong cigarettes out of his pocket and offered her one.

"No thank you," Shelagh replied.

Roger was tall and thin and in his early forties. He wore a navy-flecked jumper and black trousers and his thin, dark brown, greasy hair was combed over the top of his head. His face was pale and wrinkled and under his square, brown, tortoise shell, framed glasses, his eyes were hazy brown.

Mrs Morton was in the scullery making Roger a sandwich.

"How old are you?" he asked Shelagh.

"Nineteen," Shelagh answered.

"How long have you been engaged? He continued.

What's your boyfriend like? How old is he?

Did you enjoy your holiday?"

And so the questions continued.

When Roger seemed to be satisfied, Shelagh felt that now she could be excused, as she wanted to get ready to go out. Mrs Morton appeared in the room with a sandwich on a plate and handed it to Roger. She began to fuss around him, like Shelagh had never seen her do to anyone before.

She even smiled at Shelagh and began to sing as she sauntered back into the scullery. Roger looked at Shelagh, raised his eyebrows and grinned. Shelagh relaxed knowing that if Mrs Morton was in an excellent mood, she would not start to shout at her today.

One Saturday night, a few weeks later, Shelagh arrived home at around eleven o'clock. The house was in darkness; she breathed a sigh of relief knowing Mr and Mrs Morton had gone to bed and that she would not be subjected to a breath test in the middle of the doorway.

Even though she was nineteen years old, she still was not allowed to drink alcohol. Climbing the two flights of stairs into the attic, she soon fell into a deep sleep.

In the early hours of the morning, something disturbed her, causing her to wake. She could not make out what it was. She lay motionless, not daring to move. Her heart was thumping in her chest. Something was not right. After a few minutes, as her eyes became adjusted to the dark, she looked around the attic as best as she could. There was a strong smell of alcohol in the air. Suddenly she became very frightened and fear flooded her body making her stomach churn. Then she felt a thud on top of her bed and then another. Now she was shaking and terrified. She grabbed the blankets with both hands and held them tightly under her chin. Then another thud sounded on top of the bed. Shelagh very slowly moved to the edge of the bed and peered over the side.

Lying on the floor beside her was the figure of a man. He lifted up his head, stared into her frightened face and thumped the bed again. It was Roger.

"What do you want?" Shelagh asked, not thinking about what she was saying.

"You," Roger answered, his breath stinking of beer.

The thought of him anywhere near her, repulsed her.

"You're drunk," Shelagh said disgustingly. "Go away and leave me alone. I'll tell your mother," she threatened.

"You'll tell my mother," Roger laughed. "And what good do you think that will do? I'll just deny it ever happened." His voice was slurred and he was beginning to roll from side to side.

"She'll always believe me before she believes you," he jeered, "so come on." He thumped the bed again and attempted to get up from the floor.

An overwhelming fear filled her body, and the dark secret that she had held for years within her surfaced. The memories of that night came flooding back. The man in question then, was also drunk. She was trapped in a bedroom, and he was downstairs in a room below her. Now, another drunken man was laid on the floor beside her. Her blood ran cold. The fear she felt at that time, all those years ago, was nothing compared to the fear she was now feeling.

"If you don't go away, I'll scream and we'll see who believes who then," Shelagh threatened, trying to bluff him, "I'll scream so loud, everybody in the street will hear me, including your mother before you even have the chance to get to the bottom of the stairs," she persisted, suddenly finding the courage in her voice to stand up to him, "so try me." She still lay in bed holding onto the blankets and too scared to move.

"You wouldn't dare," Roger slurred.

"Wouldn't I, try me," Shelagh threatened again.

Then, with an increasing sense of control, she suggested to him,

"If you go away and leave me alone, I won't say anything."

Reluctantly Roger slid towards the top of the attic steps, banging each step as he slithered down to the bottom. How he did not wake Mr and Mrs Morton, Shelagh never knew. She lay for the rest of the night listening and watching through the banister at the top of the attic, wondering what to do. To make thing worse there was no door at the bottom of the steps.

"Shall I tell Mrs Morton?" she thought. She would say I must have encouraged Roger and then she would throw me out. Where, would I go?"

she pondered. Should I tell Peter? What if he came down, and had it out with Roger? Peter would be no match for Mrs Morton. She would eat him alive. I could not put him through that." Shelagh's head was exploding with thoughts of what to do. "What if I did tell Peter the truth? He might not believe me, and think I was hiding something, what will I do then? I would be out on the streets and have nowhere to go." She decided once again to keep it a secret, alongside the other secret. Hoping once again, that if she did not talk, or think about it, it would go away.

For days afterwards, Roger never spoke to, or made eye contact, with Shelagh. His mother must have been blind, or she deliberately chose not to notice the atmosphere between them. In the weeks that followed Shelagh never felt comfortable or safe in the attic.

Occasionally, those dark secrets would surface, leaving her cold. Once again, it would be many years, before she could speak of the incidents. And when she eventually did, she would realise and accept that she was in no way responsible, or to blame, for the reactions of drunken men.

Chapter 55

One Friday after work, Shelagh was tired and not feeling very well. She sat quietly in the sitting room. Roger was out, and Mr and Mrs Morton were talking in the scullery.

"Are you going out tonight?" Mrs Morton asked Shelagh, as she appeared in the doorway.

"Not sure," Shelagh answered, I don't feel very well, I ache everywhere, I must be coming down with the flu and I might have an early night. I've not decided yet," she added.

"Well don't be surprised if one night when you get back the locks have been changed and you can't get in," snapped Mrs Morton, as unfeeling as ever. "You're never in on a weekend. You spend more time at his house than you do here. So I don't know why you don't clear off and have done with it? I can soon get someone else in your place. Girls like you are ten a penny." Shelagh hung her head and looked down at the carpet.

"I can't take much more of this," she thought.

Mrs Morton's voice was getting louder and louder, causing Shelagh's head to thump as she listened to her rantings.

"In fact, if you go out tonight, don't bother coming back," she screeched.

Shelagh felt as if her head was about to explode. Suddenly finding courage and strength, though her legs felt weak, she stood up, sighed and walked across the room to take her coat off the hook, grabbed her handbag and opened the outside door.

"And where do you think you're going," Mrs Morton demanded.

"I'm leaving," Shelagh replied, "I can't take this anymore."

"Well I'll help you," Mrs Morton shouted, pushing her out of the door.

"Good riddance," she shouted, as she put one foot on the outside step. Shelagh walked down the cobbled street, crossed the road and joined the queue at the bus stop, which was visible from the doorway of the house.

"You'd better get back here, there are jobs for you to do before you leave," Mrs Morton screamed, continuing to swear and shout verbal abuse.

"And you owe me some money for this week."

Passers-by watched horrified, surprised by the abuse and language that was coming out of the mouth of such a small woman. The people in the bus queue were shaking their heads in disgust at Mrs Morton, and feeling very sorry for Shelagh, who was bravely trying to ignore the stinging comments. Shelagh's face was bright red with embarrassment, and she was very relieved when the bus eventually arrived. After a short journey up Roundhay Road, she joined another queue outside the Fforde Green Public House.

"I've just walked out and I've got nowhere to live," she thought suddenly, as she waited in the queue. "What am I going to do? Where am I going to live?"

Tears were already welling up in her eyes as she boarded the bus and sat on a seat at the front. She began to weep silent tears as she looked out of the window, sobbing quietly so as not to draw attention to herself. Soon the bus arrived at her stop. As she was about to step off the bus, the driver leaned forward and gave her a clean white handkerchief that he took from his trouser pocket.

"I've been watching you out of my mirror," he said kindly. What ever it is that is troubling you, don't worry, it will all work out in the end. Nothing is ever as bad as it seems."

"Nothing could be worse than being homeless," Shelagh thought, as she walked the short distance along the Avenue, wiping her eyes and face on the handkerchief the bus driver had given to her and giving her nose a good blow. Trying to compose herself, she knocked on the front door of Peter's house.

"You're a bit early," Peter greeted her, opening the front door and looking into her tear-stained face and swollen eyes, "what's the matter?"

"I've just walked out," Shelagh blurted out. "I've left Mr and Mrs Morton."

Peter put his arm around her shoulder, took her inside the room and sat her down on the settee.

His mother appeared from the kitchen and stood inside the door, wiping her hands on a tea towel.

"What's all this about?" she asked curiously.

"I've walked out and now I've got nowhere to live," said Shelagh, with an empty look on her face.

"I don't understand," said Hilda, walking across and sitting beside her, "why would you want to do that? Explain to me what all this is about," she said, with a puzzled look on her face.

Shelagh began to tell her in quiet, broken voice, things that she had never told Peter.

"Why didn't you tell me about this woman and how unhappy Shelagh's been," said Hilda, turning round and looking at her son. "I always felt there was something, but I could never put my finger on it. Now I understand why. Why didn't you tell me?" she asked Peter again.

"It's the first time I've heard about this," replied Peter truthfully. "She never talks about her home life and I don't ask." Hilda shook her head.

"Just like a man," she remarked.

"Will you help me look for somewhere to rent tomorrow?" Shelagh asked Peter. "I'll have to find somewhere to live."

He nodded his head.

"You make her a strong cup of tea," Hilda instructed Peter. "I won't be long." Then she disappeared out of the front door.

"What am I going to do?" is all Shelagh could say, "I've left all my clothes and everything behind, what am I going to do?" she repeated to herself again and again.

A short time later, Hilda returned. "Problem solved," she announced, "well for the moment. Our friends over the road are going on holiday in the morning. They have a spare bedroom and they've said you can stay there until they come back from their holidays."

"But they don't know me," said Shelagh.

"No they don't," replied Hilda, "but they know you are engaged to my son, and I've told them all about you."

"You mean you've told them all about me and they still say I can stay there until they come back from their holiday?" Shelagh asked disbelievingly.

Hilda shook her head, looked at Peter, and then back at Shelagh.

"Have a little more faith in people," she urged. "People like that woman are rare. So come on, I'll take you to meet our friends." Shelagh followed Hilda out of the front door and across the road to the house opposite. Hilda knocked, opened the door and walked into the front room, with Shelagh, rather nervously, close behind her. Mr and Mrs Tate were sitting on two large armchairs in the middle of the room. The atmosphere was warm and friendly.

"Pleased to meet you," said Mrs Tate, in a kind voice, "come and sit down," beckoning them to sit on the settee.

Mrs Tate was of medium height and in her late forties. She was wearing a pink twin set and a black skirt and her brown permed hair was full of tiny curls. She had kind eyes and a soft face.

"You are welcome to stay here until we get back from our holidays in two weeks time," she said warmly. "Our daughter Elaine will be here, so you'll be able to keep her company. Come on I'll show you around," she invited, with a sparkle in her eye. Shelagh followed her up the stairs.

Back downstairs, Mr Tate was taking a key off a bunch of keys in his hands and talking to Hilda.

"She might as well have my key until we come back," he offered.

Mrs Tate showed Shelagh the small light bedroom, which contained a single bed, a chest of drawers and a small wardrobe. Floral patterned curtains hung at the window that looked across at Peter's house and pretty pictures adorned the walls. When they rejoined Mr Tate and Hilda downstairs, Mr Tate handed over his front door key to Shelagh.

"Thank you," Shelagh said, feeling very humble and grateful.

As Hilda and Shelagh were about to leave, Elaine, Mr and Mrs Tate's daughter came rushing into the room from work. Mrs Tate introduced her to Shelagh and explained that she would be staying while they were on holiday, and that she would be using the small bedroom.

Elaine was in her mid twenties, and was tall, slim and dressed very smartly. Her eyes danced and sparkled.

"I'll see you later," she shouted in a friendly voice to Shelagh as they left.

Later that night, Shelagh and Elaine sat chatting and drinking tea until the early hours of the morning.

She briefly told Elaine the reasons why she had left home and had nowhere to live. Elaine was horrified listening to her story. Shelagh managed to turn around the conversation and ask Elaine about herself and her job. She told Shelagh that she worked as a secretary in the city.

"I always wanted to be a secretary," sighed Shelagh, "but Miss Lewis said I didn't speak proper English, and was always clipping my words, and that I had a strong Yorkshire accent."

Elaine laughed.

"Miss Lewis would have liked you," Shelagh continued, "because she would have said you speak the Queen's English."

Elaine laughed again.

"Who's Miss Lewis," she asked, so Shelagh explained.

Elaine was fascinated hearing about Shelagh's life and those of her brother and sisters. Eventually, in the small hours of the morning they went to bed, Shelagh fell asleep wondering where she would live when Mr and Mrs Tate returned home from their holiday.

Around dinnertime the next day, Shelagh went over to Peter's house, where she found him in the back garden tinkering with his bike. Pat, Peter's sister, always visited on a Saturday and had arrived some time earlier. Hilda was telling her the story of the previous night.

"What are you going to do about your clothes?" Pat asked Shelagh.

"I'll have to buy some more," Shelagh answered, shrugging her shoulders, "I can't go back there."

"Yes you can," Pat replied encouragingly, "because I'll go with you."

Shelagh's face went white with fear at the thought of facing Mrs Morton.

"I won't be a minute," said Pat. "You go and get your coat while I go to the 'phone box at the end of the street and 'phone for a taxi. I'll be back in a minute and we'll both go together," she called, with a determined look on her face.

"Don't look so worried," Hilda assured, looking at Shelagh's worried face. "You'll come to no harm if our Pat's with you."

Soon they were on their way back to Mrs Morton's, and when they arrived, Pat asked the driver to wait, explaining that Shelagh would not be long as she had left home and was returning to collect her clothes and belongings. The driver just smiled and got out of the taxi, opening the boot ready to be filled. Then he lit up a cigarette, crossed his legs and leant against the car. Pat stood beside Shelagh as she knocked timidly at the door. After a few moments, Mrs Morton opened it, a look of fury on her face.

"What do you want?" she shouted, staring at Shelagh.

"I've come for my things," Shelagh stammered nervously.

"And who are you?" Mrs Morton asked Pat. "I'm Peter's sister," Pat answered defiantly, "and I've come to help her."

Grabbing Shelagh by the shoulders and pulling her through the door, Mrs Morton shouted,

"you can come in; you've got ten minutes to get your things out."

Then turning to Pat and slamming the door in her face, she said coldly,

"I don't know you; you're not welcome in my house."

"Nice one," called the taxi driver as he watched.

Shelagh ran as fast as her legs would carry her, stumbling up the two flights of stairs to the attic. She began to throw everything she owned into a large, grey suitcase, fearing that Mrs Morton might follow her and in such a small room, she would have no escape. Pat meanwhile was still standing in shock, gazing at the door that had been slammed in her face. She looked across at the taxi driver with her hands on her hips. He nodded at her and pointed to the door, encouraging her to knock again. She did so, but this time opened the door and stepped inside, leaving it wide open.

"I told you, you wasn't welcome in my house," Mrs Morton shouted at Pat. "Now get out."

"I'm not leaving until Shelagh's safely out of this house and away from you," Pat replied bravely.

Mr Morton was sitting in the armchair holding his hands together and staring at the floor nervously, not daring to intervene. Pat was also a little apprehensive, fearing for Shelagh if she was left on her own. After a few trips up and down the stairs, Shelagh had collected all her belongings and thrown them into the open boot of the taxi.

"Before you leave my house you owe me some money, I want this week's board," Mrs Morton shouted again at Shelagh as they were leaving. Shelagh and Pat ignored her demand and they climbed into the back seat of the taxi.

"Good riddance to bad rubbish," Mrs Morton shouted after them. "I can soon get someone in your place. Girls like you are ten a penny."

The taxi driver was staring with his mouth wide open in utter amazement as Mrs Morton continued to hurl abuse at Shelagh.

"Well I'm shocked," he remarked, "I've never heard such an acid-tongued woman in all my life. What a horrible woman she is. You are well out of it. I don't know about good riddance to you, it's good riddance to her."

Shelagh's face was white with fear and her body was trembling. Sitting beside her, Pat wrapped both her hands around Shelagh's shaking hands as she could see that she was trembling, and visibly distressed by the whole incident. Tears began to roll slowly down Shelagh's cheeks

"Will you take us back home please?" Pat asked the taxi driver.

"Are you alright love?" the taxi driver asked in a deep Yorkshire accent, as he stretched his neck into the air to look at Shelagh through the rear view mirror.

Shelagh looked at him and nodded, her eyes now swollen with crying and feeling very embarrassed and ashamed that he had witnessed the events of the last hour.

"Cheer up lass," he continued, "at least you don't ever have to face that dreadful woman again. Look out of the window," he encouraged, "even the sun has come out and is smiling down on you. So come on cheer up and give us a smile."

Periodically, he kept on looking at Shelagh through the mirror, and then began to sing, his shoulders rocking from side to side.

"Smile though your heart is aching,
Smile even though it's breaking.
When there's a cloud in the sky, you'll get by,
If you smile through your tears and sorrow,
Smile and maybe tomorrow,
You'll see the sun come shining through for you."

Pat then joined in the singing.

"Light up your face with gladness,
Hide every trace of sadness,
Although a tear may be ever so near,
If you smile, you must keep on trying,
Smile what's the use of crying,
You'll find that life is still worthwhile,
If you just smile."

"We're going home," Pat said again, leaning forward and staring into Shelagh's face.

"Home," thought Shelagh. A ring of warmth, comfort and happiness seemed to circle around the word 'home.' "Home," she thought again. "Yes, that sounds nice." Gradually the fear that had engulfed her body little by little began to disappear slowly to be replaced by thoughts of hope and happiness.

In the next few weeks, Shelagh and Elaine got to know each other very well. Elaine told Shelagh that her oldest sister was married with two young children and that her older brother had married only a few months ago and now lived in Hull. Elaine was a bright, bubbly and friendly girl, full of life, and was always singing and laughing. She reminded Shelagh of her younger sister, who was of the similar character. She felt very relaxed and comfortable in Elaine's company, to the point of telling her about her life in care and the reasons why she had walked out of her foster home. No longer did she feel afraid or embarrassed.

Two weeks later, when Mr and Mrs Tate arrived home from their holiday, they told Shelagh that she was welcome to stay as long as she wanted. They included her in the general running of the house to the point of even asking her what she would like for dinner. She became like one of the family.

Mrs Tate taught her to cook, bake and even decorate. No longer did she fear going home. She even got a lift to and from work on the back of Peter's Lambretta scooter. Life was better than it had ever been for years. She would always be forever grateful to Mr and Mrs Tate.

One day, as Peter was riding home from work with Shelagh, sat pillion behind him, he suddenly took a different route and ended up in the small yard at the front of Corpus Christi Church.

"What are we doing here?" Shelagh asked, frowning and looking puzzled.

Peter took her by the hand and led her to a low wall, beckoning her to sit down.

"A few days ago, I made an appointment for us to see Father Brannigan," he informed her.

Shelagh's face beamed from ear to ear.

"I didn't tell you because I wanted it to be a surprise," he said carefully. "When do you want us to get married? We need to know before we go inside."

Shelagh slid from the wall and began to jump up and down with excitement.

"Well Mary got married last month!" she said excitedly, "and she said if you get married in the month of April or October, you get a big tax rebate. It's too soon for April so why don't we go for next October? Then it will give us a year to save for a house, some furniture and for our wedding."

"OK," Peter answered, grinning like a Cheshire cat.

Father Brannigan asked them in and showed them to a small waiting room where he invited them to sit around a polished table in the middle of the room.

After a long chat, they decided that the twelve of October sounded a good day.

"Seeing as you are not a good Catholic girl," said Father Brannigan to Shelagh, "you will need to come and see me for two hours a week for six weeks so I can explain to you all you need to know about the Catholic Faith. You will also need permission from your parents to get married as you will still be under twenty one years old."

He handed her a consent form.

"I don't know where they are," Shelagh explained, looking worried. "I was brought up in a children's home." That was something she hadn't thought about.

"If you cannot get parental consent," Father Brannigan told her, "then you will have to get permission from the Courts in Leeds. Either way you must get written consent, as the law of the land requires that you do so."

"If you have to go to court, I'll go with you," Peter assured her as they left the church.

"I don't fancy going to court. I have another idea. I'll try that first," Shelagh answered, not saying any more than that.

As soon as it was possible, Shelagh visited her aunt and uncle in Beeston. When she arrived, her aunt was hanging out washing.

"Is uncle Harry in?" Shelagh asked, as she unlocked the gate and stepped into the back yard.

"I think he's in the front room," her aunt replied.

Shelagh ran up the steep steps, through the kitchen and into the front room.

Her uncle was kneeling on the floor, surrounded by sheet music that he had taken out of the piano stool under the piano.

"Hello," he said, pleasantly surprised to see her, "I'm just having a tidy."

"I've come to ask you two things," Shelagh said.

"My, that sound serious," he replied, standing up and sitting on the arm of one of the easy armchairs.

"Me and Peter have set a date to get married next year," she said proudly, "will you give me away please?"

Uncle Harry covered his face with his hands, then peeped at her through his open fingers and smiled.

"I would be delighted," he cried, standing up and giving her a hug. "Wait till I tell Ethel," his eyes sparkled.

"There is one more thing," Shelagh said quietly. "I need permission from a parent, because I'll still be under twenty one, or I'll have to go to Court, and I don't really want to do that. So if you have my mother's address will you give it to me please? It's really important."

Her uncle stood for a moment, staring at her and not saying a word. Then he rubbed his chin in his hands.

"Please, please," Shelagh pleaded, "all I want her to do is sign a piece of paper. Please, she begged, looking into his eyes.

"Well," he sighed at last, "I'm not sure that it's a good idea that you see her. I don't want you getting upset."

"Please," Shelagh begged again with increasing desperation.

"Well," he sighed again. "I suppose one day it had to happen, and it is for a very special occasion." He hesitated for a moment. "Alright," he said with a look of concern on his face, not sure that what he was doing was the right thing, "I'll give it to you later."

As Shelagh returned home, she kept gazing at the piece of paper her uncle had given her, wondering why he had not given her, her mother's address before. She had asked him many, many times over the years, so much so that she had finally stopped asking him. All the time her uncle had known where her mother lived. "Why wouldn't he tell her?" Shelagh thought, feeling puzzled. He must have had his reasons. Could it be that her uncle had not wanted her to get upset by seeing her mother after all these years, or even worse, could it be that her mother really did not want to see her at all, and he knew this? "I'll soon find out," Shelagh thought. She decided that she would wait for the right time to visit her mother and not to tell anyone, least of all Peter. Shelagh was not certain what kind of reception she would receive when she met her mother after so many years, so to save any embarrassment on both sides, she decided that it would be best to visit her on her own and keep it a secret.

Chapter 56

One evening, a few weeks later, Mrs Tate and Shelagh were sitting at the kitchen table having their evening meal. Mr Tate was working a late shift and Elaine, their daughter, had gone out to tea.

"Aren't you very well?" Mrs Tate asked Shelagh, "you've picked and picked at your meal and you've hardly said a word, and it's not like you. Is there something wrong?"

"Well, I wasn't going to tell anybody," replied Shelagh, "I've decided to go and see my mother tonight. I need her to sign a consent form so that I can get married next year."

"Is Peter going with you?" Mrs Tate asked, looking concerned.

"No," Shelagh answered, "he's going with his dad to watch Leeds United at Elland Road. I haven't told him, on purpose. I've been waiting for the right time and tonight is a good opportunity."

"Would you like me to come with you?" Mrs Tate asked, looking a little worried and concerned.

"No not really," said Shelagh gratefully, "I don't know how she will react when she sees me after all these years. This is something I have to do on my own. But thank you."

"Be careful in the dark and good luck to you," said Mrs Tate a little later. "I'll be thinking of you and waiting for you when you get back home."

Early one cold, November night, Shelagh took a bus to the city centre. As she was getting off the bus, she asked the driver the number and where she could get a bus to the address she showed him.

He pointed to a bus only yards away, so Shelagh ran and caught the bus just as it was about to leave, asking the driver if he would give her a shout when she got to the bus stop nearest to the address she had been given. The bus travelled along roads and streets that she had never been on before and, just as she thought the driver had forgotten her, he turned around and gave her a shout. When she got off the bus, she looked around in all directions, not knowing which way to turn. She began to meander through the narrow streets looking for that all-important name high on a wall, lit up by the streetlights. An elderly man came walking towards her, walking his dog on a leash.

"Could you please tell me where this street is?" she asked him.

He pointed her in the right direction, so thanking him; Shelagh followed the route he had indicated. Suddenly, after all these years, she was standing in front of her mother's house. She stood still for a moment, reflecting. What would her mother look like? Shelagh had only briefly seen her once in fifteen years. Then plucking up courage, she walked down the short path towards the door. She hesitated for a moment with her clenched fist raised ready to knock at the door. Feeling extremely nervous, Shelagh gently knocked at the door and then stepped back. After a few moments, she knocked at the door again, this time a little harder. She could see a light behind the closed curtains. Suddenly Shelagh noticed a shadow of someone coming towards the door. With knots in her stomach and her heart beating, she heard a key being turned on the other side of the door. Then her mother appeared standing in the doorway.

Shelagh would have recognised her anywhere. Her heart melted and she wanted to cry. She held her hand to her mouth, trying to contain her feelings. She felt extremely shocked that her own mother did not recognise her.

"Can I help you?" her mother asked, holding on to the side of the door and looking into Shelagh's face.

"I'm Shelagh, your oldest daughter," Shelagh said, in a trembling voice. "I've come to ask you to sign a consent form for me so I can get married."

Alice leaned forward and looked up and down the street to see if anyone was about, then invited her inside, pointing to a wooden chair at the far side of a table in the middle of the room. As Alice made her a cup of tea and buttered her a slice of oven bottom cake, Shelagh could feel the tension between them. She gave her mother the form and a pen, which would give the consent she wanted so desperately. Alice's hand was trembling as she slowly signed the form.

"The three girls are in bed and Robert's out chumping," her mother said. "If he comes in, please don't tell him who you are."

Shelagh estimated that her brother Robert would be around fourteen years old. As it was the night before Bonfire Night, she could imagine him 'chumping', collecting wood for the fire. Her mother never once enquired about the welfare of Tony, Pat or Joyce, leading Shelagh to wonder if she was too embarrassed or too ashamed to ask about them. Instead, she began to tell her mother all about her sisters and brother, and of her own plans to get married the following year. Shelagh felt that her mother was uneasy and very uncomfortable in her presence. She seemed even more nervous at the thought of Robert, or one of the girls, appearing and whether Shelagh would reveal her identity to them. It was quite clear that Alice was not going to talk about the past. Perhaps she did not want to remember her former life. Shelagh thought it was best to leave, as she had achieved her main objective.

"I'll walk you to the bus stop," her mother said, putting on her coat and wrapping a scarf around her head, fastening it under her chin.

Standing at the bus stop, with the streetlights shining down on them, estranged mother and daughter were lost for words. The lights of the bus could be seen in the distance approaching them.

"Goodbye," Shelagh said, as she boarded the bus. Her mother's eyes filled with tears.

Through the misty window, Shelagh could see that the tears continued to stream down her mother's face as she waved, watching the bus drive away until it was out of sight.

On her journey home, Shelagh could not make any sense of her feelings. Mixed up emotions and thoughts were exploding inside her head. She especially felt a deep hurt inside her body, knowing her mother still didn't, or want to acknowledge that she, her sisters or her brother existed. Shelagh had secretly hoped that her mother might want to meet them all after such a long time. It seemed that she still did not want to know them. A lifetime of rejection is sometimes too hard to bear.

When Shelagh arrived home, Mr and Mrs Tate were waiting anxiously for her. Shelagh hung her coat on a wall at the bottom of the stairs and joined them in the living room.

"Come and sit down and get yourself warm lass," said Mr Tate invitingly, "It's a cold night out there."

His wife hurried into the kitchen, appearing a few moments later with a mug of steaming hot cocoa.

"Here get that down you and tell us all about your meeting with your mother," Mrs Tate said eagerly.

Shelagh spent the next hour or so telling them all about her mother, and how hurt she felt, knowing that her mother still refused to accept that they existed, even to the point of asking her not to tell her own brother who she really was.

As gentle as ever, Mrs Tate put her arm around her shoulder.

"This may be something you might have to accept, even though you don't understand why," she said wisely. "For your mother, who was pregnant, to put her four young children into a home and leave you there, and then to go and give birth to a son who doesn't even know of the existence of his other sisters and brother to this day, well words fail me. There must have been a reason why, all those years ago," she said in a soft voice.

"The fact remains," remarked Shelagh, sounding angry and hurt, "she did abandon us and leave us. Not a birthday card or even a Christmas card to any one of us. She will never know how hard it's been for us living a life in care, feeling unwanted and unloved."

"Yes you're right," agreed Mrs Tate, "and you have every reason to be angry and hurt. But by the same token, you will never know how she felt having to do what she did. I'm not trying to make excuses for her," she added hastily, taking hold of both Shelagh's hands.

"Your mother must have thought that what she did all those years ago was in your best interest. What I don't understand, for the life of me as a parent, is why she, or anyone else, never came to see you. It's as though 'out of sight out of mind', and while ever she doesn't have to talk about it, it doesn't exist. My advice to you is to stop trying to make sense of it all. One day, however long it takes, those children are bound to find out about you all."

"I hope so," sighed Shelagh, "I sincerely hope so."

"And when that happens," Mrs. Tate continued, "Your mother will have to confront those dark, deep, hidden secrets, she holds inside her. Until then, stop trying to get to the bottom of something you may never understand, or you'll make yourself ill. Now you must concentrate on organising your own wedding and looking for a house of your own."

"Mrs Tate was right," thought Shelagh, as she lay in bed later that night. One day she sincerely hoped that, however long it took; she would meet her brother and her three half sisters.

One day.

Chapter 57

One Saturday, several weeks later, Shelagh set off to visit Joyce at Keldholme
Children's Home in Headingley. She had decided not to mention to Pat and
Joyce, of her visit to their mother. They had never seemed interested enough
to ask about her in the past. Along with the usual sweets and comics for her
younger sisters, Shelagh was taking a present for Joyce's fifteenth birthday.
Firstly, she called for Pat, and as they walked together through the cobbled back
streets and ginnels, Pat told her that she was still enjoying her work at Reynolds
and Bransons. Soon they had reached Woodhouse Ridge, descending the small
stream towards Keldholme. Joyce, as usual was waiting for them, hoping for
a birthday present from both her sisters. After sharing out the sweets, Joyce
opened her presents, a white lace suspender belt and a pair of nylon stockings
from Shelagh, and a second pair of nylons from Pat. Joyce was ecstatic, as it
was her first pair of suspenders and stockings.

"I've left Mrs Morton's," Shelagh told Pat and Joyce.

"And not before time," Joyce exclaimed. "I don't know why you've waited
all this time. I don't how you've stuck it. I tell you what," Joyce said, with an air
of confidence in her voice. "Soon I'll have to find a job, and I'll have to be found
a foster home when I leave here at Christmas in a few months time, and if I've
to live with anyone like her, I'll run away again."

Shelagh and Pat looked at each other, laughing at the indignant expression
on Joyce's face.

Joyce did leave school in the December of nineteen sixty-two, and spent her last Christmas in Keldholme Children's Home.

In the following January, she was found a foster home with a Mrs Moss, who lived in the Middleton area of Leeds, in a three bed roomed flat.

Mrs Moss was a pensioner who had applied to the Children's Care Office in Woodhouse Lane, to foster a working girl. She wrote on her application form that she was keen to give a home to a needy girl, and eager to have company since the death of her husband a few months previously. She thought a young teenager would bring some life and laughter into her home; someone else to look after would help her to come to terms with her grief. Mrs Moss added that it would also help financially, as her state pension of two pounds, seventeen and sixpence, did not go very far.

Joyce was offered employment as a full time packer with a company called, Central Agencies, in the centre of Leeds, earning three pounds, seventeen shillings and sixpence per week.

From her wage, she would be required to pay Mrs Moss two pounds, ten shillings boarding out allowance. Her weekly pocket money would be ten shillings, which included a weekly bus fare allowance.

The rest would be put back into her wage packet and given to Miss Fowler, her Care Officer, at Head Office, who would put aside twelve shillings and sixpence for her clothing allowance, and any surplus money would be saved for her.

Every three months, a full clothing allowance would be sent direct to Mrs Moss to buy Joyce any clothing that she might need.

One cold, Saturday morning in January, Miss Fowler went to collect Joyce on the day of her discharge from the Children's Home. It began to snow as Joyce watched nervously through the window for her to arrive. Inside a suitcase next to Joyce, were all her clothes and her worldly possessions. Her stomach was churning at the thought of leaving all her friends in the home and entering a world that she knew little about. Joyce had spent nearly all her life in children's homes, apart from the few months that she had lived with Shelagh at the Morton's, which had been a complete disaster. That unfortunate chapter in her life was almost four years ago.

Now at fifteen years old, Joyce was expected to work and make her own way in life.

It was snowing heavily by the time Miss Fowler arrived at Keldholme. She pushed open the gate and hurried down the garden path and into the home. Her nose was red and she was rubbing her cold hands together. Mrs Hall, the Matron, offered to make her a hot cup of cocoa before Joyce began her next journey. The rest of the children were taking advantage of the thick carpet of snow that lay on the top of the front garden, encouraging Joyce to build a snowman with them before she left. In no time at all a good-sized snowman appeared. The younger children made eyes from small sprouts, using a long thin carrot for a nose and small stones shaped to make a mouth. One of the younger boys ran inside the house and returned with a red party hat. Joyce lifted him up to put the hat on top of the snowman's head. Christine, one of Joyce's friends took a multicoloured striped scarf from around her neck and wrapped it around the snowman. Then an organised snowball fight began, boys against the girls.

Miss Fowler, her hands firmly wrapped around a mug of hot cocoa, stood beside Mrs Hall. As they watched the children through the bay window, both women smiled at their loud, raucous laughter.

Eventually Joyce, wearing a very sad expression, trailed behind Miss Fowler down the garden path, dragging her feet and suitcase through the snow, leaving tracks behind her. With her case safely in the boot, a dejected look on her face, she sat down on the front seat, next to Miss Fowler.

"Don't forget to come back and see us will you," shouted one of the older boys, throwing a snowball at the car.

"I won't," Joyce called back, as they drove away and headed towards her new foster home.

Joyce was understandably apprehensive and nervous as Miss Fowler drove to Middleton, a suburb in the south of Leeds. When they arrived, Mrs Moss was waiting for them, eager to meet Joyce. She showed Joyce to her bedroom, leaving her to unpack her case while she went back to have a chat, and finalise some paperwork with Miss Fowler. Sometime later, as Miss Fowler was about to leave, Joyce came back into the room grinning like a Cheshire cat.

"I've got a bedroom all of my own," Joyce said proudly, "and there's a wireless in my room." There was excitement in her voice, and a pleased look on her face.

Satisfied with everything, Miss Fowler smiled and left the two to get acquainted, saying that she would be back in a month's time to check on Joyce's progress, and that if there were any problems not to hesitate, but ring her immediately.

A month later, on her first visit, Mrs Moss met Miss Fowler at the door.

"You have brought a breath of fresh air into my home," she cried, "I haven't laughed as much in years. Joyce is a Godsend." Inviting Miss Fowler into the living room, she continued, "I'm loving every minute of taking care of her," beaming from ear to ear. Joyce appeared from the kitchen carrying a tray of china cups and saucers, a large matching teapot full of freshly made tea, and a plate covered with fairy cakes and jam tarts that she had made herself. She handed Miss Fowler a cup of tea and offered her a cake or a jam tart. It was obvious to her that Joyce had settled in very quickly. She looked so happy and content.

"Mrs Moss lets me bake at the weekends, and next time you come, I'll make you a cake," Joyce promised. "I visited Miss Ratcliffe last week and took her a home-made Victoria sandwich sponge cake. She loved it."

Nothing or anyone would ever stop Joyce from visiting her beloved Miss Ratcliffe. Miss Fowler left knowing that Joyce was happy and settled, and that Mrs Moss seemed to be a changed, happier woman.

Every month Maureen, a young woman from the Prudential Insurance Company, called at Mrs Moss' house for her monthly payment. Maureen commented on the loud music coming from one of the bedrooms.

"It's like that every night," remarked Mrs Moss, covering her ears with both hands.

"Every night after tea, Joyce takes herself into her bedroom and plays Radio Luxemburg on the wireless. I'm sure she has the volume on full blast. It's driving me mad. She never goes out during the week."

"Sounds to me that she's bored," commented Maureen, "she needs something to do on an evening to occupy her mind."

"She's come to live with me straight from living in a children's home," replied Mrs Moss, "so she doesn't have any friends and I don't know what to say without upsetting her," Mrs Moss held her hands in the air and sighed deeply.

"Perhaps I can help," said Maureen, "I've got an idea. Why don't you ask her to come and join us and I'll have a talk to her. I've got a suggestion to make to her."

"Anything's got to be better than that noise every night," remarked Mrs Moss, "I'll go and get her."

Joyce entered the room slowly behind Mrs Moss, and looked at Maureen curiously and apprehensively.

"I belong to a youth club just down the road at the local Baptist Church," Maureen said cheerfully. "There are a lot of youngsters around your age, and we have loads of fun. Why don't you join?" she asked, "what do you think?" Joyce shrugged her shoulders.

"Don't know anyone," she muttered, hanging her head and holding both her hands together in front of her.

"I'll call for you one night," persisted Maureen, "and I'll introduce you to all my friends. It's not good for a young girl like you not to have any friends. You need to mix more. It'll do you good and get you out of the house. I promise you will love it. What do you think?"

Joyce shrugged her shoulders again and ran back towards her bedroom. Mrs Moss was sitting in an armchair, nodding and agreeing with every word, and before Maureen left, she arranged for her to call for Joyce a few nights later.

True to her word, Maureen retuned and took Joyce down to the local Baptist Church Youth Club, introducing her to the leaders and then all of her friends, who were all around the same age as Joyce.

It did not take long for Joyce to make friends, as during the many years that she had spent in children's homes, she had mixed with children of all ages and backgrounds.

In the next few weeks, Joyce fitted in so well she planned to join the Church and become a Sunday School Teacher.

321

Within weeks of going to the Youth Club, she met a young seventeen-year-old boy named Terry Kelly. He was of medium height and frame, with blond hair. Behind his 'Buddy Holly' glasses, were soft, friendly, blue eyes. He always dressed immaculately, wearing crisp neatly ironed cotton shirts, and smartly pressed trousers. He had been a member of the Youth Club for a number of years, a born organiser, always holding the welfare of others close to his heart. Terry immediately took Joyce under his wing. She never left his side, so much so that they began to go out with each other. Alongside Terry, Joyce sparkled and began to take on an active role in the Youth Club. Joyce now spent most of her evenings with Terry, and although Mrs Moss had encouraged Joyce to join, she was not very happy at the thought of her having a boyfriend, and that at fifteen years of age, she was far too young to be seriously involved with a young man who, in her opinion, was filling Joyce's head with religious nonsense. She even complained to Miss Fowler, who stated that she was not unduly concerned, and thought that no harm would come to Joyce under the roof of a church.

Joyce, being Joyce, always listened but never took any notice. She thought the world of Terry, and he, in turn, thought a lot about her.

Agreement of Foster Parent

1. I _Mrs._ _____ of _____
   Leeds 10.

   do hereby agree with the Council of the County Borough of Leeds that

   (a) I will receive _Joyce Gregson_ _____ into my home, feed, clothe
       and look after her and bring her up as carefully and kindly as I would a child of my
       own.

   (b) I will help her to become a good citizen, send her to school - work - and to Church -
       Chapel, and arrange for recreation suited to her age.

   (c) I will look after her health and consult the doctor whenever the child is ill, and
       in the event of her serious illness or accident, I will also notify the Council
       immediately.

   (d) I will provide for the cleaning, mending and renewal of her clothing and its proper
       care.

   (e) I will at all times permit any person authorised by the Home Office or by the Council
       to see the child and her home and clothing, and I will attend to the advice of any
       such person.

   (f) I will allow her to be removed from my home when required by any person so authorised

   (g) I will notify the Council within two weeks if I change my address.

2. I make this agreement with the Council in consideration of my receiving the sum of
   _£2 - 10/-_ per week for maintenance, plus _10/-_ per week for pocket
   money, and clothing allowance at the rate of _12/6_ per week paid quarterly.

3. I acknowledge having received _Joyce Gregson_ _____ into my home
   on the _26.1.63_ and agree that she brought with her the following articles
   of clothing and personal possessions:-

Clothing	Number Bought	Brought	Clothing	Number Bought	Brought
Coat	1	1	Suspender Belt	1	1
Hat			Brassiere	2	2
Raincoat			Stockings/Socks	3	3
Blazer			Handkerchiefs		
Shoes	2		Overall/Pinafore		1
Slippers		1	Gloves		1
Wellington Boots	1		Scarf		
Dress	1	2	Brush and comb		1
Skirt	2	1	Toothbrush		1
Gym Slip			Suitcase	1	
Blouse & Tee Shirt		3	Sandals		
Jersey	1		Cardigan	2	2
Pyjamas/nightdress	1	2	Vest	2	
Underskirt or Set	3	3	Knickers	2	3

Doctor's Card ✓   Personal Savings ✓ 15/- + 17/6 in p.w

Signature of foster parent _____
Address _____   _Leeds 10_ _____

Witness _PWest_
Address _229 Woodhouse Lane   Leeds 2_
Date _26.1.63._

Chapter 58

One day, several months later, as Peter and Shelagh were travelling to work; Shelagh noticed a house for sale. The house, a semi-detached, not too far away from where Peter's mother and father lived, was all they could have wished for. At one side of the long back garden stood a plum tree, while on the other side a rhubarb patch, a blackberry bush and gooseberry bush. In the centre of the lawn stood a pear tree. Shelagh and Peter offered the full asking price, which was accepted, and began to decorate the rooms inside the house. In the next few weeks, they began to plan their wedding

Pat continued to be happy in her work and contented at the Woods. Of the three sisters, Pat had been fortunate enough to be fostered into a secure, happy family, and had lived with them for almost five years. She had been immediately accepted and loved as one of the family, from 'day one'.

Tony and Shelagh continued to write regularly to each other. Her brother was now stationed with the army in Germany.

Joyce's romance with Terry blossomed more than ever.

Late one Saturday morning, the three sisters met at the front of Marks and Spencer in the centre of Leeds. They bought something to eat at the snack bar in the basement of the store and then sat at one of the empty tables.

"Do you remember when we used to get all the sandwiches and cakes that were left over on a Saturday night and pick them up at the back entrance?" Shelagh remarked, unwrapping a cheese and lettuce sandwich.

"I remember that's all we had to eat for tea for the next few days until every one had been eaten," answered Pat, taking a bite out of a ham salad sandwich.

"Well, I got sick of eating sandwiches, so that's why I've got this," said Joyce, biting into a thick cream cake causing the cream to squelch onto her cheeks. Shelagh and Pat both laughed as they saw her cheeks covered in cream. Joyce was the one with a sweet tooth, and was the joker among the three girls. They sat at the table for hours, occasionally replenishing their drinks and talking of the past, present and future.

Shelagh gave Pat and Joyce instructions of how to get to the church where she and Peter were to be married in a few weeks time. She also informed them that Tony had been given special leave for her wedding and that he would meet them at the church. Joyce talked non-stop of Terry, the love of her life, and of her involvement with the Baptist Church.

"And I've got something to tell you," said Pat, sheepishly.

Shelagh and Joyce looked at each other wondering what it could be.

"I've met someone," Pat said shyly. His name's David and he's eighteen years old, a year and a half older than me. I've been going out with him for a few weeks. I met him at the Methodist Youth Club. He works in the printing industry, the same as you," she said, turning her head and looking at Shelagh.

"Well, that's a coincidence," remarked Joyce, "I met Terry in a youth club. Have you met his mother yet?" she added, raising her eyebrows.

"Yes I have," Pat replied, "Why?"

"Well I hope she didn't say to you, what Terry's mother said to me," remarked Joyce in a concerned voice. "The first thing she said to me was, so you're Joyce! You're the young girl that Terry's started to go out with. He said he felt sorry for you because you'd been brought up in children's homes."

Shelagh and Pat laughed at the expressions on Joyce's face as she spoke, then she too, joined in the merriment. Their laughter was so loud that other customers in the snack bar began to stare at them.

"We've been sitting here hours," Shelagh remarked. "We'd better leave. It's time we were making our way home."

The sisters climbed the stairs and said their goodbyes at the entrance of the store. Shelagh watched as Pat and Joyce separated and made their different ways home, their heads bobbing up and down in the crowds of shoppers. Just before they were out of sight, they turned around, held their arms high in the air and waved to her. She always watched and waited, and then waved back. There had been too much waving over the years for her liking. She kept an eye on them until they were out of sight. She would have loved them to stay with her the night before her wedding, but that was for normal families, and they did not have a normal family background. Never mind. The most important thing was that, despite everything, they had all remained very close to each other, and that was something of which she was very proud.

Chapter 59

It was a long, long time ago since I was separated from my brother and sisters at the Children's Home in Street Lane. I can remember Miss Baker, my Care Officer, taking me by the hand and telling me that she was taking me to Rothwell Children's Home for Girls. We should not have been separated. I was four years old at the time, and as the eldest, I was supposed to be the one who would look after the family and keep us together. That was the day all those years ago, when Tony, Pat and I had been playing together in the playroom with lots of other children, and having the time of our lives with all the toys that were available for us to play with. Joyce, who was only nine months old, had been sitting in her pram, vigorously rocking backwards and forwards and occasionally throwing her toys over the side and onto the floor. I remember the tears rolling slowly down my cheeks as I had reluctantly waved goodbye to them, not knowing how long it would be before I saw them again. Looking back, they must have wondered why I was being taken away from them. With puzzled looks on their faces, they had waved half-heartedly back at me. My eyes still fill with tears and I can still see a blurred vision of their hands in the distance as I was led away. So much has happened to us since that day.

It was like looking down a long tunnel once again, watching the little hands of my brother and sisters waving goodbye. As I blinked away the tears that blurred my vision, I realised the hands had become one large hand, moving up and down in front of my eyes. Startled, I moved back as the fingers of the hand brushed away the tears on my wet cheeks. Someone shaking my shoulders brought my reverie back to the reality of my wedding day. This event would mark the ending of the first chapter of my life. Now, with Peter, I faced a new one, one that was to bring me more contentment and joy than I had ever thought possible.

It was Peter, my brand new husband, who was standing by my side, bending forwards and looking concerned into my eyes. The tears that had been running down my face were no longer tears of sadness, but tears of joy. This was my wedding day, the best day of my life.

"My, you were miles away," he whispered. "Everybody's waiting for you to make a speech."

He took me by the elbow and helped me to my feet. It took me a few moments to get my thoughts back together. I didn't know where to begin. I had so many people to say thank you to. Nervously, with all eyes upon me, I thanked, firstly, my uncle Harry for giving me away. Then I expressed my gratitude to Peter's mother and father for paying for our wedding reception, and for caring about me and making me one of their family. A special thanks was given to Mr and Mrs Tate and Elaine, who had taken me into their home when I had nowhere to go and made me feel that I mattered. I could feel my face blushing with embarrassment, and hear my heart pounding, as everyone looked and listened to me.

"Thank you to everybody for coming and all the wonderful wedding presents," I concluded nervously.

Turning quickly to Peter, I wrapped my hand around his that were holding onto a large sharp knife, and together cut deeply into the bottom tier of our wedding cake then quickly sat down again.

"Would you like me and my mother to cut the cake and pass it around?" Pat, my new sister-in-law, offered, leaning forwards and whispering down the table towards me.

"Yes please," I whispered back, gratefully.

As the plates containing the small pieces of wedding cake were being handed around the tables, I propped my elbows comfortably on top of the table and held my face between my hands.

I began to look around at my many friends, and my new extended family, that were busily eating and enjoying themselves.

My eyes wandered around the church hall, catching sight of Tony, Pat and Joyce. Tony and Pat were doubled up with laughter, as whatever Joyce was saying to them must have been highly amusing. I smiled to myself. Joyce was definitely the comedienne of the family. My heart skipped a beat. I was so proud of them. It had been a long, bumpy road. There had been many days of darkness since the day that we had been abandoned and taken into care.

"You're doing it again," Peter said, as his eyes followed my gaze to where I was staring once again at my brother and sisters.

"You're miles away again," Peter continued. "Where are you? What are you thinking?"

"I was just thinking," I answered, still staring at them.

"So much has happened to us since the day we were all left in Street Lane Children's Home and put into care. We've come through alright haven't we?"

"You certainly have," he answered, putting his arm around my shoulder and giving me a squeeze.

"There is so much to tell," I whispered, still staring at them.

"One day I will write a book and tell everyone our story."

"And one day, God willing, I hope my brother and sisters will be as happy as I am."

The End

Pat, Peter, Shelagh, Tony and Joyce
12 October 1963

Epilogue

Shelagh and Peter have been very happily married for nearly forty-three years. They are the very proud parents of their son Darren and daughter Adele and a very special daughter-in-law Christine.

Joyce did marry Terry, 'the love of her life'. They too have been very happily married for almost forty years. They are also the very proud parents of their son Neil, daughter Angela and son-in-law Robert. They are devoted grandparents to their grandson Alex and granddaughter Isabelle.

Pat did marry David. They have a son Ian and a daughter Tina. Pat is very proud of them both. Pat and David divorced after twenty-three years of marriage. Pat is now happily married to Mel and has lived in Eastbourne for nearly fifteen years. She is the proud grandmother of two grandsons Conner and Jack. Tina, Ian, her daughter-in-law Jan and her grandchildren, live not too far away.

During the nine years that Tony was in the army, he regularly visited Peter and Shelagh whenever he was on leave. Married in his twenties, he took his wife and two small sons Jason and Neil to live and work in Johannesburg, South Africa. Gradually he and Shelagh lost touch with each other.

Shelagh Flynn

Many years later when legislation allowed all children, that had been 'in care' to obtain access to any documentation about them, Pat wrote to Leeds City Council's, Social Services Department, asking if there were any documents written about her.

A Social Worker, Sharon McCormack, was given Pat's case. After tracing our notes, Sharon wrote to Pat stating that she would need the consent of both her sisters, as their names were incorporated in her file. Joyce and I wrote a letter of consent to the appropriate department and a date and time was made for all three of us to meet Sharon at her office.

A few days before our appointment, Sharon 'phoned asking if she could see all three of us a day earlier. We were all a little puzzled as to why she wanted to see us, and when she duly arrived at my house voiced her concerns to us.

"Did we realise that what we were about to read could affect us emotionally and mentally?" she asked, "and did we realise we could be opening a can of worms?"

Sharon, a kind and very caring young woman, informed us that our notes dated back to nineteen forty seven, and that there were letters, notes, documents and a monthly account on our progress written right up to the time of our passing out of care when we had reached eighteen years of age. She was very concerned and continued to stress that reading our notes would take us back to the day when we had been abandoned and left in a children's home. Sharon asked whether we really wanted to go back to a place that held such traumatic memories for us.

Not realising just what she meant, all three of us, nevertheless, met her the following day at her office, each with an open mind.

Our individual files had been placed each on top of a small work surface, so we each sat on a high buffet and began to read our respective files. Sharon made us large mugs of tea and then sat in the corner of the room, on hand in case we needed to ask any questions. She continued to show concern about how we were responding to the classified information that we were reading. After reading a few pages, Joyce began to sigh quietly, holding her chin in her hand and shaking her head. A few more pages later, she began to cry and could not read anymore. Sharon ran quickly to comfort her in her distress. Joyce left the building, not having read her notes, with a banging headache and the keys to

332

my house. Pat and I continued to read the files, and I too, at various stages of reading, became increasingly upset.

"Do you know," I remarked to Sharon, "I always said whenever I was telling my children, nieces and nephews stories about when we were in the orphanage, that one day I would write a book."

"Yes you should," replied Sharon, "all the social workers here have read all your files over and over again, and several have suggested that someone should just do that, write a book. It needs to be told how things were in the nineteen forties and onwards, and," she paused for a moment, "it's called social history, and you'll be surprised how big an interest it will be to hundreds of readers, especially those who have been in care."

We were not allowed to take our original files home, as they have to be kept in the archives for a hundred years before they can be destroyed. However, we were allowed to have copies of every page including documents, headed forms and letters. Sharon promised each of us an individual copy of the files.

In the next few days, when Pat had signed and received hers, she read them again and again before leaving them with me, giving her consent for me to use them.

A few weeks later, Joyce and I went down to Sharon's office, where we each signed and received our files.

"Write that book," Sharon encouraged me, as we left her office.

We took our files back to our respective homes, read, and re-read and re-lived our strange but true childhoods. Later, Joyce gave me her files and consent to use them.

For weeks, I read and re-read our notes, and somewhere in the background, I could hear Sharon's voice saying,

"Write that book."

So, one day, I sat at the dinning room table, surrounded by paper, pencils, rubbers and paper clips, and of course, the three large thick documented files of our life, dating back to nineteen forty seven, and began to write.

As I started to write our story, I began to wonder how Tony was, and where in the world he and his family might be. Consequently, I wrote to the Salvation Army in London, sending a photograph that had been taken of him in the army many years ago, and asked if it would be possible to trace him. I had not seen him in thirty-two years.

On the day of my sixtieth birthday, as I was sitting writing another chapter of our story, I received a telephone call from a Major in the Salvation Army in London informing me that they had traced Tony to a small remote village on the northern west coast of South Africa. I immediately rang and spoke to him. It was so wonderful to hear his voice after so long. He told me that he and his first wife had divorced many years ago, and that she had returned to England with their two sons. He also said that after the divorce, he travelled around, taking work when and where he was able.

In time, he met and married Jane, a very attractive South African woman and together they have a beautiful teenage daughter, Samantha. Tony invited us to stay with him if we could manage to get there, so Peter and I decided to visit him the following year. In the months before we visited, Tony sent a letter to the appropriate authorities in Leeds giving me consent to acquire his file and take it to him. Months later, with his case notes safe in my hand luggage, Peter and I set off on the long journey to see him. What a long journey that was. We travelled from Leeds to London, followed by a seven-hour wait in Heathrow airport, then the long flight from London to Cape Town. Tony, his wife Jane, his daughter Samantha, and some of Jane's family, met us at the airport.

It was a very emotional reunion. Tony then drove another eight hours to the quiet, secluded area of McDougal Bay where he lives, only yards away from the Atlantic Ocean. During the three weeks of our stay, he drove us into the nearest small village, Port Nolloth, where he works part time. Employment in the area is very low. Jane's family live in the village and Samantha attends school there. Tony's friends and work colleagues greeted us very warmly, and his boss, Grazia, invited us to tea where we were treated like royalty. Grazia said that we could not return to England without taking in the sights of Cape Town. Grazia very kindly let us stay at one of her apartments in Cape Town.

Thank you, Grazia.

While we were there, we visited several tourist attractions; Peter and I even took the ferry to Robben Island where Nelson Mandela had spent many years in jail, alongside many other political prisoners.

One day Tony hopes to visit England. He has not seen Pat or Joyce for almost forty years. Who knows, one day he might even meet the younger brother he never knew.

Robert, our brother also joined the army at a very young age and noticed the surname that he had always used was not the same one on his birth certificate. Puzzled, he asked why this was, and was eventually told that he had three older sisters and an older brother. Years later, he emigrated to Australia where he has lived for nearly thirty years.

Robert, and Alice's three daughters from her second marriage, were brought up in a normal, happy, family environment, and were unaware of Shelagh, Tony, Pat and Joyce's existence until many years later.

One day, God willing, all the sisters and brothers will meet up with each other.

Wouldn't that be something?

At the beginning of 2006, Tony booked a flight to England to be re-united with his family.

When the day finally arrived for him to set off from the small village, where he lives in South Africa, for the long journey that lay ahead of him. He was very nervous and at the same time excited at the thought of seeing his family. He had not seen or spoken to them in decades.

Jason, the eldest of his two sons, met him at Heathrow airport; he had not seen them in over 20 years.

Tony stayed with Jason at his home in Norwich, where he lives with his partner Lizzie and their two young children, Ella and Bill. He then stayed with Neil, his youngest son, who also lives in Norwich.

A re-union party was held for Tony, Joyce, Pat and I at Joyce and Terry's home. It was the first time we had all been together in 43 years.

Jason, Lizzie and their children joined us at our celebration party.

Jason met his aunties, uncles and cousins for the first time. It was truly a very emotional day.

However, there is still one small piece of our story missing. Robert, who now lives in Australia and our three younger sisters were not there.

One day all eight of us may meet, and when that day happens, there could be another book on the horizon.

Pat, Joyce, Tony and Shelagh. May 2006

During the months it took for my manuscript to be published and made into a book, a lot has happened to our family.

My nephew Neil and his lovely partner Sarah have become the proud parents of a son, Thomas William Kelly. Welcome to our family.
Sarah already has a delightful daughter Sophie from her first marriage

My brother-in-law Mel, Pat's husband died after a very short illness.
The day after Mel died, my beloved husband Peter suddenly collapsed and died. I miss him every minute of every day. He was my rock, my life and my world. I thank Peter for sharing his life with me.

Printed in the United Kingdom
by Lightning Source UK Ltd.
120270UK00001B/175-210